A Short
Old French Dictionary
for Students

Saorla ó Corráin
Cork 22/04/01

A Short
Old French Dictionary
for Students

Edited by
Kenneth Urwin

BASIL BLACKWELL

First published 1946

Reprinted 1949, 1963, 1972, 1990
First published in paperback 1985

Basil Blackwell Ltd
108 Cowley Road, Oxford OX4 1JF, UK

Basil Blackwell Inc.
3 Cambridge Center
Cambridge, MA 02142, USA

ISBN 0 631 07970 X

Printed in Great Britain

FOREWORD

In compiling this glossary for University students of Old French, Dr. Urwin has performed a useful and by no means easy task. The difficulties of selection must have been considerable if the work was to satisfy the legitimate demands of the student and at the same time to remain within the reach of his usually rather slender purse. There were difficulties, too, of a higher order. A dictionary, even of a living and standardized language, can no more produce an impression of its complex organic life than a directory can portray the busy life of a civic community; and the linguist who sets out to compose a short dictionary of Old French must be painfully conscious of the impossibility of conveying any adequate impression of its great variety of forms and its remarkable fertility in word-formation. The observant user of Dr. Urwin's dictionary will, however, receive more than an inkling of this variety and fertility. He will, moreover, receive a useful introduction to French Etymology. The derivations given have been scrupulously chosen and are neither over-conservative nor over-venturesome. When the author himself does not feel convinced, he does not fear to let it be known. Finally, Dr. Urwin leaves a great deal for the student himself to do—and that, in a student's manual, is an essential virtue : it should encourage as well as sustain; it should not be a mere prop, but a pole, urging him to leap. I wish the work well.

JOHN ORR.

HOW TO USE THIS DICTIONARY

THIS dictionary is limited to common Old French words which might present difficulties to the University student : for that reason easily recognizable words are omitted, unless needed for cross-reference. Meanings are given for the forms most frequently found in prescribed texts or in works often used as sources of " Unseens," dialect or " literary." No attempt has been made to list them under the corresponding Central French form : the student seldom knows enough to be able, at a glance, to trace the corresponding Francien spelling.

FORMS.

All forms cannot be included in a short dictionary. It must be remembered that, in medieval times, there were many ways of spelling a word. Common interchangeable spellings are given at intervals throughout the work, and should be carefully noted. Within the dictionary the usual abbreviations are used; e.g., *sm.* = masculine substantive. Note, however, that *pr.* = present indicative, and that *pft.* = perfect (i.e., past definite, past historic).

An elementary knowledge of morphology is assumed. Thus *murs* is the case in -*s* (nominative singular or accusative plural) of *mur.* Students would do well to study a work such as A. Ewert's *The French Language* (Faber and Faber).

Many omissions are due to war-time paper shortage. Suggestions for other words or forms to be included if a further edition becomes necessary would be welcomed. The work as it stands must not be expected to do more than it claims to do. It will not solve every problem, and use of the reference dictionaries [1] in the University Library will be necessary for some words. Intelligent use of the present work will sometimes furnish information, even where the specific form is not given. Thus, the meaning of the adverb *soutivement* can be found from that of the adjective *soutif.* Similarly, the meanings given to *marrir* and *marrement*

---

[1] e.g., Godefroy ; Meyer-Lübke ; Gamillscheg ; von Wartburg (*A-F*) ; Tobler-Lommatzsch (*A-De*) ; Clédat ; Hatzfeld, Darmsteter et Thomas.

-would suggest that *marrison, sm. & f.*, will be " grief," " affliction " ; and the sense of *departie, sf.*, can be guessed on examining
département and *departir*.

ETYMOLOGIES.

The etymologies given here are mainly those of the Bloch-
Wartburg school of philology. In many cases, however, there is
no general agreement, and, if your professor prefers another
etymology, this can be written in the margin. Latin words are
usually given in the accusative, except for those in *-a* : meanings
of the source are not given where they are virtually the same as the
Old French.

Etymologies are given in italics, and, unless otherwise indicated,
are Latin (an asterisk before a Latin word indicates an unattested
Popular Latin form). Again, in Latin words long vowels only are
shown, except that $\bar{a}$ is not marked, $\check{a}$ and $\check{a}$ having coalesced in
Popular Latin. Thus *cooperire* should be read as *cŏŏpĕrĭrĕ*. A
question-mark following an etymology means that it is dubious,
but tentatively accepted.

The following abbreviations are used :—

alter. = alteration ; **Arab.** = Arabic ; **b.** = borrowed from (i.e.,
" learned " or " retarded " forms) ; **Carol.** = Carolingian ; **Celt.** =
Celtic ; **CL.** = Classical Latin ; **dimin.** = diminutive ; **Eccl.** =
Ecclesiastical ; **Eng.** = English ; **etym. obsc.** = etymology obscure
(i.e., the suggestions so far made present great difficulties) ;
Fk. = Frankish ; **Flem.** = Flemish ; **G.** = German ; **Gaul.** =
Gaulish ; **Germ.** = Germanic ; **Gk.** = Greek ; **Goth.** = Gothic ;
Icel. = Icelandic ; **infl.** = influenced ; **intens.** =intensive ; **Ir.** =
Irish ; **L.** = Latin ; **LG.** = Low German ; **LL.** = Low Latin ;
Med. = Medieval ; **Medic.** = Medical ; **Merov.** = Merovingian ;
MHG. = Middle High German ; **Netherl.** = Netherlandish ;
n.pl. = neuter plural ; **obsc.** = obscure ; **OHG.** = Old High
German ; **onom.** = onomatopæia ; **O.Pr.** = Old Provençal ;
orig. = origin ; **O.Sc.** = Old Scandinavian ; **perh.** = perhaps ;
Pers. = Persian ; **PL.** = Popular Latin (attested) ; **Sk.** =
Sanskrit ; **Sp.** = Spanish ; **var.** = variant ; **W.** = Welsh ; **+** =
crossed with *or* plus.

Language is creative. It constantly adds to itself by forming
new words, verbs on nouns, nouns on verbs, nouns on other nouns,
etc. The cross-references given will help to show how French
developed its own resources. A list of common prefixes and
suffixes used in word-building is given at the end of the Introduction.

HOW TO USE THIS DICTIONARY

Once a word is in a language it develops as an individual. Clashes with other words, confusions between forms popularly supposed to be connected, contact with the written language—all these things help a word to develop on its own, both for sense and for sound. Phonology is but the beginning of language-study : philology is essentially the study of man thinking and speaking, and is closely linked with his sociological and mental development. It is therefore a living subject of interest to all cultured men.

COMMON PREFIXES AND SUFFIXES USED IN WORD-FORMATION

PREFIXES :—

A- (*ad-* & *ab-*).
AN- (*ante-*).
BES- (*bis-*).
CON- (*cum-*).
DES- (*dis-*).
EM- (*im-*).
EN- (*inde, in-* & *im-* & cf. AN-).
ENTRE- (*inter-*).
ES- (*ex-*).
FORS- (*foris* & Germ. *fur-*).
MAL- (*male-*).
MAU-, V. MAL-.

MES- (*minus* & Germ. *miss-*).
OLTRE- (*ultra-*).
OUTRE-, V. OLTRE.
PAR- (*per-*).
POR- (*prŏ-*).
PRE- (*prae-*).
RE- (*re-*).
SOR- (*super-*).
SOUS- (*subtus-*).
SOZ-, V. SOUS.
TRES- (*trans-*).
VIS- (*vice-*).

SUFFIXES :—

-ABLE (*-abilem*).
-ACE (*-acem*).
-AGE (*-aticum*).
-AIE (*-ēta*).
-AIL (*-aculum* & *-alium*).
-AILLE (*-alia*, n.pl.).
-AIN (*-anum* & *-anem*).
-AINE (*-ana*).
-AISON (*-atiōnem*).
-AL (b. *-alem*).
-ALT (Germ. *-halt*).
-ANCE (*-antia*).
-ART (Germ. *-hart*).
-ASTRE (*-astrum*).
-AUT, V. -ALT.
-É (*-atum*).
-ECE (*-itia* & LL. *-issa*).
-EE (*-ata*).
-EIE (*-ăta*).

-EIS (*-ĕ(n)sem*, Germ. *-isk*, & Græco-L. *-iscum*).
-EL (*-alem* & *-ellum*, dimin.).
-EMENT (*-amentum*).
-ENCE (*-entia*).
-ENGE (*-emia*).
-(E)OR (*-(at)orem*).
-ER (*-arem*).
-ET (*-ittum*).
-ETTE (*-itta*).
-EUL (*-iolum*).
-EURE (*-atura*).
-EUS, V. -OS.
-IE (LL. *-ía*).
-IER (*-erium* for *-arium*).
-IERE (*-eria* for *-aria*).
-IF (*-ivum*).
-ILLE (*-icula*).
-IS (*-icium*).

ix

PREFIXES AND SUFFIXES USED IN WORD-FORMATION

-ISE (-*itia?*).

-ISON (-*itionem*).

-IZ (-*icium*).

-MENT, adv. (*mente*).

-OIR (-*ŏrium*).

-OIRE (-*ŏria*).

-OIS, V. -EIS.

-OISON (-*ōtiŏnem*).

-ON (-*ōnem*).

-OR (-*ŏrem*).

-OS (-*ōsum*).

-TÉ (-*tatem*).

-U (-*ŭtum*).

The Editor wishes to acknowledge his gratitude to all those who have helped and encouraged him, and especially to Professor John Orr, Mr. L. J. D. Richardson, Professor Morgan Watkin, Professor Mary Williams, Dr. C. B. Lewis, and Mr. Evan John Jones. Their advice and suggestions have been most helpful. It must not be assumed, however, that they accept every etymology here proposed.

K. U.

A

A-. Try **Ha-.** For infinitives in **A-**, try also under the simple form, e.g. **Aflner,** v. *finer.*

Aaisler (on *aise* < *adjacēns*), *va. & rfl.* care for, rest, refresh oneself.

Aate (*aptum,* fitting), *adj.* fine, suitable, swift.

Abandonner (on *abandon,* on *bandon,* q.v.), *va.* give up ; *v. rfl.* expose oneself, offer battle. *Se mettre en abandon de :* expose oneself to, offer battle. *Mettre en abandon :* betray.

Abatre (on *batre* < **battere* for *battuere*), *va.* throw down, strike down. **Abatiéd,** 3 pft.

Abaubir (on *baube* < *balbum,* stammering), *va.* astonish, stupefy.

Abelir (on *bel,* q.v.), *vn.* please.

Abevrer (**abbiberare,* on *bibere,* drink), *va.* quench the thirst of.

Abrevie, pp. of **Abrever,** cf. *abevrer,* or v. *abrivé.*

Abrivé (on *brevem,* short), *adj.* swift.

Aceindre (on *ceindre* < *cingere*), *va.* go round, surround.

Acener (on LL. *cinnum,* sense obsc.), *va.* beckon to, point at, give.

Aceré (on LL. *aciarium,* on *aciēs,* edge), *pp. adj.* sharp, sharpened.

Acesmer (on *schisma,* division), *va.* adorn, arrange.

Achetivé (on *chaitif,* q.v.), *pp. adj.* unfortunate.

Acholson (*occasiŏnem,* oppor-tunity, with change of prefix), *sf.* occasion, chance, reason, pretext, accusation.

Acoarder, Acoardir (on *coard,* q.v.), *va. & rfl.* fear, turn coward.

Acoillir (on *coillir,* q.v.), *va.* greet, take up, continue, strike. *A . ire :* become angry. *A . en hé :* begin to hate.

Acointance (on *acointier,* q.v.), *sf.* acquaintance, friendship.

Acointe (*accōgnitum,* known), *adj.* friendly, friend, acquainted with.

Acointier (**accōgnitare,* on *accōgnitum*), *va. & rfl.* know, learn, inform, undertake, get to know, frequent.

Acoler (on *col* < *collum,* neck), *va.* embrace, put round the neck, smite.

Acomenier (on *comenier,* q.v.), *va., n. & rfl.* give communion to, receive communion. *Var. :* **Acominjer.**

Aconsivir (on *sivir,* q.v.), *va.* pursue, overtake.

Aconter (on *conter* < *computare,* calculate), *va.* count, tell.

Acorcier (on *corcier* < **curtiare,* on *curtum,* short), *va.* shorten.

Acorder (**accordare,* on *concordare,* agree), *va. & rfl.* reconcile ; *v. rfl.* accept, agree to.

Acoster (on *coste* < *costa,* rib, side), *va. & rfl.* put alongside, draw near, lean against.

Acouter (on *coute* < *cubitum,* elbow), *v. rfl.* lean (upon the elbows).

Acraventer (on *craventer,* q.v.), *va.* shatter, hurl down.

Acroire (on *croire* < *crēdere*, believe), *va. & n.* believe, buy on credit.

Adenz (*ad + dentes*, teeth), *adv.* face downwards.

Adés (*ad de + ipsum*, self), *adv.* soon, straightway, ever, now.

Adeser (**addē(n)sare*, make thick), *va.* touch, approach, fall (dew).

Adober (on **dober*, Fk. **dubban*, strike), *va. & rfl.* arm, equip.

Adresse (on *adresser*, on *dresser*, v. *drecier*), *sf.* direction, way, skill.

Aduré (on *dur* < *dūrum*, hard), *pp. adj.* hard, strong, stubborn, firm.

Aé (*aetatem*, age), *sm.* age, life.

Aemplir (on *emplir* < **implire* for *implēre*), *va.* fill.

Aerdre, Aers, v. *aherdre.*

Afaitier (**affactare*, prepare), *va. & rfl.* prepare, train, educate, arrange, dress.

Afeibleier (on *feible*, v. *foible*), *va., n. & rfl.* weaken.

Aferir (**afferire*, on *afferre*, bring), *vn.* be suitable, appertain, concern.

Afeutreüre (on *feutre*, Fk. **filtir*), *sf.* padded object, saddle(?).

Affremer = Affermer (on *fermer*, q.v.), *va. & rfl.* establish, fix, make firm, confirm.

Afiancer (on *fiance*, on *fier* < **fīdare*, entrust), *va. & n.* provide with a pledge, promise.

Afichier (on *fichier*, q.v.), *va. & rfl.* fix, make firm, resolve.

Afier (on *fier* < **fīdare*, entrust), *va. & rfl.* pledge, proclaim.

Afiert, 3 pr. of *aferir*, q.v.

Afoler (on *fol*, q.v.), *va. & rfl.* send mad, go mad, wound severely, destroy.

Afubler (**affībulare*, on *fībula*, brooch), *va.* put on, dress, cover.

Afuster (on *fust*, q.v.), *va. & n.* arrange, hide (behind tree).

Agregier (on *gregier*, q.v.), *va., n. & rfl.* weigh upon, grow more grievous.

Agu (*acūtum*), *adj.* sharp, pointed.

Ahan (orig. unkn.), *sm.* suffering, agony, toil.

Aherdre, Aherdeir (*adhaerēre*, adhere to), *va. & rfl.* seize, attach, cling.

Ahers, pp. of *aherdre*, q.v. **Aide, Aie,** v. *aiude.*

Aidier (*adjūtare*), *va.* help. *Si Dieu m'ait* : so help me God, I swear.

Aigue, v. *eve.* **Ainchies, Ainchois,** etc. v. *ançois.*

Ainques (*ainz*, q.v. + *onques*, q.v.), *adv.* never.

Aint, 3 pr. subj. of *amer* (*amare*), love.

Ainz (**antius*, compar. of *ante*, before), *prep. & adv.* before, previously, sooner ; *conj.* but.

Air (on *aïrer*, on *ire* < *īra*, anger), *sm.* anger, violence.

Aire (*area*, eyrie, + *aēr*, air, ?), *sm. & f.* birth, lineage, race.

Aise, cf. *aaisier.*

Ait (etym. unkn.) : *Ad ait :* speedily, with zest.

Aït, 3 pr. subj. of *aidier*, q.v.

Aitre (*atrium*, hall), *sm.* porch, parvis, close.

Aiude, Aide, Aie (on *aidier*, q.v.), *sf.* aid, help.

Alve, v. *eve.*

Ajorner (on *jorn,* q.v.), *vn. & impers.* dawn ; *va.* summon.

Ajoster (on *joster,* q.v.), *va. & n.* assemble, bring together in battle.

Albe (PL. *alba,* on *albus,* white), *sf.* dawn ; alb (Eccl.).

Alberc, v. *halberc.*

Alcobe (Arab. *al-goubba,* small room), *sf.* tent, canopy.

Alegier (LL. *alleviare,* alleviate), *va., n. & rfl.* alleviate, become light ; excuse oneself.

Alerion (Fk. **adalaro?*), *sm.* eagle.

Aleûre (on *aler,* etym. disputed), *sf.* speed, gait.

Algalife (Arab. *al-khalîfa*), *sm.* caliph.

Alge, 3 pr. subj. of *aler,* go.

Alier (*alligare,* bind), *va. & rfl.* join, assemble, rally.

Almosniere (on *almosne* < **alemosina* for Eccl. L. *eleemosyna,* compassion), *sf.* wallet, purse.

Aloer (on *loer* < *locare*), *va.* place, put.

Aloser (on *los,* q.v.), *va.* praise, vaunt. *Alosé,* pp. adj. : famous.

Alquant (*aliquanti,* moderate), *pron. pl.* some.

Alques (*aliquid,* something, + adv. *-s*), *adv.* somewhat, a little. *A. de :* some.

Alsi (**ale,* for *alid* + *si* < *sic*), *adv.* as, so, as much.

Alt, Aut, 3 pr. subj. of *aler,* go.

Alter (*altare*), *sm.* altar.

Altresi (*altre* < *alterum,* other, + *si* < *sic*), *adv.* also, so.

Altretel (*altre* < *alterum,* other, + *tel* < *talem*), *pron.* the same.

Altrier (*altre* < *alterum,* other, + *ier* < *heri,* yesterday), *adv.* the other day.

Alve (**alvea,* on *alveum,* trough, ?), *sf.* saddle-bow, pommel, side-bar (of saddle).

Amanantir (on *manant,* q.v.), *va.* provide with a dwelling or fief.

Amanevir, cf. *manevi.*

Amatir (on *mat,* q.v.), *va.* mate (chess), defeat.

Ambedui, Ambesdous, v. *andui, ansdous.*

Amblant (*ambulantem,* walking), *adj.* swift-moving.

Amender (alter. of *ēmendare,* correct), *va. & n.* atone for, improve, benefit.

Amentevoir (on *mentevoir,* q.v.), *va.* recall, remember, mention.

Amerrai, 1 fut. of *amener* (on *mener,* q.v.).

Amirail, Amiran, Amiré (on Arab. *amîr,* chief), *sm.* emir.

Amoine, pr. of *amener* (on *mener,* q.v.).

Amonester (**admonestare?*), *va.* admonish, advise, encourage.

Amont (on *mont* < *mōntem,* mountain), *adv.* up, on high, towards heaven.

An-, try also **En-.**

Ancele (*ancilla,* maid), *sf.* maid, servant.

Ancessor (*antecessōrem,* forerunner), *sm.* ancestor(s). *D'ancessorie :* of long standing. *Nom. sing. :* **Ancestre** (*antecessor*).

Ancienor (**antianōrum*), *adj.* old, of the ancients.

Ançois (*anteipsum*, for *ante ipsum*, or *anteidius*, for *ante + -idius*), *prep. & adv.* before, rather; *conj.* but, before.

Andier, v. *landier*.

Andul (*ambi *dui*), *pron. & adj. nom. pl.* both.

Anel (*anellum*, little ring), *sm.* ring.

Anglet (on *angle* < *angulum*, angle), *sm.* corner.

Angoissier (LL. *angustiare*, on *angustia*, distress), *va. & n.* press in upon, trouble, be in distress, be dying.

Anoel (*annualem*), *adj.* annual, high (of Church feast).

Anprés, v. *emprés*. **Ansdous**, acc. of *andui*, q.v. **Anseler,** v. *enseler*.

Ansgarde (on *garde*, q.v.), *sf.* vanguard, look-out.

Antan (*ante + annum*), *adv.* last year.

Ante (*amita*), *sf.* aunt.

Antif, form of **Anti** (*anticum*) infl. by fem., *adj.* old.

Anual, Anuel, v. *anoel*. **Anult,** 3 pr. subj. of *anuier* (v. *enuier*) or of *anuitier*, q.v.

Anuit (*hac nocte* or *ad noctem*), *adv.* to-night, in the night, to-day.

Anuitier (on *nuit* < *noctem*, night), *v.* impers. be night, become dark.

Aorer (*adōrare*), *va.* worship.

Aoster (on *aost* < **agostum*, for *augustum*, August), *va. & n.* harvest.

Apaier, cf. *paier*.

Apaisier (on *pais*, q.v.), *va., n. & rfl.* appease, reconcile, obtain reconciliation.

Apareillier (**appariculare*, get ready), *va. & rfl.* prepare, equip, arrange.

Aparmain (on *main* < *mane*, q.v.), *adv.* soon, straightway.

Apeler (*appellare*, address), *va., n. & rfl.* call, address, cite, accuse. *En a. qq'un :* address him.

Appendre (on *pendre*, q.v.), *vn.* pertain, appertain.

Aperceivre (on *perceivre*, v. *perçoivre*), *va. & rfl.* become aware of; *v. rfl.* regain consciousness.

Apert (*apertum*, uncovered), *adj.* open, clear, clever. *Also* 3 pr. of **Aparoir** (*apparēre*), appear.

Apetisser (on *petit*, q.v.), *va. & n.* make or grow smaller.

Apoier (**appodiare*, on *podium*, support), *v. rfl.* lean, recline, support oneself.

Apostle (*apostolum*), *sm.* apostle. *L'a. de Rome :* St. Peter.

Apostolle, Apostolie (Eccl. L. *apostolicum*), *sm.* Pope.

Aprimier, Aproismier (LL. *approximare*), *va., n. & rfl.* approach. *A. en :* go into.

Aprovender (on *provende*, q.v.), *va.* furnish with provisions, look after.

Apruef (*ad + prope*, after), *adv. & prep.* after.

Aquerre (**acquaerere*, for *acquirere*), *va.* acquire.

Aquiter (on *quiter*, q.v.), *va. & rfl.* redeem, ransom, fulfil (obligation), free, restore peace to. *S'a. de :* carry out.

Araisnier (on *raisnier*, q.v.).

Araisoner (on *raisoner*, q.v.),

va. exhort, address, summon, intercede with.

Arbaleste, Arcbaleste (LL. *arcuballista*), *sf.* crossbow.

Ardeir (*ardēre*), *va. & n.* burn.

Areer, Areier (**arrēdare*, on Germ. **rēd-*, means), *va.* arrange.

Arester (**arrestare*, on *stare,* stand), *va., n. & rfl.* stop, remain, stand still. *S'a. a :* remain, choose.

Arguer (*argūtare,* chatter), *va. & rfl.* press, hurry.

Ariver (**arripare,* on *rīpa,* bank), *vn.* land, reach shore, arrive.

Arme, var. of *anme* (*anima*), *sf.* soul.

Aroter (on *rote,* v. *route*), *va., n. & rfl.* band together, gather, pursue, take one's way, direct.

Arrement (*atramentum,* black fluid), *sm.* ink.

Arroi (on *arroier,* v. *areer*), *sm.* order, arrangement.

Ars, (1) pp. & 1 pft. of *ardeir,* q.v. (2) pl. of *art* (*artem*) or of *arc* (*arcum*).

Arsin (Late L. *arsiōnem,* on *arsus,* burnt), *sm.* fire, burning.

As-, try also **Es-.**

Ascolter (PL. *ascultare* for *auscultare*), *va.* listen.

Asconser (**absconsare,* on *absconsum,* hidden), *va. & rfl.* hide.

Aseeir, Aseoir (**assedēre,* on *sedēre,* sit), *va. & rfl.* place, seat, besiege, sit down. **Asis,** pp. adj. : fashioned, fixed.

Aserir (on *sērō,* late), *v. impers.* grow dark.

Aseürer (**assēcūrare,* on *sēcūrum,* care-free), *va. & rfl.* assure, reassure, ensure one's own safety, be a laggard.

Asme, v. *esme.*

Asmer (for *esmer < aestimare,* appraise), *va. & n.* think, think of, aim at, try to.

Asoldre (*absolvere,* loosen), *va.* absolve, give absolution to. **Asolu,** pp. adj. : free, blessed (of France).

Ass-, try also **As-** or **Es-.**

Assaler, v. *essaier.*

Assasé (**ad + satis + -atum*), *pp. adj.* satisfied, rich.

Assembler (**assimulare,* on *simul,* at once), *va., n. & rfl.* gather together, join battle.

Assener (on *sen,* q.v.), *va. & rfl.* guide, direct, instruct.

Assentir (on *sentir < sentire,* feel), *va., n. & rfl.* feel, agree ; *v. rfl.* decide.

Assouvir (**assōpire,* send to sleep), *va.* calm, satisfy.

Assouvir (as above, infl. by *assevir < *assequire,* follow up) *va.* finish, achieve.

Atant (on *tant,* q.v.), *adv.* thereupon, then. See also *tant.*

Atargier (on *targier,* q.v.), *va., n. & rfl.* delay, tarry, await.

Ate, v. *aate.*

Atemprer (on *temprer,* q.v.), *va.* moderate, soften.

Atorner (on *torner,* q.v.), *va., n. & rfl.* turn, arrange, adorn, equip. *A. a :* take for, interpret. *A. a deshonor a :* be dishonourable for. *A. son talent a :* set one's heart upon, begin to think of. *S'a. de :*

give one's mind to. *Mal atorné :* in a sorry condition.

Atort, 3 pr. subj. of *atorner,* q.v.

Atot (on *tot,* q.v.), *prep. & adv.* with, therewith.

Atraire, Atrere (**attragere,* attract, cf. *traire*), *va.* attract, win over, extract. **Atrait,** pp. adj. : complete.

Atrait, Atret (on *atraire,* q.v.), *sm.* provision, equipment; snare; greeting.

Au-, try also **Al-.**

Aucun (*alicŭnum), *adj. & pron.* some, someone. *A . . . . ne :* none. *Aucunement,* adv. : somewhat.

Auferrant (Arab., cf. Ar. *al-fâris,* horseman, ?), *adj. & sm.* swift, charger, valuable horse.

Aŭner (**adŭnare,* on *ŭnum,* one), *va., n. & rfl.* assemble, unite, gather; affirm; rejoin.

Aŭr, v. *eŭr.* **Aŭs, Aŭsse,** pft. & impft. subj. of *avoir (habēre).*

Autrier, v. *altrier.*

Aval (on *val < vallem,* valley), *adv. & prep.* below, down.

Avaler (on *aval,* q.v.), *va., n. & rfl.* go down, come down, fall.

Avant (Late L. *abante,* before), *adv. & prep.* before, forward. *Amener a. :* bring forward. *Ça a. :* further. *Par a. :* previously. *Parler a. :* speak out, speak first.

Ave (b. *avum*), *sm.* grandfather, ancestor.

Avenir (*advenīre*), *vn. & impers.* happen, befit. *Il leur avient bien :* they are successful. **Avenant,** pr. p. adj. : becoming, attractive.

Aventure (**adventŭra,* what is to happen), *sf.* happening, adventure, chance, fortune. *En a de :* in danger of.

Aver (*avarum*), *adj.* greedy, miserly.

Averé (on *veir < vĕrum,* true), *pp. adj.* true, verified.

Avers (*adversus,* opposed to), *prep.* near, compared with.

Avers (*adversum,* opposed), *aaj.* enemy, hostile. *La gent a. :* the pagans.

Aversier (*adversarium,* adversary), *sm.* enemy, the devil.

Avertin (on *vertīginem,* giddiness), *sm.* faintness, epilepsy.

Avesprer (on *vespre,* q.v.), *v. impers.* become dark, be evening.

Aveugler (on *aveugle < ab oculis,* without eyes,?), *va.* blind (*phys. & moral*).

Avillier (on *vil,* q.v.), *va.* abase, weaken.

Avis (for *a vis*), *sm.* opinion. *Ce m'est a. :* I think.

Aviser (on *viser < *vīsare,* intens. of *vidēre,* see), *va.* look at, recognize, watch. *Also* (on *avis,* q.v.), think of (*rfl.*).

Avoé (*advocatum,* advocate, witness), *pp. as sm.* protector, overlord, patron.

Avoiler (on *voie,* q.v.), *va.* guide, direct.

Avuler, v. *aveugler.*

B

Bacheler (Med. L. *baccalarem), *sm.* young warrior, knight aspirant, squire.

Baer (PL. *batare*, onom. orig.), *va. & n.* open (mouth), aspire; be open.

Baillie (on *baillir*, q.v.), *sf.* power, possession. *Avoir en b. :* have under one's rule or in one's keeping.

Baillier (*bajulare*, carry), *va.* carry, rule, grant, give, take. *Syn. :* **Baillir**. *Mal bailli :* in sorry plight.

Baller (LL. *ballare*), *vn.* dance.

Balt (Germ. **bald*, bold), *adj.* bold, happy.

Bandon (on Germ. **banda*, standard, band), *sm.* power, permission, discretion. *A force et a b. :* freely, powerfully. *Se mettre en b. :* advance, offer battle.

Banir (Fk. **bannjan*, give signal), *va.* proclaim, summon, banish.

Barat, *sm.*, **Barate**, *sf.* (etym. obsc.), deceit, fraud, harm, struggle.

Barde (Arab. *barda'a*, via Span. *barda*, stuffed saddle), *sf.* padded pack-saddle, breast-piece (horse).

Barge (**barica*, on *baris*, Egyptian skiff, ?), *sf.* boat.

Barnage (**barōnaticum*, on Fk. **baro*), *sm.* assembly of barons, prowess.

Barné (**barōnatum*, on Fk. **baro*), *sm.* Cf. *barnage*.

Baron (**barōnem*, on Fk. **baro*, a royal functionary), *sm.* baron, lord, knight; husband.

Bast (LL. *bastum*), *sm.* stick, staff.

Bataille (LL. *battalia*, sort of fencing), *sf.* battle, army. *Afiner la b. :* triumph. *Guer-*
B

pir b. : retreat, disengage. *Laisser b. :* retreat, disengage. *Veintre la b. :* triumph.

Baucent (on *balteum*), *adj.* white-footed, trammelled (horse).

Baudré(etym. obsc.), *sm.* baldrick.

Bayer, Beer, v. *baer*. **Behorder,** v. *border*. **Belf, Beis, Belt,** etc., pr. of *beivre*, v. *boivre*.

Bel (*bellum*), *adj.* fine, handsome, beautiful. *Estre b. a :* please, suit.

Bendé (Germ. **bindjan*), *pp. adj. Arc. b. :* bended bow. *Escu b. :* shield with diagonal lines in two alternate colours (cf. Med. L. *arma bendata*, arms bendy).

Beneir (*benedicere*, praise), *va.* bless. **Beneoit,** *pp. adj. :* blessed, sacred.

Ber(s) (Fk. **baro*), nom. of *baron*, q.v.

Bers (**bercium?*, Celt. orig., cf. Ir. *bertaim*, I shake), *sm.* cradle.

Berser (etym. unkn.), *vn.* hunt, shoot (bow & arrow).

Berseret (on *berser*, q.v.), *sm.* hunting-dog.

Besant (*byzantium*, Byzantine), *sm.* small gold coin.

Bestorner (on *torner*, q.v.), *va., n. & rfl.* illtreat, change, become corrupt, fall.

Beü, pp. & pft. of *boivre*, q.v.

Bial = *beal*, v. *bel*.

Bien (*bene*), *adv.* well, very, much; *sm.* good. *Biens*, sm. pl. : services, goods. *En bien :* favourable. *Estre b. de :* be favoured by. *Par (Por) b. :* with good intent. *Tenir b. a :* favour.

Bieneurté (on *eür*, q.v.), *sf.* happiness.

Bis (etym. obsc.), *adj.* dark grey, brown, dark?

Bisse (**bistia* for *bestia*, animal), *sf.* hind.

Blandir (**blandire* for *blandiri*, flatter), *va.* flatter, caress, care for.

Blason (etym. unkn.), *sm.* buckler, blazon; flattery, blame.

Blesmer, Blesmir (etym. obsc.), *va. & n.* blanch, turn pale; brand, be branded.

Bliaut (etym. unkn.), *sm.* under-tunic, long close-fitting tunic.

Blol (etym. obsc.), *adj.* fair, yellow, flaxen, blue(?).

Bobance, *sf.*, **Bobant,** *sm.* (etym. unkn.), arrogance.

Boce, (1) (etym. obsc.), *sf.* bump, hump, knob, boss; (2) (*bucca*), *sf.* mouth, opening.

Boceler (on *boce* 1, q.v.), *va.* cover with bosses.

Bohorder, v. *border*.

Boisdie (etym. obsc., cf. *voisous?*), *sf.* trickery, cunning.

Boisier (etym. obsc.), *va.* deceive, wrong.

Boisine, form of **Buisine** (*būcina*), *sf.* trumpet.

Boivre (*bibere*), *va. & n.* drink.

Bone (Gaul. **bodina*-, boundary stone), *sf.* limit, boundary stone.

Bore (LL. *burgum*, from Germ. **burgs*), *sm.* town.

Border (etym. unkn.), *vn. & rfl.* bésport, joust, tilt, joke, converse; *va.* mock at. *A b. :* to one's heart's content.

Boter (Fk. **bottan*, strike), *va. & rfl.* strike, push, place.

Bouguerant, Bouqueran (on *Boukhara* (town)?), *sm.* fine buckram, linen.

Brace (PL. *brachia*, n.pl. as fem. sing.), *sf.* the two arms, embrace.

Brachet (on Germ. **brakko*), *sm.* hound, hunting-dog.

Braier (on *braie*, Gaul. *braca*), *sm.* breeches.

Braire (**bragere*, orig. unkn.), *vn.* weep, howl, roar.

Brait (on *braire*, q.v.), *sm.* cry.

Brandir (on *brand*, v. *brant*), *va. & n.* brandish, fly, hurtle. *B. son colp :* brandish one's sword. *Faire b. le cors :* send toppling.

Brant (Germ. **brand*, brand, sword), *sm.* sword, blade.

Bregier, var. of **Bergier** (PL. *berbicarium*), *sm.* shepherd.

Bricon (etym. unkn.), *sm.* fool, rogue.

Brief (*brevem*, short), *sm.* letter, brief, chronicle.

Briment, var. of **Briément** (on *brief*, q.v.), *adv.* quickly, soon.

Bris, nom. of *bricon*, q.v.

Brochier (**broccare*, on *brocchus*, pointed), *va. & n.* spur on, ride.

Broigne, Bronie (Late L. *brugna*, Fk. **brunjâ*), *sf.* hauberk, byrnie, leather tunic covered with mail.

Broncher, cf. *embronchier*.

Brosder (Fk. **brozdôn?*), *va.* embroider.

Bruit (on *bruire* < **brügere*, on *rügire* + *braire*, q.v.), *sm.* noise; reputation; army.

Buc (Fk. *bûk*, belly, body), *sm.* trunk (body).

Buef (*bovem*), *sm.* ox.

Buen, var. of *bon* (*bonum*), good.

Buisine, v. *boisine.*

Burel (on **bûra*), *sm.* coarse woollen cloth.

C

Ca-, try also **Cha-** or **Che-**.

Ça (*ĕcce hāc*), *adv.* here. *En ça :* till now.

Cacier, var. of *chacier*, q.v.

Çaens, Çaiens (*ça + enz*, q.v.), *adv.* herein, inside.

Cane, v. *quene.*

Car (*quārē*, by which means), *conj.* therefore, now, because.

Carboncie (*carbunculum*), *sm.* carbuncle, ruby.

Cas (*casum*, falling), *sm.* fall, event, circumstance. *A c. :* to the ground.

Ceans, v. *çaens.* **Ceinst,** 3 pft. of **Ceindre** (*cingere*, gird).

Cel, Celi (*ĕcce illum*), *adj. & pron.* this, that.

Celeement (on *celee,* pp. fem. of *celer < cēlare*, hide), *adv.* secretly, quietly.

Celement (on *celer < cēlare*, hide), *sm.* secret.

Cendal, Cendé (LL. *cendalum,* cf. Sk. *sindhu*), *sm.* fine silk-cloth, sendal, taffeta.

Cener, cf. *acener.*

Cengle (*cingula*, girdle), *sf.* saddle-girth.

Cenglilion (on *cengle,* q.v.), *sm.* girth (strap).

Cerchier (LL. *circare*, on *circa*, around), *va.* go round, explore, seek.

Cerge (*cēreum*, waxen), *sm.* wax candle.

Certes (PL. *certas*, for *certō*, assuredly), *adv.* indeed. *A c. :* at once, assiduously.

Cescun (**cisque ūnum* for *quisque ūnum*), *adj. & pron.* each, each one.

Cest, Cesti, Cestui (*ĕcce istum*), *adj. & pron.* this.

Cha-, try also **Chai-** or **Che-**.

Chacier (**captiare*, on *captare*, hunt), *va. & n.* chase, expel, hunt.

Chadeir, Chaoir, v. *cheoir.*

Chaeignable (on *chaeine,* q.v.), *adj.* in chains.

Chaeine (*catēna*), *sf.* chain.

Chalere (*cathedra*, chair), *sf.* seat, pulpit.

Chaille, 3 pr. subj. of *chaloir,* q.v. *Ne vos en ch. :* do not worry.

Chainse (Late L. *camisia,* orig. obsc.), *sf.* linen undergarment, shirt.

Chainsil (on *chainse,* q.v.), *sm.* linen.

Chair, var. of *chaoir,* v. *cheoir.*

Chaitif (*captivum*), *adj. & sm.* captive, wretched, unfortunate.

Chalcier (*calceare,* provide with shoes), *va.* put on (gloves, spurs, etc.).

Chaleir (*calēre*, be of interest to), *v. impers.* matter, be of interest to.

Chalengement (on *chalengier,* q.v.), *sm.* challenge. *Mettre en ch. :* challenge possession of.

Chalengier, Chalongier (*calum-
niare*, for *calumniari*, attack),
va. challenge, claim, attack,
vilify. *Ch. mort et vie* : defend oneself to the utmost.

Chalt (*calidum*), *adj.* hot. *Also*
pr. of *chaleir*, q.v.

Chambre (*camera*, vaulted room),
sf. chamber, bedroom; special
province.

Champel (on *champ* < *campum*,
field), *adj.* in the field.

Chantel (on *chant* < *canthum*,
wheel, tyre), *sm.* corner, fragment. *L'escu en ch.* : the
shield to one side.

Chape (LL. *cappa*), *sf.* cloak;
cope (Eccl.).

Chapleis, Chaples(on*chapler*,q.v.),
sm. fight, slaughter, sword-play.

Chapler (LL. *capulare*, cut), *va.*
strike, hew, hack. *Var.*:
Chaploier.

Char, (1) (*carrum*, wagon), *sm.*
cart. (2) (*carnem*), *sm.* flesh,
meat.

Charchier, Chargier (*carricare*,
on *carrum*, wagon), *va.* load,
entrust.

Charier, Charoier (on *char* 1,
q.v.), *va.* cart, load.

Charn, v. *char* 2.

Chartre (*chartula*, small paper),
sf. charter, document.

Chartre (*carcerem*), *sf.* prison.

Chaser (*casare*, on *casa*, cottage),
va. enfeoff, establish.

Chastier (*castigare*), *va.* rebuke,
punish.

Chataigne (LL. *capitaneum*, adj.,
capital), *sm.* captain, leader.

Chatel (*capitalem*, relating to life),
sm. property, goods.

Chauces (*calcia*, on *calceum*, slipper), *sf. pl.* knee-piece (armour), hose, breeches.

Chaûn, v. *chedun*. **Chaut**, v. *chalt*.

Chaver (*cavare*), *va.* hollow out.

Cheance (*cadentia*), *sf.* fall of the
dice, fortune, chance.

Chedun (*cata ūnum*), *adj.* each.

Cheisil, Chesil, v. *chainsil*.

Cheitif, Chetif, v. *chaitif*.

Chenu (LL. *canūtum*, on *canus*,
white), *adj.* hoary, white.

Cheoir (*cadēre* for *cadere*), *vn.* fall,
be failing.

Cherral, 1 fut.; **Chet**, 3 pr.;
Cheü, pp. of *cheoir*, q.v.

Cherté (*caritatem*, dearness), *sf.*
value, esteem. *Avoir en ch.* ;
Faire ch. de : hold dear. Cf.
chier.

Chevalerie (on *chevaler*, on *cheval*,
< *caballum*, PL. horse), *sf.*
knightly exploit, valour. *Par
ch.* : in knightly fashion.

Chevecel ; pl. **Cheveçaus** (on
chevece < *capitia*), *sm.* head-
stall, bridle.

Cheveçuel (on *chevece* < *capitia*),
sm. bolster, pillow.

Chever, v. *chaver*. **Chevetaigne**,
v. *chataigne*.

Chief (*capum* for *caput*, head),
sm. head, leader, end. *A ch.
de piece* : again, after a time.
De ch. en altre : from end to
end. *Metre* (*Traire*) *a ch.* :
finish, accomplish. *Venir a
ch. de* : accomplish.

Chier (*carum*), *adj.* dear, valuable, fine. *Avoir ch.* : cherish.

Chiere (LL. *cara*, from Gk. *kara*,
head, face), *sf.* head, face; welcome, cheer.

Chiés (on *in casa*), *adv.* in the home of, at.

Choier (on *cadĕre* for *cadere?*), *vn.* fall, flow, subside.

Choisir (Germ. *kausjan*, taste), *va.* see, distinguish, recognize, choose.

Ciclaton, Ciglaton (on *cycladem*, female robe of state), *sm.* robe of silken cloth, the cloth itself (with a border of purple or gold).

Cierge, Cirge, v. *cerge*. **Cil,** nom. of *cel*, q.v.

Cinee (connected with *cento*, a covering of rags,?), *sf.* rag, tatter.

Cinne, Cisne (PL. *cicinum*, for *cycnum*), *sm.* swan.

Cist, nom. of *cest*, q.v.

Claim, 1 pr. of *clamer*, q.v.

Clamer (*clamare*, shout), *va. & rfl.* call, call oneself. *C. sa colpe :* say one's " mea culpa." *C. quite :* renounce all claim upon, absolve. *Se c. par :* call upon.

Cliner (*clinare*), *vn. & rfl.* bow, bow down, bend down. *Syn. :* **Cligner.**

Clo (*clavum*), *sm.* nail. *Hence* **Cloer,** to nail, and **Clofis** (*clavum + fixum*), *adj.*, nailed on.

Clore (*claudere*), *va., n. & rfl.* close.

Clos, pp. & pft. ; **Closisse,** impft. subj. of *clore*, q.v.

Coarder (on *coart*, q.v.), *v. rfl.* turn coward, behave like a coward.

Coardie, Codardie (on *coart*, q.v.), *sf.* cowardice.

Coart, Codart (on *coe*, q.v.), *sm.* coward.

Coe (*cōda*), *sf.* tail.

Cogn-, try **Con-.**

Coi (**quētum*, for *quiētum*, peaceful), *adj.* silent, calm.

Coigniee (PL. *cuneata*, on *cuneum*, wedge), *sf.* hatchet, axe.

Coillir (*colligere*, collect), *va., n. & rfl.* gather, seize. *C. en haür, en hé :* conceive hatred for.

Cointe (*cōgnitum*, known, proved), *adj.* clever, refined, friendly, pleasant ; *fem. often* pretty.

Cointise (on *cointe*, q.v.), *sf.* skill, sense, understanding; elegance.

Coite (on *coitier*, q.v.), *sf.* A *c. d'esperon :* spurring fast, in haste. *Also* fem. of *coi*, q.v.

Coitier (**coctare*, on **ccactare*), *va., n. & rfl.* spur on, hasten.

Colchier (*collocare*, put), *va., n. & rfl.* put to bed, lay, lie, go to bed.

Colee (on *col < collum*, neck), *sf.* blow on the neck, blow (in general).

Colp (**colpum* for *colaphum*), *sm.* blow. *A c. :* suddenly. *Grand c.*, *adv. :* much.

Colpe (*culpa*), *sf.* fault, sin, the " mea culpa." *Clamer sa c. :* v. *clamer. Moie c. de :* I repent of. *N'i avoir c. :* be innocent.

Colvert (*collibertum?*, freedman), *sm. & adj.* wretch, base, coward.

Com-, try also **Con-. Com,** v. *come.*

Commander (**commandare*), *va.* order, entrust, recommend.

Faire c. : put in command.

Comandé, *sm. :* good vassal.

Comant (on *comander,* q.v.), *sm.* order. *A vostre c. :* as you command. *Also* pr. & pr. subj. of *comander,* q.v.

Comble (*cumulum,* heap), *sm.* top, crest.

Come (LL. *quŏmo* for *quŏmodo,* how), *adv. & conj.* as, how, when. *Si c. :* just as, when. *Si . . . c. :* as . . . as. *Tant . . . c. :* as . . . as.

Comenier (Eccl. L. *commūnicare*), *va. & n.* communicate, receive communion.

Comm-, try Com-.

Comovoir (on *movoir,* q.v.), *va. & rfl.* raise, shake, stir up.

Compagne, Compaigne (**compania,* on *cum + panem*), *sf.* company, body of soldiers.

Compaing, Compain (**companio*), nom. of **Compagnon** (**companiŏnem,* cf. *compagne*), *sm.* friend, companion, fellow-knight.

Comparrai, 1 fut. of **Comparer** (*comparare*), compare, or of *comperer,* q.v.

Compasser (**compassare,* on *passum,* step), *va., n. & rfl.* measure, construct, arrange, control oneself. *A compas, adv. :* exactly, skilfully. **Compasseûre,** *sf.* construction, enclosure.

Comperer (**comperare* for *comparare,* settle), *va.* pay for.

Comunel (on *comun < commūnem,* common), *adj.* common, united.

Con-, try also **Com-.**

Condulre (*condūcere,* lead together), *va. & rfl.* lead, accompany, depart.

Coneû, pp.; **Coneûs,** pft. of *conoistre,* q.v.

Confaitement, Confetement (on *faitement,* q.v.), *adv.* how.

Confire (**confecere,* for *cŏnficere,* finish), *va.* make, compose, finish.

Confondre (*cŏnfundere,* mix), *va. & rfl.* destroy, ruin, embarrass.

Confort (on *conforter,* LL. *confortare,* on *fortem,* strong), *sm.* encouragement, help. (**Not** comfort, well-being.)

Congeer (on *congié,* q.v.), *va.* grant leave, dismiss, expel.

Congié (*commeatum,* leave of absence), *sm.* permission, leave. *Doner le c. :* allow to depart. *Prendre c. :* take one's leave.

Conissez, 5 pr. of *conoistre,* q.v.

Conjoïr (on *joïr,* q.v.), *va. & n.* greet, welcome, entertain.

Conme, v. *come.*

Conoistre (*cognŏscere*), *va.* know, get to know, recognize.

Conplie (Eccl. L. *complēta* (*hŏra*)), *sf.* compline.

Conraer, Conreer (on Germ. **rêd-,* v. *areer*), *va. & rfl.* fit out, see to, prepare, arm, attend to.

Conroi (cf. *conreer*), *sm.* care; armour; service. *Faire c. a :* take care of. *Prendre c. de :* see to.

Conseil (*cŏnsilium,* deliberation), *sm.* deliberation, opinion; secret; intention; aid. *A c. :* secretly. *Avoir c. :* deliberate. *Metre c. que :* decide to.

Prendre c. a : seek advice from. *Prendre c. que :* decide to. *Tenir c. de :* consider.

Conseü, pp. of *consivre,* q.v. **Consevir, Consivir,** v. *consivre.*

Consivre (**consequere* for *cōnsequī,* follow), *va.* follow, follow up, reach, strike down.

Conte (*comitem,* associate), *sm.* count, peer.

Conte (on *conter < computare,* calculate), *sm.* story, account.

Contendre (*contendere,* strive), *va. & n.* fight, contest, dispute.

Contenance (on *contenir,* q.v.), *sf.* bearing.

Contençon (on *tençon,* q.v.), *sf.* striving, rivalry, quarrel; zeal.

Contenement (on *contenir,* q.v.), *sm.* bearing.

Contenir (on *continēre,* contain, curb, infl. by *tenir,* q.v.), *v. rfl.* behave; contain oneself; stay.

Contoier (on *conter < computare,* calculate), *va. & n.* tell, speak, recount.

Contraire (*contrarium*), *adj.* opposite, contrary ; *sm.* difficulty, misfortune, unpleasantness.

Contrait (*contractum,* drawn in), *adj.* contracted, crippled, deformed.

Contralie (on *contraloier,* q.v.), *sf.* contradiction.

Contralier (LL. *contrariare,* on *contrarium*), *v. rfl.* quarrel, dispute.

Contraloier (**contrarizare?*), *va.* resist, contradict, annoy.

Contre (*contra,* opposite), *prep.* opposite, towards, at the time of.

Contrecengle (*contre,* q.v. + *cengle,* q.v.), *sf.* girth leather.

Contredeignier (on *deignier < dignare,* consider worthy), *va.* esteem.

Contremont (*contre,* q.v. + *mont, < montem*), *adv. & prep.* aloft, up towards.

Contrester (on *ester < stare,* stand), *va., n. & rfl.* resist, withstand, avoid.

Contreval (on *val < vallem,* cf. *contremont*), *adv. & prep.* below, down, downwards.

Conv-, try also **Cov-,** e.g. **Convenir,** v. *covenir.*

Contechier (on *teche,* q.v.), *va. & n.* please, suit ; earn.

Converser (**conversare* for *conversari,* frequent), *vn.* dwell, live.

Convine (on *convenir,* v. *covenir*), *sf.* behaviour.

Convoier (**conviare,* on *via,* way), *va.* accompany.

Cop, v. *colp.*

Copé (on *cop,* q.v.), *pp. adj.* hollowed (of horse's hoof).

Corage (**corem + -age < -aticum*), *sm.* heart, soul, intention, mind. *Torner le c. de :* change one's attitude towards.

Cordoan (Sp. *cordobán,* via O. Pr. *cordoan*), *adj.* of Cordova ; *sm.* leather.

Corn, var. of **Cor** (*cornu*), *sm.* horn.

Coroné (*corōnatum,* or on *corone < corōna*), *pp. adj.* crowned ; tonsured.

Coroz (on *corrocier,* q.v.), *sm.* anger, grief.

Corre (*currere*), *vn.* run. *Laissier c. :* charge, give a horse its head.

Corrocier (*corruptiare, on *cor ruptum*), *va.* grieve, anger; *rfl.* become angry.

Cors, (1) (*corpus*), *sm.* body, person, corps. *Mon c. :* myself, my body; (2) (*cursum*, running), *sm.* course, race. *Le c.*, *adv.* : running. *Plein c. :* running; (3) nom. of *corn*, q.v.

Cort, (1) (PL. *curtem* for *cohortem*), *sf.* court, domain; (2) (*curtum*), *adj.* short.

Cortine (LL. *cortina*), *sf.* curtain, tapestry, tapestried room.

Coru, pp.; **Corul,** 1 pft. of *corre*, q.v.

Costoier, Costeer, Costier (on *coste* < *costa*, rib, side), *va. & n.* skirt, go by the side of, coast.

Cote, Cotte (Fk. *kotta), *sf.* close-fitting tunic.

Cou (*coquum*), *sm.* cook.

Coulte, Coute (*culcita*), *sf.* mattress, pillow, cushion.

Courre, v. *corre.* **Cov-,** try also *Conv-.* **Covei-,** v. *Covoi-.*

Covenant (pr. p. of *covenir*, q.v.), *sm.* agreement, vow. *Avoir en c. que :* promise, vow that.

Covenir (*convenire*, come together), *vn. & rfl.* meet, agree, suit; *impers.* must, is fitting.

Covent (*conventum*, agreement), *sm.* meeting, agreement; monastery, convent. *Avoir en c. :* promise, agree. *Par tel c. :* on the condition that. *Tenir c. :* keep one's promise.

Coverture (on pp. of *covrir* < *cooperire*, envelop), *sf.* covering, roofing; trickery.

Covir (*cupire for *cupere*, long for), *va.* desire, covet.

Covoitos (*cupidietōsum for *cupidum*), *adj.* covetous, desirous. *Estre c. :* desire, covet.

Craventer (*crepantare, on pr. p. of *crepare*, break with a crash), *va.* strike down, crush, shatter.

Creance, Credance (*crēdantia, or on *creire* < *crēdere*, believe), *sf.* faith, confidence.

Creanter (on pr. p. of *creire* < *crēdere*, believe), *va. & n.* pledge, swear, grant.

Crei, Creis, pr. of *creire* (*crēdere*), believe.

Creindre (*cremere for *tremere*), *va. & n.* fear.

Creissole, 1 impft. of *croistre*, q.v.

Crem-, forms of *creindre*, q.v.

Cremor (*cremōrem for *tremōrem*, trembling), *sf.* fear, awe.

Creole, 1 impft.; **Crerral,** 1 fut. of *creire* (*crēdere*), believe.

Crespi (on *cresp* < *crispum*, curly), *pp. adj.* in ringlets, curling, lined (face).

Crestiener (on *crestien* < Eccl. L. *christianum*, Christian), *va.* baptize.

Creüsse, impft. subj. of *croire* or of *croistre*, q.v.

Crever (*crepare*, break with a crash), *va., n. & rfl.* kill, destroy, dawn (day).

Criem-, forms of *creindre*, q.v.

Crient, 6 pr. of *crier*, q.v. or 3 pr. of *creindre*, q.v.

Crier (*critare for *quiritare*, shriek, ?), *va. & n.* call. *Estre* *crié de :* be accused of. *C. le ban :* proclaim.

Crignels (on **crinium*, on *crinem*), *sm. pl.* hair.

Croissir (**corruscire*, throw out sparks), *va. & n.* break, grate, grind.

Croistre (*crescere*), *vn.* grow.

Crolleis (on *croller*, q.v.), *sm.* shock; quagmire.

Croller (etym. doubtful, perh. **corotulare*), *va. & n.* wave, brandish, tremble.

Croute (*crypta*), *sf.* grotto, crypt.

Cruissir, v. *croissir.* **Cuels, Cuelt,** pr. of *coillir,* q.v.

Cuens (*comes*), nom. of *conte* (*comitem*), q.v.

Cuer (**corem* for *cor*), *sm.* heart.

Cuevre, pr. of *couvrir* (*cooperire,* envelop), cover.

Cuidier (**cugitare* for *cō-*, reflect), *vn.* think, expect, wish. *Au mien c. :* in my opinion. *C. enragier :* go nearly mad. *C. prendre :* be about to take, try to take.

Cuil-, try **Coil-.** **Cuit,** 1 pr. of *cuidier,* q.v. **Cuivert,** var. of *colvert,* q.v.

Cuivre (**coprium* for *cyprium* (*aes*), copper), *sm.* copper, copper-bowl.

Cure (*cūra*), *sf.* care. *Avoir c. de :* worry about, care for, take care to, desire. *Tenir c. de :* notice.

Curios (*cūriōsum*), *adj.* careful, anxious.

D

Dahet, v. *dehait.* **Dalez,** v. *delez.*

Dam, (1) (*damnum,* injury), *sm.*

harm. *Estre en d. a :* be detrimental to; (2) (*dominum,* lord, with special devel. of *o*), *sm.* lord, sir.

Damagier (on *damage,* on *dam* 1, q.v.), *va.* harm, wrong.

Dame (*domina,* cf. *dam* 2), *sf.* lady, or var. of *dam* 2, q.v.

Damedé, Damedieu, Damnedieu (*dominum deum*), *sm.* the Lord, God.

Dan, v. *dam* 2.

Dancel (**dom(i)nicellum,* on *dominum,* lord, infl. by *dan,* q.v.), *sm.* squire, youth.

Dangier (**domniarium,* power, infl. by *dan,* q.v.), *sm.* prerogative, power, resistance, whim; difficulty, peril.

Dansel, var. of *dancel,* q.v. **Dant,** v. *dam.* **Davant,** v. *devant.* **De-,** try also **Des-.**

Dé, var. of **Dieu** (*deum*), God.

Debatre (on *batre,* cf. *abatre*), *va., n. & rfl.* beat, oppose, resist, contest.

Debonaire (*de + bon + aire,* q.v.), *adj.* high-born, noble, good.

Deça (*de + ça,* q.v.), *prep. & adv.* this side (of).

Decevoir (**dēcipēre,* for *-ere*), *va.* deceive, disappoint, desert.

Deceivre (*dēcipere*), *va.* deceive, surprise.

Dechacier (on *chacier,* q.v.), *va.* chase, exile.

Deci (*de + ci,* PL. *ecce hic*), *prep.* from here, from now. *D. a ; D. en ; D. vers .* as many as, as far as. *D. en avant ; D. mais :* henceforth. *D. que :* until, as far as.

Decoste (on *coste* < *costa*, rib, side), *prep.* by the side of, along with.

Dedesoz (on *desoz*, q.v.), *adv. & prep.* beneath, below.

Deduire (*dēdūcere*, bring), *va., n. & rfl.* lead ; *rfl.* go away, amuse oneself.

Deduit (on *deduire*, q.v.), *sm.* amusement, sport, love-making, pleasure.

Def-, try also **Desf-**.

Defaillir (on *faillir*, q.v.), *vn.* fail, be missing.

Defaute (on *faute* < **fallita*, failing), *sf.* lack, want.

Defenir (on *fenir*, q.v.), *va. & n.* finish off, die.

Deffaé, v. *desfaé*.

Deffremer (*de* < *dis* + *fermer*, q.v.), *va.* open.

Defois (LL. *dēfē(n)sum*, forbidden), *sm.* fief, private territory; enclosure.

Defoler (on *foler*, q.v.), *va.* crush, ruin, lay waste to.

Defors (LL. *dēforis*, on *foris*, outside), *adv. & prep.* out, outside.

Degaster (**dewastare*, cf. *gaster*), *va.* ravage, destroy, ruin.

Degitter, v. *dejeter*.

Deguerpir (on *guerpir*, q.v.), *va.* abandon.

Dehait (*dé* < *deum* + root of Fk. **hatjan*, hate) : *D. ait* : cursed be.

Dehait (on *hait*, q.v.), *adj.* happy, cheerful.

Del-, try also **Dol-**. **Deis**, 2 pft.; **Deisse**, 2 impft. subj.; **Deistes**, 5 pft. & impft. subj. of *dire* < (*dīcere*), say.

Dejeter (on *jeter*, q.v.), *va., n. & rfl.* cast out, reject, hurl down, fall; *rfl. also* writhe.

Dejoste, Dejuste (on *joste*, q.v.), *adv. & prep.* near, alongside.

Delaier (on *laier*, q.v.), *va.* delay.

Deleit, v. *delit*.

Delez (on *lez*, v. *les*), *adv. & prep.* by the side of, alongside.

Delgié (*dēlicatum*, soft, delicate), *adj.* slender, tender.

Delit (*dēlictum*, crime), *sm.* fault, crime.

Delit (on *delitier*, q.v.), *sm.* delight, charm, pleasure.

Delitable (*dēlectabilem*), *adj.* delightful, agreeable.

Delitier (*dēlectare*), *va. & rfl.* delight, charm, rejoice. *Se d. en* : delight in.

Delivre (**dēliberum*, on LL *dēliberare*, free), *adj.* free, freed, agile. *Adv.* : **Delivrement**.

Delivrer (LL. *dēliberare*, free), *va.* free, deliver, empty, accomplish, pay for; *vn. & rfl.* hurry.

Demaine, pr. of *demener*, q.v., or var. of *demeine*, *adj. & sm.*, q.v.

Demeine (*dominicum*, lordly), *adj.* princely, personal, very. *Homme d.* : vassal; *sm.* domain; liegeman. *Also* pr. of *demener*, q.v.

Demener (on *mener*, q.v.), *va.* display, utter, shake, control; *vn. & rfl.* behave, go, writhe. *D. un propos* : discuss. *D. une feste* : celebrate a feast.

Dementer (**dēmentare*, on *mentem*, mind), *vn. & rfl.* lament, go mad. *Se d.* : lament bitterly.

Dementieres (*dum interea* + adv.
-s), *adv.* meanwhile, then.

Dementres (*dum interim* + adv.
-s), *adv.* meanwhile, then. *D.
que* : whilst.

Demeur (on *demorer*, q.v.), *sm.*
delay, stay.

Demeure (on *demorer*, q.v.), *sf.*
delay. *Faire d. a* : be slow
to.

Demeurer, v. *demorer*. **Demoine**,
pr. of *demener*, q.v. *Also* var.
of *demeine*, adj. & sm., q.v.

Demorer (*dēmorare* for *dēmorari*,
remain, delay), *va.*, *n.* & *rfl.*
remain, delay, be late. *Se d.* :
be late; remain alive. *D. de* :
give up the idea of. *N'iert
demoré* : it will not be long,
soon.

Demostrer (on *mostrer*, q.v.), *va.*
show.

Dent (*dentem*), *sm.*, later *sf.*
tooth. *A denz*, v. *adenz.
Entre ses denz* : inaudibly,
quietly.

Denz (LL. *de intus*), *adv.* & *prep.*
in, inside. *Also* form in -s of
dent, q.v.

Department (on *departir*, q.v.),
sm. share; departure.

Departir (on *partir*, q.v.), *va.*, *n.*
& *rfl.* separate, cut, share,
distribute; end, give a verdict;
depart; *sm.* departure.

Depecer, v. *despecier*. **De-
plaindre** = *plaindre*, q.v. **De-
plaint** = *plaint*, q.v.

Deport (on *deporter*, q.v.), *sm.*
amusement, pastime, joy.

Deporter (*dis* + *portare*), *va.*, *n.*
& *rfl.* amuse, distract, spare,
treat kindly; denounce; bear.

Depreindre (*dēprimere*, press
down), *va.* depress, make low.

Deproier (on *proier*, q.v.), *va.* &
n. beseech, pray, call upon.

Deputaire (*de* + *put*, q.v. + *aire*,
q.v.), *adj.* vile, low, low-born,
bad.

Deramer (*disramare*, sever
branches), *va.* tear, rip.

Derompre (on *rompre* < *rumpere*,
break), *va.*, *n.* & *rfl.* break,
tear, rout, break up.

Derot (on *ruptum*), *pp.* of *derompre*, q.v.

Derrain, Derrien (*dēretranum*,
on *dēretrō*, behind), *adj.* last.

Derriere (*dēretrō*), *adv.* behind.
En d. : later.

Derver, Desver (etym. obsc.), *vn.*
go mad. *Avoir le sen desvé* :
be mad.

Des-, try also **De-**.

Desacointier (on *acointier*, q.v.),
va. embroil, set at variance.

Desaffrer (on *saffre*, cf. *safré*), *va.*
take the yellow varnish off
(shield).

Desarmer (on *armer* < *armare*,
arm), *va.* help off with armour,
disarm, uncover (head).

Deschaus (*discalceum*, unshod),
adj. barefoot.

Desclore (on *clore*, q.v.), *va.* & *rfl.*
open, reveal.

Descoloré (on *color* < *colōrem*, colour), *pp. adj.* pale, wan.

Descombrer (on *combre*, cf. *encombrer*), *va.* & *rfl.* clear, free.

Desconfire (on *confire*, q.v.), *va.*
break, destroy, harm, vanquish.

Desconoistre (on *conoistre*, q.v.),
va. fail to recognize, not to
know; disguise.

Desconseillier (on *conseillier* <
cōnsiliare, for *cōnsiliari*, take
counsel), *va.* advise badly, deprive of advice or protection.
Desconseillé, pp. adj. : forlorn.

Descorder (*discordare*, cf. *acorder*), *va.* embroil, set at variance.

Descuevre, pr. of **Descovrir** (LL.
discooperīre, uncover), *v.a.*
disclose, uncover, discover ; *v.
rfl.* reveal one's secret.

Deserte (on *deservir*, q.v.), *sf.*
deserts, merit, value. *Sans
d.* : undeservedly.

Deservir (*dēservīre*, serve zeal-
ously), *va.* deserve, earn ; repay.

Deseur (on *seur*, v. *sor*, *sore*), *adv.
& prep.* on, upon, above, over.

Desevraille (on *desevrer*, q.v.), *sf.*
separation, difference.

Desevrer (on *sevrer*, q.v.), *va. &
rfl.* separate, sever, part.

Desf-, try also **Def-**.

Desfaé (on *fai* for *fei*, q.v., infl.
by *fatum*), *pp. adj.* infidel,
faithless.

Desfaire (on *faire*, q.v.), *va. & rfl.*
make reparation, undo ; bring
low, kill.

Desfier (on *fier*, q.v.), *va.* defy,
indicate hostility to, challenge.

Desfubler (on *fibula*, cf. *afubler*),
va. & rfl. undress, remove one's
cloak.

Desguaster (on *guaster*, q.v.), *va.*
lay waste.

Desirier (*dēsiderare*, long for), *sm.*
desire. *Selon mon d.* : ac-
cording to my wishes.

Desloer (on *loer* 1, q.v.), *va.*
blame, dissuade ; *v. rfl.* be
dissatisfied.

Desloer (*dislocare*, on *locum*,
place), *va. & rfl.* dislocate.

Desloier (on *loier* 2, q.v.), *va.*
loosen.

Desloier (on *loi*, q.v.), *v. rfl.* be
disloyal, be unworthy.

Desmaillier (on *maille*, mail,
q.v.), *va.* break the mail of
(armour).

Desmentir (on *mentir*, q.v.), *va.
& n.* belie, contradict, disown,
break.

Desmesure (on *mesure* < *mē(n)-
sūra*, measure), *sf.* excess. *A
d.* : extraordinarily, excessively.

Desnoer (on *noer*, q.v.), *va.* untie,
reveal.

Desnoier (on *noier* 1, q.v.), *va. &
n.* deny, declare untrue.

Desor, Desour, Desore (on *sor*,
sore, q.v.), *adv. & prep.* above,
over, on.

Desore, Desor (*des* < *dē ex*, + *ore*
< *hōra*), *adv.* from that moment.
Also var. of *desor*, *desour*, q.v.

Desoz, Desouz (on *soz*, q.v.),
prep. under, beneath.

Desparsement (on *despars* <
disparsum, scattered), *adv.* in
disorder.

Despecier (on *piece*, q.v.), *va. &
n.* break to fragments, stop,
separate.

Despendre (*dispendere*), *va. & n.*
spend, distribute largess.

Despire (*dēspicere*), *va.* despise.

Despit (*dēspectum*, looking down),
sm. scorn, shame. *El d. de* :
in scorn of, in order to shame.

Despoillier (*dēspoliare*, plunder),
va. & rfl. unclothe, undress ;
despoil.

Desprisier, Desproisier (on *proisier*, q.v.), *va. & rfl.* depreciate, scorn.

Desque (var. of *jusque*, infl. by *des < dě sx*), *prep.* as far as, until.

Desraisnier (on *raisnier*, q.v.), *va. n. & rfl.* dispute, explain, defend, relate, speak to.

Desreer (on Germ. *rêd-, cf. *areer*), *va.* throw into confusion; *v. rfl.* become disordered, be too impetuous.

Desrober (on *rober*, q.v.), *va.* rob, despoil.

Desroi (on *desreer*, q.v.), *sm.* disorder, confusion, harm, wickedness, pride.

Desrouter (on *route*, q.v.), *va., n. & rfl.* scatter, disband.

Dess-, try also **Des-**, e.g. **Dessaffrer**, v. *desaffrer*.

Dessi, v. *deci*.

Dessirier (on Fk. *skîran, scratch), *va.* tear.

Destor (on *destorner*, on *torner*, q.v.), *sm.* hidden spot, detour; combat (infl. of *estor*, q.v.).

Destorber (*disturbare*, throw into confusion), *va.* confuse, trouble, interfere, prevent; *sm.* (often **Destorbier**) difficulty.

Destordre (on *tordre*, q.v.), *va., n. & rfl.* twist, torture, turn from, unfurl, writhe.

Destors (pp. of *destordre*, q.v.), *pp. & adj.* unfurled.

Destre (*dextrum*), *adj.* right; *sf.* (*dextra*), right hand.

Destreindre (*distringere*, stretch), *va. & rfl.* torture, mortify, fast.

Destreit (*districtum*, pp. of *distringere*, stretch, tighten), *adj.*

narrow; distressed; harsh; *sm.* defile; distress. *En d. :* in custody.

Destresse (*districtia, on *districtum*, v. *destreit*), *sf.* narrow passage; distress; harshness.

Destros, var. of *destors*, q.v.

Desus (on *sus*, q.v.), *adv. & prep.* on, thereon, up.

Desuz, var. of *desoz*, q.v. **Desver**, var. of *derver*, q.v.

Desvoier (on *des < dis*-, + *voie < via*, way), *va. & n.* mislead, remove; lose oneself, stray.

Det-, try also **Dest-**.

Detenir (on *tenir*, q.v.), *va.* retain.

Deterrai, 1 fut. of *detenir*, q.v.

Detraire (*dětragere for *dětrahere*, remove), *va.* pull, drag, tear out.

Detrenchier (on *dětruncare*, cut off, with obsc. vowel change), *va.* cut to pieces, cut.

Detrés (*de + tres*, q.v.), *prep.* behind.

Deugié, v. *delgié*. **Deūs, Deūsse,** etc., pft. & impft. subj. of **Devoir** (*děběre*).

Devaler (on *val < vallem*, valley), *va. & n.* descend.

Devancer, Devancir (on *devant*, q.v.), *va.* precede, forestall.

Devant (*de + avant*, q.v.), *adv. & prep.* before (time & place).

Devenres (*diem Veneris*), *sm.* Friday.

Devers (on *vers*, q.v.), *prep.* towards, near, by.

Deveurent, pr. of *devorer* (*děvorare*), *va.* consume, devour.

Devier (on *vie < vîta*, life), *va. & n.* kill; die.

Deviner (*dīvīnare*, foretell), *va.* tell, talk of, mean, wish.

Devis (on *deviser*, q.v.), *sm.* division, desire, beauty. *A d. : Par d. :* well-planned, marvellously, beautifully.

Devise (on *deviser*, q.v.), *sf.* separation, division, talk, arrangement, device (on shield). *A d. :* according to plan.

Deviser (**dīvīsare*, on pp. of *dīvidere*, divide), *va. & n.* divide, discuss, decide, imagine, expound, speak, suggest, plan.

Dewaster, var. of *desguaster*, q.v.

Dex, Diex, case in -*s* of *deu, dieu* < *deum, sm.* God.

Di (*dīem*), *sm.* day. *Toz dis :* always.

Die, pr. subj.; **Di,** 1 pr.; **Dient,** 6 pr. of *dire* < *dīcere*, say.

Diemenche (**dīa dominica*, the Lord's day), *sm. & f.* Sunday.

Disent, Distrent, 6 pft.; **Disimes,** 4 pft.; **Disis,** 2 pft.; **Disisses,** 2 impft. subj. of **Dire** (*dīcere*), say.

Disme (*decima*), *sf. & sometimes sm.* tithe.

Dit (*dictum*, saying), *sm.* speech, tale, exposition.

Dobler (LL. *duplare*, double), *va.* line. *Halberc doblé :* lined or double-mailed hauberk. *Doblé en treis :* triple, triple-mailed.

Doel, var. of *duel*, q.v.

Doëlise (on *dōtalem*, relating to a dowry), *sf.* gifts, dowry.

Doi, nom. of *dous,* q.v. **Doigne,** pr. subj.; **Doin,** 1 pr.; **Doinse,** 1 pr. subj.; **Doinst,** 3 pr. subj. of *donner* < *dōnare*, give.

Doit (**ditum* for *digitum*), *sm.* finger.

Dol, var. of *duel*, q.v.

Dolent (**dolentum* for *dolentem*), *adj.* grieving, sorrowful, unfortunate.

Doloir (*dolēre*, suffer), *va., n. rfl. & impers.* suffer, complain, regret, grieve.

Doloser (connected with *dolēre*, suffer), *va., n. & rfl.* afflict, lament for, grieve.

Domagier, var. of *damagier*, q.v.

Don (*dōnum*), *sm.* gift. *Par vostre d. :* by your leave.

Donc (LL. *dunc*, from *dumque?*), *adv. & conj.* then.

Donge, 3 pr. subj. of *donner* < *dōnare*, give.

Donjon (**dominiōnem*), *sm.* chief hall of the castle, the lord's tower.

Donoiement (on *domina*, lady), *sm.* dalliance, amorous pastime.

Donques, var. (infl. by *onques,* q.v.) of *donc*, q.v. **Donrai,** 1 fut. of *donner* < *dōnare*, give.

Dont (*dē unde*, whence), *adv. & pron.* whence, of which, how. *Also* var. of *donc*, q.v.

Dorrai, v. *donrai*.

Dotance (on *doter*, q.v.), *sf.* fear, doubt, suspicion.

Doter (*dubitare*), *va., n. & rfl.* fear. *Se d. que :* fear that.

Dotos (on *doter*, q.v.), *adj.* redoubtable, timorous.

Dou-, try also **Do-**.

Doubtance, Doubter, v. *dotance, doter.* **Dougié,** var. of *delgié,* q.v. **Douneer,** var. of *donoier,* cf. *donoiement*.

Dous (*duos*), *num*. two.

Doüsse, etc., v. *deüs, deüsse*.

Dout, 1 pr. of *doter*, q.v.

Dreeier (*dīrēctiare, on *dīrēctum*, straight), *va., n. & rfl.* raise, prop up; *v. rfl.* rise.

Dreit (*dīrēctum*), *adj.* right, just, fitting; *adv.* straightway; *sm.* (LL. *dīrēctum*), right. *Avoir d. :* be in the right. *Avoir d. dans un país :* be the country's lawful ruler. *Faire d. a :* make amends. *Jugier le d. de :* judge a claim. *Ni a d. ni a tort :* without reason. *Par d. :* as is right. *Rendre son d. a :* give (him) his due, behave properly towards.

Droiture (on *droit*, v. *dreit*), *sf.* right, justice, reparation. *A d. :* outright, rightly.

Droiturier (on *droiture*, q.v.), *adj.* rightful.

Dru (Gaul. **druto-*, strong), *adj.* luxuriant, strong, gay, agile, favourite, lover.

Druerie (on *dru*, q.v.), *sf.* love-making, love, love-token, illicit love. *Mener d. :* practise love-making, make love.

Du-, try also **Do-**.

Dueil, Duel, Duelent, Duelt, pr. of *doloir*, q.v.

Duel, Dueil (3rd c. L. *dolum*, on *dolēre*, suffer), *sm.* grief, pain, loss, affliction. *A d. :* painfully, sorrowfully. *Faire, Mener d. :* display grief, be sorrowful.

Duerrai, 1 fut. of *durer* < *dūrare*, endure. **Dui**, var. of *doi*, q.v. or 1 pft. of *devoir* < *dēbēre*, owe, **be** obliged to.

Duire (*dūcere*, draw, lead), *va. & n.* lead, please, suit, stroke.

Duit (pp. of *duire*, q.v.), *adj.* skilled, clever.

Durement (on *dur* < *dūrum*, hard), *adv.* roughly, violently, hotly.

Durrai, 1 fut. of *durer* < *dūrare*, endure, or of *donner* < *dōnare*, give.

Dusque (*de* + *usque*), *prep.* as far as, until.

E

E = Et, and, *or* var. of *es*, lo !, q.v.

Eage (*aetaticum, on *aetatem*), *sm.* age, life, old age.

Edé, Eé, v. *aé*. **Edrant, Edrer**, v. *errant, errer* (travel). **Eff-**, try also **Esf-**. **Effant**, var. of *enfant* < *infantem*, child. **Efforcier**, v. *esforcier*.

Egal, v. *ivel*.

Egroté (*aegrōtatum*, sick), *adj.* stricken with illness.

Eidre, pr. & pr. subj. of *errer* (*iterare*), q.v., or var. of *oirre*, q.v.

Einchies, Einçois, Enchois, v. *ançois*. **Eins, Einz**, v. *ainz*. **Einsi**, v. *ensi*. **Eir**, v. *hoir*. **Eirre**, pr. & pr. subj. of *errer*, q.v., or var. of *oirre*, q.v. **Eirsoir**, v. *ersoir*. **Eis**, pr. of *issir*, q.v., or var. of *es* < *ĕcce*, q.v. **Eissi, Eissine**, v. *ensi*. **Eissi, Eissir, Eist, Eistrai**, forms of *issir*, q.v.

El (*en* + *le*), *art. contr.* in the, on the.

El (*ale for *alid*), *pron.* something else, other.

Ele (*ala*), *sf.* wing.

Elgal, v. *ivel.* **Elme**, v. *helme.*

Els (*illos*), *pron.* them. *Also art. contr.* = *en les*, in the.

Em-, try also **En-**.

Embasmer (on *basme* < *balsamum*, gum of the balsam-tree), *va.* embalm.

Embatre (on *batre*, cf. *abatre*), *va., n. & rfl.* plunge, penetrate; *v. rfl.* rush, hurl oneself. *Embatié*, 3 pft. *Embatre* also var. of *esbatre*, q.v.

Embler (*involare*, attack, seize), *va. & rfl.* steal; flee. **Emblant**, *pr. p. adj. :* furtive.

Embraeier (on *bras* < *brachium*, arm, or on *brace*, q.v.), *va.* take in the arms, take on the arm, hold against the breast (shield).

Embronchier (on *bruncare, stumble?), *va. & rfl.* bow, bend, fall forward, cause to fall forward. **Embronchié**, pp. : hidden, deep.

Embuschier (on *busche* < *búska for Germ. **búsk-*, stick), *va., n. & rfl.* ambush, hide, lie in wait. **Embuschié**, *pp. adj. : sometimes*, in a wood.

Emmi, v. *enmi.*

Empaindre (*impangere for *impingere*, strike), *va., n. & rfl.* thrust, launch, pierce, strike down, blow (horn), rush. *E. en mer; S'e. en mer :* embark, 3 pft. : **Empainst**.

Empainte (on *empaindre*, q.v.), *sf.* attack.

Empeindre (*impingere*), v. *empaindre.*

Empeirier (on *peior*, q.v.), *va., n. & rfl.* spoil, become worse, lay waste to, injure, slander.

Empené (on *pene* I, q.v.), *pp. adj.* feathered.

Emperedor, v. *emperĕor.*

Emperedre, Emperere (*imperator*), nom. of *emperĕor*, q.v.

Emperĕor (*imperatŏrem*, commander), *sm.* emperor.

Empeschier (LL. *impedicare*, trap), *va. & rfl.* take in a trap, trouble, hinder, prevent.

Empirier, v. *empeirier.*

Empleier (*implicare*, enfold), *va.* plunge, place, make use of, lay on (blows).

Empor (*en + por*, q.v.), *prep.* in order to, on account of, for.

Emprendre (on *prendre*, q.v.), *va., n. & rfl.* undertake, take, begin.

Emprés (on *pres*, q.v.), *adv. & prep.* near to; afterwards, then.

Empresser (on *presser*, q.v.), *va. & n.* press, press closely, hurry.

Empris, pp. of *emprendre*, q.v.

Emprise (pp. fem. of *emprendre*, q.v.), *sf.* enterprise, adventure.

En-, try also **Em-**.

En-. For verbs, try also the simple form, e.g. **Enoindre**, v. *oindre.*

En (*in*), *prep.* in, on.

En (*inde*), *adv. & pron.* from thence, thereof, of it, of him.

En, var. of *on*, v. *hom.* **Enceis**, v. *ançois.*

Encensier (on *encens* < Eccl. L. *incēnsum*, incense), *sm.* censer, thurible.

Encerchier (on *cerchier*, q.v.), *va.
& n.* search, seek, pursue, examine.

Enchalcier (on *calceum*, slipper),
va. pursue; *vn.* hurry.

Enchals (on *enchalcier*, q.v.), *sm.*
pursuit, urgent request. *A e. :*
with zeal, speedily.

Enchargier (on *chargier*, q.v.), *va.
& n.* take or put on the back
or in the arms, entrust, lay on
blows, attack; *vn.*, also, bear (a
child).

Enclin (on *encliner*, q.v.), *adj.*
bowed, sad, submissive.

Encliner (*inclinare*, incline), *va.,
n. & rfl.* bow down, bend for-
ward, greet, go down, put
down.

Encoi, v. *encui.* **Ençois,** v. *ançois.*

Encombrer (on *combre*, Gaul.
**comboro(s)*, pile of felled
trees), *va., n. & rfl.* hinder,
burden, prevent, tie up; *sm.*
misfortune, difficulty. *En-
combré,* pp. adj.: hesitant,
embarrassed.

Encontre (on *contre*, q.v.), *adv. &
prep.* against, towards, opposite, by comparison with.
Cheoir e. terre : fall heavily to
the ground. *Respondre e. :*
retort.

Encoste (on *coste*, cf. *decoste*), *adv.
& prep.* at the side of, along-
side.

Encoudre (on *coudre* < *côsere
for *cônsuere*, sew together), *va.
& rfl.* stitch, attach, sew up,
thrust in.

Encovir (on *covir*, q.v.), *va. & n.*
covet, try to obtain, select.

C

Encroier, Encroer (on *croc*, O. Sc.
krôkr, hook), *va., n. & rfl.*
hang, attach. *Espaules en-
croees :* round shoulders.

Encroser (etym. obsc.), *va. & rfl.*
plunge, plant.

Encui (*hinc hodiē*), *adv.* this very
day.

Encuser (*incûsare*, blame), *va.*
accuse.

Endemain (on *demain*, on *main* <
mane, q.v.), *sm.* the day following, morrow.

Endementieres, Endementres, cf.
dementieres, dementres.

Enditier (on *ditier* < *dictare*, re-
peat), *va. & n.* expound, indicate, dictate, compose, instruct.

Endormie (on *endormir* < *indor-
mire*, go to sleep), *sf.* sleeping-
draught.

Endreit (on *dreit*, q.v.), *adv. &
prep.* towards, opposite, in the
direction of, exactly. *E. sei :*
on his own side, for his part.
E. none : about 3 p.m. *Ici
e. :* right here. *Or e. :* this
very moment, at once; *sm.*
place, way, manner.

Endroit, v. *endreit.* **Endui,** v.
andui.

Eneslepas (*in ipsum + le pas,*
sm., q.v., but cf. *isnel*), *adv.*
immediately.

Enfance (*infantia*, childhood), *sf.*
childhood, folly, childishness.

Enfer(m) (*infirmum*, weak), *sm.*
cripple, sick man.

Enfes (*infans*), nom. of **Enfant**
(*infantem*), *sm.* child.

Enforcier (*infortiare, strength-
en), *va., n. & rfl.* strengthen,

grow strong, make great efforts; violate. **Enforcié,** pp. adj.: powerful, mighty, plentiful, well-endowed. *Var.:* **Enforcir.**

Enformer (*informare*), *va.* shape, instruct, inform; *v. rfl.* take shape, dress.

Enfouer, var. of **Enfouir** (**infodire* for -*ere*), *va.* bury, inter.

Enfrener (on *frener*, q.v.), *va.* furnish with reins; rein in, repress, prevent.

Enfuïr, var. of *enfouir,* v. *enfouer.*

Engaignier, v. *engeignier.*

Engan (var. of *engin*, q.v.?), *sm.* trick, deceit, roguery; toil.

Enganer (on *engan*, q.v.), *va., n. & rfl.* deceive, irritate, annoy.

Engeignier (on *engein,* v. *engin*), *va. & rfl.* deceive, torment.

Engeindre (*ingignere*, implant, infl. by *gignere*, beget), *va.* beget.

Engener, v. *engeignier* and *enganer.* **Engien,** v. *engin.* **Engignier,** v. *engeignier.*

Engin (*ingenium*, cleverness), *sm.* skill, cunning, deceit, trick, expedient.

Enginner, v. *engeignier.*

Engouler (on *goule,* v. *gole*), *va.* swallow, gulp down, thrust into the throat.

Engreignier (**ingrandiare*, on *grandiōrem* or *grandem*), *va. & n.* increase, grow greater.

Engrés (on *agrestem*, wild, ?), *adj.* impetuous, fiery, difficult, violent, wicked. *E. de :* desirous of, yearning to.

Engroté, v. *egroté.*

Enguardes (on *guarde*, q.v.), *sf. pl.* vanguard. *Faire les e.:* act as vanguard.

Enheldir, Enheudir (on *helt*, q.v.), *va.* provide with a hilt; incite.

Enherber (on *herbe* < *herba*, herb), *va.* poison.

Enjan, v. *engan.*

Enjusque (on *jusque*, q.v.), *prep. & conj.* until, as far as.

Enluminé (pp. of *enluminer*, on *inlūmināre*, make light), *pp. adj.* illuminated, glittering.

Enmi (*in medium*), *adv. & prep.* in the middle (of).

Enne, *interj. & interr. particle*, indeed; did (I) not. . . .

Ennubler (on *nubler*, q.v.), *va. & rfl.* cover with clouds, obscure.

Ennuit, v. *anuit.*

Enorter (**enortare*, on *hortari*, urge), *va.* exhort.

Enosser (on *os* < *ossum*, bone), *va. & rfl.* get a bone lodged in the throat, choke, strangle, kill.

Enpevrer (on *peivre* < *piper*, pepper), *va.* pepper, season (food).

Enprés, v. *emprés.*

Enque (LL. *encautum*, red ink), *sf.?* ink.

Enquenuit (*hinc* or *hanc* + *noctem*), *adv.* this very night, to-day.

Enquerre (**inquaerere* for *inquīrere*, interrogate), *va.* ask, inquire about, seek.

Enqui, Enquoi, v. *encui.*

Enqui (*hinc* + *hūc?* or var. of *encui*, qv.), *adv.* there. *D'e. en avant :* thenceforward.

Ens, v. *enz.* **Ensample,** v. *essemple.*

Enseeler (on *seeler*, q.v.), *va.* seal up.

Enseigne (*insignia*, distinguished by a token, *adj.* as *sf.*), *sf.* banner, war-cry, signal. *E. avoir de crier :* have as rallying-cry.

Enseignier (**insignare* for *insignire*, point out), *va.*, *n. & rfl.* point, point to, point out, reveal; teach, learn; bless, make the sign of the cross over.

Enseler (on *sele* < *sella*, seat), *va.* saddle.

Ensemble (*insimul*, at the same time), *adv. & prep.* together, with. *E. o*(*od*) *:* together with.

Ensement (*ensi*, q.v. + *-ment*), *adv.* in the same way, thus, equally.

Ensevre, v. *ensivre.*

Ensi, Ensinc (etym. obsc.), *adv.* thus. *E. que :* so that, whilst.

Ensient, v. *escient.*

Ensivre (on *sivre*, q.v.), *va.*, *n. & rfl.* follow, continue, happen.

Ensoignier, Ensonnier (on *soing*, q.v.), *va.*, *n. & rfl.* occupy, trouble, excuse oneself.

Ensorquetot (*in* + *super* + *quam* + **tottum* for *totum*), *adv.* moreover, above all.

Ensuivre, v. *ensivre.* **Ent,** v. *en*, adv.

Entaille (on *taillier*, q.v.), *sf.* carving, window-opening, window, vizor; quality.

Entalenté (on *talent*, q.v.), *pp. adj.* willing, eager.

Entechier (on *teche*, q.v.), *va.* endow (with good or bad qualities).

Entendre (*intendere*, extend, direct the thoughts to), *va. & n.* attend, listen to, hear, understand, intend; stretch. *E. a :* give heed to, give in to, be intent upon.

Entente (*intenta*, pp. fem. of *intendere*), *sf.* intention, meaning, care, thought, attention. *A vostre e. :* as you understand, of course, as you wish. *Metre s'e. :* concentrate (on).

Ententif (on *entente*, q.v.), *adj.* attentive, intending to, careful to.

Entercier (**intertiare*, sequestrate, on *tertium*), *va.* seize, seek out, pick out, recognize.

Enterin (on *entier* < *integrum*, whole), *adj.* complete, pure, loyal; *sm.* whole.

Enterrai, 1 fut. of *entrer* < *intrare*, enter.

Entoischier, Entoschier (Med. L. *intoxicare*, on *toxicum*), *va.* poison.

Entor, Entour (on *tor* 3, q.v.), *adv. & prep.* around, towards. *A l'e. :* around.

Entre-. In refl. verbs, *s'entre-* = one another.

Entre (*inter*, between), *prep.* between, among. *Entre . . . e :* both . . . and.

Entrelacier (on *lacier*, q.v.), *va.* interlace, lace.

Entremés (on *mes* < *missum*, put), *sm.* argument; amusement; medium, entremet.

Entremetre (on *metre*, q.v.), *va. & rfl.* place amid, mingle; concern oneself with.

Entrepris (pp. of *entreprendre*, on *prendre*, q.v.), *adj.* seized, embarrassed, in sad plight, ill, surrounded.

Entreque, Entresque (on *intrō +usque*, or on *tresque*, q.v.), *prep.* up to, until.

Entroblier (on *oblier*, q.v.), *va.* forget.

Entrues, Entruef (on *entresque?*), *adv. & prep.* during, meanwhile.

Enuier (LL. *inodiare*, on *in odio esse*, to be hated), *va., n., rfl. & impers.* trouble, grieve, harm.

Enuit, v. *anuit*, or 3 pr. subj. of *enuier*, q.v.

Envale (pp. fem. of *envaïr < *invadire* for *invadere*, invade), *sf.* invasion, attack, assault.

Enveillier (on *veillier*, q.v.), *va., n. & rfl.* awake.

Enveillir (on *vieil*, q.v.), *vn.* grow old.

Entrevenir (on *venir*, q.v.), *v. rfl.* attack each other, come together.

Envers (on *vers*, q.v.), *prep.* towards, compared with.

Envis (*invitus*), *adv.* against one's will, with difficulty, with regret. *Syn.* **A envis.**

Envoisier (on *voisier < vitiare*, corrupt), *vn. & rfl.* amuse oneself, be gay.

Envoleper (on *voloper*, etym. unkn.), *va.* envelop.

Enz (*intus*), *adv. & prep.* in, inside. *E. en :* inside.

Er, Erent, fut.; **Ere, Erent,** impft., of *estre < *essere*, be. **Erité,** v. *herité*. **Ermin,** v. *hermin*. **Erragier,** v. *esragier*.

Erranment, Erraument (on *errant*, q.v.), *adv.* at once, straightway.

Errant (*iterantem*, on *iter*, journey), *adv.* at once, straightway.

Erre, v. *oirre*.

Errement (on *errer < iterare*), *sm.* habit. *Also* var. of *arrement*, q.v.

Errer (*errare*, stray), *va. & n.* deceive, stray, sin.

Errer (*iterare*, on *iter*, journey), *va., n. & rfl.* travel, wander; proceed, act ; *sm.* journey.

Ersoir (*ier < heri*, yesterday, *+ soir < sēro*, late), *adv.* last night.

Ert, 3 impft. or fut. of *estre < *essere*, be.

Es-. For verb forms, try also the simple infinitive.

Es (*ĕcce*), *prep.* here is, lo, behold.

Es (*en les*) *art. contr.* in the.

Esbaïr (on *baer*, q.v., with change of conjug.), *va., n. & rfl.* astonish, frighten.

Esbaldir (on *balt*, q.v.), *va. & rfl.* embolden, rejoice, enjoy oneself, display joy ; *pp. also =* violent.

Esbanier, Esbanoier (etym. obsc.), *va., n. & rfl.* amuse, amuse oneself.

Esbatre (on *batre*, cf. *abatre*), *va. & rfl.* beat ; amuse. *S'e. sor :* fall upon, attack.

Esbaudir, v. *esbaldir*. **Escalgaite,** v. *eschargaite*. **Escanteler,** v. *eschanteler*.

Escachier, Escacier, var. of *esquacier*, q.v.

Escarimant (etym. unkn.), *adj. & sm.* silken cloth.

Escarlate (Pers. *saqirlât*, from Arab. *siqillat*, cloth decorated with seals), *sf.* fine cloth, probably of reddish-blue.

Eschacier (on *eschace*, wooden leg, Fk. **skatja*), *adj.* lame, limping.

Eschaitif (on *chaitif*, q.v.), *adj.* miserable, bereft of help, captive.

Eschaitiver (on *chetiver* < LL. *captīvare*, take captive), *va.* take prisoner, enslave, despoil.

Eschange (on *eschangier* < **excambiare*, exchange), *sm.* exchange, substitute. *Avoir e. de :* have a substitute for. *Doner e. de :* replace. *Doner e. efforcé de :* give a better substitute for. *Prendre e. de :* accept in exchange.

Eschanteler (on *chantel*, q.v.), *va., n. & rfl.* break into fragments.

Eschar(n) (on *escharnir*, q.v.), *sm.* taunt, mockery, shame.

Eschargaite (Fk. **skârwahta*, on **skâra*, troop, + **wahta*, watch), *sf.* watch (people or action), watch-tower.

Eschari (etym. obsc., perh. on *eschar*, q.v. or *eschars*, q.v.), *adj.* small, wretched, few, sparsely populated, with few companions (of a knight, etc.).

Escharnir (Fk. **skernjan*), *va., n. & rfl.* mock at, taunt.

Escharpe (Fk. **skerpa*, satchel), *sf.* bag, pocket, pilgrim's purse ; *rarely* scarf.

Eschars (**excarpsum* for *excerpsum*, tight), *adj.* miserly.

Eschas (on Arabo-Pers. *shâh*, king), *sm. pl.* chess.

Eschele, v. *eschiele.* **Eschelgaite,** **Eschergaite,** v. *eschargaite.*

Eschevi, Eschewid (on Fk. **skafjan*, shape, ?), *adj.* slender.

Eschiec (Fk. **skak*), *sm.* booty. *Also* var. of *eschas*, q.v.

Eschiele, Eschiere (Fk. **skâra*, troop), *sf.* band of armed men, division, battalion.

Eschiez (Germ. *skip, skif,* boat), *sm.* warships.

Eschif (Germ. **skiuh,* cf. *eschiver*), *adj.* hostile, discontent, bereft, difficult. *E. a ; E. de :* unwilling to.

Eschignier, cf. *reschignier.*

Eschiver (Germ. **skiuhan,* fear, shy), *va. & rfl.* avoid, escape from, prevent. *E. sa voie :* lose one's way.

Escient (*sciente*). **Esclentre** (*scienter*). *A e. :* voluntarily, wittingly. *Par mien e. ; Mien e. :* from, to, or with my knowledge.

Esclace (onom.?), *sf.* splash, gushing.

Esclachier (onom. ?), *va. & n.* break.

Esclairier (**exclariare*, on *clarum,* clear), *va., n. & rfl.* clear up, explain, solace, light, enlighten, shine ; *v. impers.* lighten.

Esclarcir (**exclaricire*, on *clarum,* cf. Late L. *claricare*, shine), *va. & n.* lighten, become light, shine, explain. *S'e. vers :* smile upon. *Haubert esclarci :* thinly-mailed hauberk.

Esclargier (**exclaricare*, on Late L. *claricare*, shine), *va.* lighten.

light up, declare. *Var. :*
Esclargir.

Esclicier (on *esclice* < **slitia*, on
Fk. **slîtî*, slit), *va., n. & rfl.*
break to fragments, splinter.

Esclot (Germ., cf. Icel. *sloth*), *sm.*
shoe, horseshoe, track, trail,
hoof (animal). *Changier es-
clos :* change course.

Escoer (on *coe*, q.v.), *va.* cut the
tail off.

Escolte (on *escolter* for *ascolter*,
q.v.), *sm.* spy.

Escombatre (on *combatre* < **com-
battere* for LL. *combattuere*), *va.,
n. & rfl.* fight, conquer in
battle. *S'e. de :* prevent.
Escombatu, pp. : vanquished.

Escomengier, Escomunier (Eccl.
L. *excommūnicare*), *va.* excom-
municate.

Escondire (LL. *excondicere*, on
condicere, agree), *va.* exculpate,
defend; refuse, reject; *v. rfl.*
excuse oneself, justify oneself.

Esconser, v. *asconser.*

Escorcier (on *corcier* < **curtiare*,
on *curtum*, short), *va. & n.*
shorten; *v. rfl.* lift up the
hem of the dress.

Escorcier (on *corse*, on pp. of
currere, run), *va., n. & rfl.* run,
spread.

Escorre (on *corre*, q.v.), *vn.* run,
run away, hurl oneself.

Escorre (*excutere*, shake out), *va.*
shake.

Escremir (Germ. **skirmjan*, protect), *va., n. & rfl.* fence, defend
oneself.

Escrever (on *crever*, q.v.), *va., n.
& rfl.* break, burst, dawn (day).

S'e. a plorer ; S'e. de plorer :
burst into tears.

Escrier (on *crier*, q.v.), *va., n. &
rfl.* call, call upon, call out.

Escrisis, 2 pft. of **Escrire** (*scri-
bere*), *va. & n.* write.

Escu (*scūtum*), *sm.* shield. *E.
bendé,* v. *bendé. E. voti :*
arched or curved shield.

Esculer (*scūtarium*, shield-bear-
er), *sm.* squire, shield-maker
(*rare*).

Esforcier (on *forcier* < **fortiare*),
va., n. & rfl. seize, violate;
make an effort, regain strength,
strengthen. *Eschange esfor-
cié :* advantageous exchange.
Cité esforciee : powerful city.

Esfort (on *esforcier*, q.v.), *sm.*
armed force, reinforcement.
A e. : with speed, in great
force. *Par e. :* powerfully.

Esfraer, Esfreer (**exfridare*, on
Germ. **fridu*, peace), *va. &
rfl.* disturb, perturb, frighten,
anger.

Esfrei (on *esfreer*, q.v.), *sm.* fight,
commotion, rage.

Esgarder, v. *esguarder.*

Esgarer (on *garer*, Fk. **warôn*,
take care), *va.* put aside, repel,
dismay, lose. *Esgaré*, pp. adj. :
alone, abandoned, distressed,
embarrassed.

Esgart (on *esgarder*, q.v.), *sm.*
look, sight, opinion; conduct;
care. *En e. de :* intent upon.
Faire e. : decide, consider.
Par e. ; Por e. : justly.
Prendre e. : reach a conclu-
sion. *Se metre en e. de :* submit to. *Tenir l'e. :* deliberate.

**Esgraignier, Esgriner, Esgruig-
nier** (etym. unkn.), *va.*, *n. &
rfl.* break, break to fragments,
notch, destroy.

Esguarder (on *guarder*, q.v.), *va.
& n.* look, look at, examine,
seek, choose, decide, decree,
take heed.

Eslais (on *eslaissier*, q.v.), *sm.*
dash, gallop. *A e. ; D'e. :* at
full speed. *Le grant e. :* at
full gallop.

Eslaissier (on *laissier*, q.v.), *va.,
n. & rfl.* gallop, ride full gallop,
rush forward. *Eslaissé*, pp.
adj. : speedy, galloping. *S'e. a:*
rush forward, let oneself go.

Eslongier (on *long*, v. *lonc*), *va. &
n.* remove to a distance, expel,
leave behind, leave ; lengthen.

Esmaier (*exmagare*, render in-
capable, on Germ. *magan*, be
able), *va., n. & rfl.* dismay,
discourage, disturb, frighten ;
be troubled, etc. *S'e. de parler :* be afraid to speak, worry
about speaking.

Esmal (Fk. *smalt*), *sm.* enamel,
varnish.

Esmarir, Esmarrir (on *marrir*,
q.v.), *va., n. & rfl.* trouble,
grieve, distress, disconcert,
frighten.

Esme (on *esmer*, v. *asmer*), *sm.
& f.* value, opinion, plan, ges-
ture, aim. *Dire son e. :* speak
one's mind. *Estre a e. de :* be
about to. *Faillir a son e. ;
Perdre son e. :* miscalculate.
Par e. : approximately.

Esmer, v. *asmer*.

Esmeré (on *mier*, q.v.), *adj.* pure,
refined.

Esmolu (on pp. of *exmolere* for
ēmolere, grind away), *pp. adj.*
pointed, sharpened.

Esmovoir (*exmovēre* for *ēmovēre*,
set in motion), *va. & rfl.* set in
motion, start, move, incite. *E.
une querelle :* start or reopen
a quarrel.

Espaenter (*expaventare*, on *pa-
ventem*, fearing), *va.* terrify ;
v. rfl. be afraid.

Espardre (*spargere*), *va., n. & rfl.*
scatter, spread, disperse.

Espars, pp. of *espardre*, q.v.

Espartir (on *partir*, q.v.), *va., n.
& rfl.* part, separate, split.

Espartir (on *espart* for *esparc*,
Germ. *sparke*, spark, crackle),
v. impers. lighten.

Espaventer, v. *espaenter*.

Especiaument (on *especial* < *spe-
cialem*, particular), *adv.* especially.

Esperitable (on *spīritum*, breath
of life, + *-abilem*), *adj.* spirit-
ual.

Espié, Espiel (Fk. *speut*, hunt-
ing-spear), *sm.* spear, lance,
pike, stake.

Espleit (*explicitum*, accomplish-
ment), *sm.* success, diligence,
advantage, exploit, income.
A e. : energetically, at full
speed. *Faire e. :* be successful. Cf. also *esploitier*.

Esploitier (*explicitare*, perform
successfully), *va., n. & rfl.* succeed, carry out, accomplish,
act (well, badly, vigorously,
cleverly), hasten, travel. *Bien
e. :* do well. *L'e. :* succeed.
Mal e. : do wrong.

Espoenter, v. *espaenter*.

Espoir (*spēro*, I hope), *adv.* perhaps, about. *Al mien e. :* in
my view. *Also* 1 pr. & pr.
subj. of **Esperer** (*spērare*), hope.

Esponde (*sponda*, bedstead), *sf.*
edge (of bed, table), rampart,
support.

Espondre (*expōnere*, set out), *va.*
explain, reveal; abandon; *pp.*
Espost (*expositum*).

Esprendre (on *prendre*, q.v.), *va.,
n. & rfl.* light, set fire to; catch
fire, be inflamed, be aflame
with desire.

Espringuer (Fk. *springan*), *va.
& n.* leap, gambol, dance.

Esprins, pp. of *esprendre*, q.v.

Esprevier, var. of **Espervier**
(Fk. *sparwâri*), *sm.* sparrow-
hawk.

Esquacier (on *quacier* < *quassare*,
shake), *va.* crush, break.

Esquier, v. *escuier.* **Esquif**, v.
eschif.

Esrachier (*exradicare* for *ēradī-
care*, uproot), *va. & n.* tear,
carry off by force; be uprooted.

Esragier (on *rage* < *rabia* for
rabies, madness), *vn. & rfl.*
go mad, rage, rave. *Also* var.
of *esrachier*, q.v.

Essaier (*exagiare*, weigh), *va. &
rfl.* try, test (valour, etc.).
S'e. a : make an attempt at.
Essaié, pp. adj. : proven,
valiant.

Essart (LL. *exsartum*, on *sarire*,
hoe), *sm.* cleared land, burnt
clearing, tilled land, destruction, slaughter.

Essaucier (on *haucier*, q.v.), *va.,
n. & rfl.* raise, exalt, add to the
reputation of, accomplish.

Essemple (*exemplum*), *sm.* ex-
ample, model, tale, illustra-
tion. *Also sf.* (*exempla, n. pl.*
as *sf.*), *in the same sense.*

Essient, v. *escient.*

Essil (*exilium*, exile), *sm.* exile;
destruction, ruin; misery.

Essilier (on *essil*, q.v.), *va. & rfl.*
exile, ravage, ruin, destroy,
bring harm to; suffer exile.

Essoigne, Essoine (on *soing*, q.v.),
sf. excuse, obstacle, difficulty,
danger.

Estache (Germ. *stake*), *sf.* stake;
fig. support.

Estachier (Germ. *stakôn*), *va.,
n. & rfl.* fasten, fix, attack;
pierce; be fixed, planted.

Estage (*staticum*, on *stare*), *sm.
& f.* dwelling, abode, stay;
state, rank; stage. *Chascun
en son e. :* each one. *En e. :*
standing. *Estre en son e. :*
stand, stay still. *Prendre son
e. :* stop. *Tenir en son e. :*
hold sway over.

Estal (Fk. *stall*, position, abode),
sm. place, stake, dwelling,
platform. *Donner e. :* stand
firm against. *En e. ; A e :*
firmly, in the same place.
Faire e. ; Se metre a e. : stop.
Livrer e. : give battle. *Muer
e. :* move, yield a position.
Prendre e. : take one's stand,
take up position. *Remaindre
en e. :* stand firm. *Rendre e. :*
re-attack. *Se tenir en e. :*
stand firm. *Tenir e. :* stand
firm.

Estance (*stantia*, on *stare*,
stand), *sf.* dwelling, place, stop,
situation. *En e. :* standing.

Estanchier (etym. obsc.; *ex* +
LL. *stancare* for *stagnare*, over-
flow,?), *va., n. & rfl.* stop, close,
prevent, dry up, finish, fall
exhausted.

Estant (*stantem*, pr. p. of *stare*,
stand), *adj.* standing; *sm.*
position. *Estre en e. :* remain
standing, stand. *Remaneir en
e. :* remain standing.

Ester (*stare*, stand), *vn. & rfl.*
stand, be, be quiet, remain,
stop, dwell. *E. bien a :* suit,
please. *Laissier e. :* let be,
leave in peace, be quiet. *S'e. :*
stop, stand. *Se dresser en e. :*
rise, get to one's feet.

**Esteûmes, Esteûs, Esteûsse, Es-
teûst,** pft. & impft. subj. forms
of *ester*, q.v. or of *estoveir*, q.v.
Estez, imper. pl. of *ester*, q.v.
Estiquier, v. *estachier*.

Estoire (*historia*), *sf.* story, his-
tory.

Estoire (Med. L. *storium*, on Gk.
stolos), *sm. & f.* fleet, army.

Estolt (*stultum*, fatuous), *adj.*
proud, violent, arrogant,
heroic.

Estoltie (b. *stultitia*, folly), *sf.*
reckless courage, recklessness,
folly.

Estoner (**extonare* for *attonare*,
stun), *va., n. & rfl.* daze,
deafen, shake; resound; be
stunned, be frightened.

Estont, 6 pr. of *ester*, q.v.

Estor (Fk. **sturm*, storm), *sm.*
combat, battle, assault, engagement, joust. *Faire e. :*
give battle. *Rendre l'e. a :*
give battle to. *Vaincre l'e. :*
win the battle.

Estordre (**extorcere* for *extorquēre*,
wrest), *va., n. & rfl.* twist,
overthrow, drag out, escape,
come out; *vn. & rfl., usually,*
escape, twist out of.

Estore, v. *estoire*.

Estorer (*instaurare*, prepare, begin anew), *va. & rfl.* construct,
establish, govern, furnish, prepare.

Estoveir, Estovoir (infin. on
estuet < est opus, impers.,?), *v.
impers.* be necessary, need, be
fitting; *sm.* needs, necessity,
duty. *Par e. :* of necessity.

Estovra, 3 fut. of *estoveir*, q.v.
Estragnier, v. *estrangier*. **Es-
trai,** 1 fut. of *estre < *essere*,
be.

Estraier (on *strata*, pavement),
vn. stray, wander; *pp.* wandering freely.

Estrain (*stramen*), *sm.* straw,
litter.

Estraindre, v. *estreindre*.

Estrait (*extractum*), pp. of **Es-
traire** (**extragere* for *extrahere*,
extract), born, descended.

Estrange, Estragne (*extraneum*),
adj. foreign.

Estrangier (on *estrange*, q.v.), *va.,
n. & rfl.* estrange, remove, put
on one side, alienate; *vn. &
rfl.* go away, estrange; *sometimes* alter.

Estre (*ext(e)ra*, outside), *sm.*
place, position, room, garden;
pl. surrounds. *Also* **Estre**
(subst. infin., **essere*, be), *sm.*
being, manner, nature, custom.

Estre (*extra*), *prep.* outside, in
addition to, without. *E. mon
gré :* against my will.

Estree (*strata*, pavement), *sf.* way, road ; journey (*rare*).

Estreindre (*stringere*), *va.*, *n. & rfl.* clasp, embrace, press, tighten, seize (love, fear, etc.), constrain, control. *E. les denz :* grit the teeth. *S'e. de :* be obliged to.

Estreit, v. *estroit.*

Estreu, Estrieu (Fk. **streup,* strap), *sm.* stirrup.

Estril (var. of *estrit,* Fk. **strîd-*), *sm.* quarrel, dispute, struggle, strife, distress.

Estriver (Germ., cf. G. *streben*), *va. & n.* strive, contest, rival, quarrel.

Estroer (on *troer,* q.v.), *va.* pierce. *Estroé,* pp. adj.: pierced, worn out, full of holes.

Estroit (*strictum,* tight), *adj.* narrow, in close array ; *adv.* tightly, closely ; *sm.* defile.

Estros (on *estrousser,* q.v.), *adj.* resolute. *A e. :* ardently, completely, at once, insistently. (*Syn. :* **Estroussement,** *adv.*)

Estrousser (**extorciare* for *extorquère,* twist), *va.* break, interrupt, promise.

Estuece, pr. subj. ; **Estuet,** pr. of *estoveir,* q.v.

Estuier (etym. obsc.), *va.*, *n. & rfl.* sheath, shut up, save.

Esturent, 6 pft. of *ester,* q.v. **Estut,** 3 pft. of *ester,* q.v., or of *estoveir,* q.v.

Esvertuer (on *vertu,* q.v.), *va. & rfl.* fortify, strengthen, make a great effort.

Esvuidier (on *vuidier,* q.v.), *va.*,

n. & rfl. empty, quit, nullify (intention). *Var. :* **Esveudier.**

Eue, v. *eve.* **Eulz,** etc., v. *ueil.*

Eür (**agŭrium* for *augurium,* omen), *sm.* chance, fortune.

Eüré (on *eür,* q.v.), *pp. adj.* fortunate, happy.

Eüsse, etc., impft. subj. of *avoir* < *habēre,* have.

Eve (*aqua*), *sf.* water, stream.

Evel, v. *ivel.*

Ex (*oculos*), *sm. pl.* eyes (*pl.* of *ueil,* q.v.).

Exil, Exill, v. *essil.*

F

Face, Fache, Faiche, pr. subj. of *faire,* q.v.

Fade (**fapidum* or *vapidum + fatuum?*), *adj.* weak, insipid.

Faé (pp. of *faer* < **fatare,* on *fatum,* destiny), *pp. adj.* enchanted, bewitched.

Fael, v. *feeil.*

Faeler, Faieler (etym. obsc.), *va.* split, crack.

Faillance (on *faillir,* q.v.), *sf.* lack, weak point, weakness, wrong. *Ne faire f. :* not to fail. *Sans. f. :* without fail, assuredly.

Faille (on *faillir,* q.v.), *sf.* lack, deceit. *A f. :* in vain, to no effect. *Faire f. a :* lose. *Sans f. :* without fail.

Faillir (**fallīre* for *fallere,* deceive), *va.*, *n.,* *rfl. & impers.* fail, cease, lack ; *v. impers.* be necessary. *Failli,* pp. adj.: weak, coward, wicked.

Fain, var. of *fein,* q.v., or

of Faim (*famem*), *sf.* hunger.
Faindre, v. *feindre.*

Faire (*facere*), *va., n. & rfl.* do,
make, act. *Coment le fet :*
how is . . .? *F. a :* deserve,
occasion, be wise to. *F.
d'armes :* prove oneself a warrior. *Fet escolter :* it is necessary to listen to, it is wise to
listen to. *F. que :* behave
like. *F. tant que :* see to it that,
act in such a way that. *Se f. :*
become, turn.

Fais (*fascem*, bundle), *sm.* burden,
bundle, grief. *A f. :* all together, at once, suddenly, with
regret. *A un f. :* all together,
at once, suddenly. *Se metre
a f. :* undertake, take upon
oneself.

Faitement (on *faite*, pp. fem. of
faire, q.v.), *adv.* in this way,
how. *Com f. :* how, in what
way. *Si f. :* how, in the same
way.

Faiteur (Eccl. L. *factōrem*), *sm.*
the Creator. *Also* doer (CL.
factōrem).

Faitis (*facticium*, artificial), *adj.*
well-made, elegant, handsome.
F. a, pour : designed for,
suited to.

Faitre (Eccl. L. *factor*), nom. of
faiteur, q.v.

Faiture (*factūra*, fabrication), *sf.*
doing, face, form, creature.

**Faldestoed, Faldestoef, Falde-
stoel** (Fk. *faldistôl*, folding
chair), *sm.* chair of state.

Faldrai, 1 fut. ; **Falent,** 6 pr. of
faillir, q.v.

Fame (*fama*), *sf.* reputation,
renown, rumour.

Fanc (etym. obsc., perh. Germ.,
cf. Goth. *fani,* mud), *sm.* mire,
mud.

Fauc (LL. *falco*), nom. of **Falcon**
(LL. *falcōnem,* perh. of Germ.
orig.), *sm.* falcon; small can-
non.

Faudestuef, v. *faldestoef.* **Fault,**
pr. of *faillir,* q.v.

Faus (*falsum*), *adj.* false. *Also*
var. of *fols,* nom. of *fol,* q.v.,
or var. of *fauc,* q.v.

Fausser (LL. *falsare*), *va.* falsify,
accuse of falseness, damage,
tear (armour).

Fautre, v. *feltre.*

Feable (*fei,* q.v. + *-abilem*), *adj.*
faithful, loyal.

Fealté (*fidēlitatem*), *sf.* loyalty,
sincerity, homage due to an
overlord.

Feeil (*fidēlem*), *adj.* faithful,
loyal; *sm.* loyal servant, subject.

Fei (*fidem*), *sf.* faith, loyalty,
pledge. *Par f. :* truly, indeed.

Feimenti (*fei,* q.v. + *menti,* pp.
of *mentir,* q.v.), *adj.* perjuror,
one who breaks his sworn
word.

Fein (*fēnum*), *sm.* hay.

Feindre (*fingere,* fashion, invent),
va., n. & rfl. pretend, dissimu-
late. *Se f. :* hesitate, pretend
to be, be faint-hearted.

Feinsis, Feinst, 2 & 3 pft. of
feindre, q.v. **Feis,** 2 pft. ;
Feismes, 4 pft. ; **Feïsse,** impft.
subj. of *faire,* q.v. **Feitis,** v.
faitis.

Feiz (*vicem,* change, turn), *sf.*
time. *A ceste f. :* now, for
now, on this occasion.

Fel (Carol. L. *fello*), nom. of
Felon (*fellōnem*, perh. of Germ.
orig.), *adj. & sm.* cruel, harsh,
pitiless, wicked, perfidious, furious, terrible, traitor.

Felenie, Felonie (on *felon*, v. *fel*),
sf. wickedness, cruelty, treachery.

Feltre (Fk. **filtir*), *sm.* felt.

Fenir (*finīre*), *va. & n.* finish,
die.

Feoil, v. *feeil.*

Ferain (on *fier* 1, q.v., or on L.
fera, wild beast), *adj.* wild;
sm. wild beast.

Ferarmé (*fer < ferrum*, iron, +
armé < armatum, armed), *adj.*
barded with iron, clad in
armour.

Fereïs (on *ferir*, q.v.), *sm.* strik-
ing, blow, clash.

Ferir (*ferīre*), *va., n. & rfl.* strike,
knock, plunge, spur on. *F.
en :* enter into. *Se f. (en) :*
rush (into).

Fer(m) (*firmum*), *adj.* firm, strong,
fortified.

Fermail (on *fermer*, q.v.), *sm.*
clasp, brooch, bolt.

Fermer (*firmare*, strengthen), *va.
& rfl.* strengthen, fix, fasten,
fortify. *F. le heaume :* lace
the helmet on the head. *Gonfanon fermé :* gonfalon fast-
ened to the end of the lance.

Fermeté (on *ferme*, cf. *ferm*), *sf.*
fortification, fortress, firmness.
A f. : assuredly, certainly.

Ferons, 4 pr. of *ferir*, q.v., or 4
fut. of *faire*, q.v.

Ferrant (pr. p. of *ferrer < *fer-
rare*, on *ferrum*, iron), *adj.* grey,
greying ; *sm.* grey horse, horse.

Ferté (*firmitatem*), cf. *fermeté* for
sense. **Feru,** pp. of *ferir*, q.v.

Fervestu (*fer < ferrum*, iron, +
vestu, v. *vestir*), *adj.* iron-clad,
clad in armour.

Fes, v. *fais.* **Fesimes, Fesis,** 4 &
2 pft. of *faire*, q.v.

Feste (*festa* (*dies*)), *sf.* feast,
festival. *F. anoel :* high
feast. *Faire f. a :* welcome
with joy.

Feste (on *fest,* sm., Fk. **first*), *sm.
& f.* crest, summit, top. *As
festes :* aloft, on high.

Festiier, Festoier (on *feste*, feast,
q.v.), *va., n. & rfl.* feast,
celebrate, entertain sumptu-
ously.

Festu (**festūcum* for *festūca*), *sm.*
straw.

Feu, v. *fiet* or *fou* 1. **Feus,** form
in *-s* of *fel*, q.v.

Fevre (*fabrum*, worker), *sm.* arti-
san, blacksmith.

Fi (*fīdum*, faithful, true), *adj.*
certain, sure, confident. *De
fi :* certainly, for sure. *Also*
1 pr. & pr. subj. of *fier* 2,
q.v.

Fiance (on *fier* 2, q.v.), *sf.* assurance, guarantee, confidence,
homage, fealty. *Avoir f. de ;
Prendre f. de :* receive a
pledge from, receive someone's
submission. *Donner f. de :*
promise, pledge, submit.

Fiancier (on *fiance*, q.v.), *va.*
promise, swear, pledge. *F.
prison :* give one's parole; set
free on parole. *Fiancier,* adj. :
confident, trusting, certain.

Fichier (**ficcare* for **figicare*, on
figere, attach), *va. & rfl.* fix,

set up, plunge, pierce. *F. l'esgart :* give attention to, fix the eyes upon. *Se f. :* pass through.

Fie, Fiee (**vicata* on *vicem*), *sf.* time. *A la f. :* at last. *Alcune f. :* some day. *Par f. :* sometimes.

Fieble, v. *foible.* **Fief,** v. *fiet, fieu.*

Fieffer (on *fief*, q.v.), *va.* enfeoff, bestow, grant.

Fiens (**femus* for *fimus*), *sm.* dunghill.

Fier, (1) (*ferum*, wild), *adj.* ferocious, haughty, ruthless, daring ; (2) (**fidare*, entrust), *va. & rfl.* trust. *Se f. de :* trust in ; (3) 1 pr. of *ferir*, q.v.

Fierge, pr. subj. ; **Fiert,** 3 pr. of *ferir*, q.v.

Fiet, Fieu (Fk. **fēhu*, cattle,?), *sm.* fief, privilege.

Fieus, nom. of *fil*, q.v., or of *fieu*, q.v. **Fiever,** v. *fieffer.*

Fil (*filium*), *sm.* son.

Filolage (on *filleul < filiolum*, little son), *sm.* heritage of an adopted son.

Fin (**finum*), *adj.* fine, delicate, sincere. *En f. :* truly.

Finer (on *fin < finem*, end), *va. & n.* end, kill, die ; reach ; desist. *Estre finé de mort :* be killed. *Finer de :* pay off.

Firie (**fidicum*), *sm.* liver.

Fisent, 6 pft. of *faire*, q.v. **Fiu,** v. *fiet.* **Fius, Fix,** form in *-s* of *fil*, q.v.

Flaeler, Flaieler (*flagellare*), *va.* scourge, whip, punish.

Flairier (**flagrare* for *fragrare*, be fragrant), *va. & n.* smell sweetly, smell, scent ; breathe.

Flambe, Flamble (*flammula*, little flame), *sf.* flame.

Fleble, v. *foible.*

Flori (pp. of *florir < *flōrīre* for *flōrēre*, bloom), *pp. adj.* hoary (beard, head) ; covered with flowers.

Flun (*flūmen*), *sm.* river, stream.

Foeillie, v. *fueillie.*

Foible (*flēbilem*, lamentable), *adj.* weak.

Fole, v. *fie.* **Foimenti,** v. *feimenti.* **Fois,** v. *feiz.* **Foit,** v. *fei.*

Fol (*follem*, bag, balloon), *adj.* foolish, mad ; *adv.* madly.

Folage (on *fol*, q.v.), *sm.* folly ; shame.

Foldre (*fulgur & fulgura*), *sm. & f.* thunderbolt.

Fole (on *foler < *fullare*, q.v.), *sf.* crowd, press.

Foleier (on *fol*, q.v.), *vn. & rfl.* be mad, commit folly, stray ; *va.* lead astray.

Foler (on *fol*, q.v.), *va.* mislead ; *vn.* become mad.

Foler (**fullare*, to full cloth), *va.* beat, ill-treat.

Folie (on *fol*, q.v.), *sf.* folly. *Also* var. of *fueillie*, q.v.

Folier, v. *foleier.*

Folor (on *fol*, q.v.), *sf.* folly.

Fondre (*fundere*, pour out), *va. & n.* overthrow, destroy ; crumble, fall, be destroyed, sink.

Fonz (Eccl. L. *fontes*), *sm. pl.* baptismal font. *Lever sur les f. :* stand godfather to. *Also sm. sing.* (*fundus*), bottom.

Forain (LL. *foranum*), *adj. & sm.* foreign, outer, foreigner. *Gent f. :* strangers.

Forcele (*furcella*, little fork), *sf.* stomach, chest, throat. *Entre les dous f. :* full in the breast, across the breast. *Les dous f. :* the collar bone and midriff.

Forçor (*fortiŏrem*, stronger), *adj.* stronger, greater.

Forfaire (*fors*, q.v. + *faire*, q.v.), *va., n. & rfl.* transgress, violate, wrong, act wrongly towards; stray from the path of duty; become a criminal.

Forjugier (*fors*, q.v. + *jugier*, q.v.), *va.* banish, deprive, condemn (justly or unjustly).

Forlignier (*fors*, q.v. + *lignier*, on *ligne*, q.v.), *va., n. & rfl.* degenerate, shame.

Formener (*fors*, q.v. + *mener*, q.v.), *va. & rfl.* withdraw, mislead, torment, tire, ill-treat.

Forment (on *fort*, q.v.), *adv.* strongly, greatly, much, sorely.

Fornir, v. *fournir*.

Forostagier (*fors*, q.v. + *ostagier*, q.v.), *va. & n.* leave (be left) as hostage without protection.

Forpasser (*fors*, q.v. + *passer*, q.v.), *va. & n.* pass beyond.

Forrer (on *fuerre* 2, q.v.), *va. & n.* forage, plunder, pillage.

Fors (*foris*, outside), *adv. & prep.* out, outside, except. *F. de :* out from, off. *F. que*, *F. tant que* (*com*) *:* except that. *Ne . . . fors* (*que*) *:* nothing . . . except, only.

Forsener (*fors*, q.v. + *sen*, *sm.*, q.v.), *vn. & rfl.* go mad, be out of one's mind with rage.

Forsfaire, v. *forfaire*.

Fort (*fortem*), *adj. m. & f.* strong, difficult. *Au f. :* indeed.

Forvoiier (on *fors*, q.v. + *voie*, q.v.), *vn.* go astray, get lost.

Fou, (1) (*focum*, fireplace), *sm.* fire. *F. grezois*, v. *grezois*. *Mal f. :* Hell. *Touchier le f. a :* set fire to; (2) (*fagum*), *sm.* beech; (3) var. of *fol*, q.v.

Foule, v. *fole*. **Four-,** try also *For-*.

Fournir (Fk. *frumjan), *va.* carry out, execute, furnish. *Fourni*, pp. adj. : strong, great, mighty.

Fourrer (on *fuerre* 1, q.v.), *va.* sheath, cover, thrust. *Also* var. of *forrer*, q.v.

Fox, form in -*s* of *fol*, q.v.

Fraile (*fragilem*), *adj.* frail, weak.

Fraindre (*frangere*), *va. & n.* break, destroy; *fig.* weaken, yield.

Frainte (on *fraindre*, q.v.), *sf.* breaking, tumult, noise, clash.

Fraisnin (on *fraisne* < *fraxinum*, ash), *adj.* of ash.

Frait (*fractum*), pp. of *fraindre*, q.v.

Franc (3rd c. L. *Francum*, on Fk. *frank), *adj.* freedman, noble.

Franchise (on *franc*, q.v.), *sf.* nobility.

Fraper (Germ., cf. Icel. *hrappr*, violent), *va., n. & rfl.* strike; *vn. & rfl.* hurl oneself.

Frapier (on *fraper*, q.v.), *sm.* flight, noise. *Metre al f. :* put to flight. *Se metre al f. :* flee, take up one's journey.

Frarin (etym. obsc., perh. on Eccl. L. *frater*, monk), *adj.* poor, wretched, weak, vile, cruel (weapon, battle).

Freindre, v. *fraindre*. **Fremaus,** pl. of **Fremail,** v. *fermail*.

Fremillon (on *vermeil*, q.v., ?), *adj.* red, bright, brilliant.

Fremir (*fremīre for *fremere*, roar), *vn. & rfl.* rattle, ring (metal), tremble, shake, be greatly agitated. *Toz li sans li fremi :* he was greatly agitated, he felt faint, he was beside himself with anger.

Fremor (*fremōrem*, murmuring), *sm. & f.* noise, tumult, shaking.

Frener (*frēnare*), *va.* bridle, rein in, curb.

Fresé (perh. on *orfreser*, v. *orfreis*), *adj.* decorated, adorned (with gold?).

Fresle, v. *fraile*. **Fresnin,** v. *fraisnin*. **Freté,** v. *ferté*.

Friente (*fremita, on *fremitum*, roar, or var. of *frainte*, q.v.), *sf.* noise (horses), clash (steel).

Froer, Froier (*fricare*, rub), *va.*, *n. & rfl.* break, strike, rub.

Frois, Froisseis (on *froissier*, q.v.), *sm.* tumult, clash, noise.

Froissier (*frustiare, on *frustum*, fragment), *va. & n.* break, shatter.

Fueillie (on *fueille*, q.v.), *sf.* leaves, bower.

Fuer (*forum*, market), *sm.* price, state; custom (*rare*). *A* (*En*) *nul f. :* in any way, at any price.

Fuerre, (1) (Fk. *fôdr, sheath), *sm.* scabbard; (2) (Fk. *fôdr, fodder), *sm.* fodder.

Fui, 1 pft. of *estre* (*essere), be.

Fuie (*fūga for *fuga*), *sf.* flight. *Doner f. :* put to flight. *Se metre en f.; Torner en f. :* flee, take flight.

Fuildre, v. *foldre*. **Fuillie,** v. *fueillie*.

Fuir (*fūgīre for *fugere*), *vn.* flee; *va.* scatter (*rare*).

Fuitif (*fūgitīvum for *fū-*), *adj.* wandering, vagabond; *sm.* wanderer, fugitive.

Fule, v. *fole*.

Fum, Fun (*fūmum*), *sm.* smoke. *Syn.* (on *fum*) : **Fumiere,** *sf.*

Furnir, v. *fournir*.

Fust (*fūstem*, staff), *sm.* wood, wooden part of a shield, shaft (lance), cudgel, barrel, plank, tree. *L'arbre de mal f. :* gallows.

G

Gaaignier (Fk. *waidanjan, obtain food, booty), *va. & n.* capture, procure, win, seize, till (ground), work in the fields.

Gaaing (on *gaaignier*, q.v.), *sm.* gain, booty, crop, harvest.

Gab (O.Sc. *gab*, jest), *sm.* jesting boast, joke. *A* (*En*) *g. :* jestingly. *Tenir a* (*en*) *g. :* regard as a joke, make mock of.

Gabeis, v. *gabois*.

Gaber (O. Sc. *gabba*, mock), *va.*, *n. & rfl.* brag, make fun of.

Gaberes, nom. of **Gabeor** (on *gaber*, q.v.), *sm.* mocker, joker.

Gabois (on *gab*, q.v.), *sm.* joke, jest, jesting. *Faire g. :* make merry.

Gaegnier, v. *gaaignier*.

Gagier (on *gage*, Fk. *waddi), *va. & n.* pledge, give or take a pledge.

Gaignart (on *gaigner*, q.v.), *adj.* robber, thief, violent, cruel.

Gaigner, v. *gaaignier*.

Gaillard (etym. obsc.), *adj.* lusty.

Gaimenter (on *guai*, alas !, Germ., cf. OHG *wê*, + infl. of *lamenter*), *va.*, *n. & rfl.* lament, weep, complain.

Gain, Gainer, v. *gaaing, gaaignier*. **Gaires**, v. *gueres*.

Gaite (on *gaiter*, q.v., or Fk. **wahta*), *sm.* watchman.

Gaiter (Fk. **wahtôn*, watch), *va. & n.* wake, watch over, lie in wait for, eye. *Se g. de :* be on one's guard against.

Gal, v. *jal*. **Galee**, v. *galie*.

Galie (Med. L. *galea*), *sf.* ship, galley.

Galoner (etym. unkn.), *va. & rfl.* bind the head with golden threads, plait the hair with ribbons.

Gambison (Germ., cf. OHG. *wamba*, belly, ?), *sm.* padded undertunic worn under the mail.

Gamenter, v. *gaimenter*.

Gandir (Fk. **wandjan*, go), *vn.* flee, escape, avoid.

Gant (Fk. **want*, glove), *sm.* glove (also as token of one's personality or person), authority, jurisdiction.

Garandir (*garant*, q.v.), *va.* guarantee the safety of, protect.

Garant (Germ., cf. OHG. *wĕrento*, pr. p., providing a guarantee), *sm.* guarantee, witness, proof, evidence, warranter, protector. *Avoir g. de :* have protection against. *Estre g. a :* be of avail to, protect, aid.

Garde (on *garder*, q.v.), *sf.* guard, precaution, care, fear. *Avoir g. de :* have need to fear. *Se donner* or *prendre g. de :* attend to, look after.

Garder (Fk. **wardôn*, care for), *va. & n.* take care of, protect, hold to, observe, look, look at, see to, keep. *G. a :* see to. *G. que :* see to it that . . ., take care that. *Se g. :* be on one's guard, protect oneself. *Se g. de :* protect oneself against, notice.

Garét, v. *guarét*.

Garir (Fk. **warjan*), *va.*, *n. & rfl.* heal, save, defend, be saved, take refuge, recover, resist. *Se g. :* take care of oneself, equip oneself.

Garison (on *garir*, q.v.), *sf.* healing, cure, protection, salvation, safety, provisions.

Garnement (on *garnir*, q.v.), *sm.* protection, armour, equipment, attire.

Garnir (Fk. **warnjan*, refuse), *va.*, *n. & rfl.* fortify, equip, supply, garrison, warn ; *v. rfl.* protect oneself, provide oneself with. *Garni*, pp. adj. : rich, powerful, ready.

Garral, 1 fut. of *garir*, q.v.

Gast (**wastum*, on *vastum*, deserted, devastated, + Germ. **wost-*), *sm.* pillage, waste land, moor ; *adj.* devastated, ruined, abandoned, bereft, deserted, empty.

Gastelet (on *gastel*, Fk. **wastil*, food), *sm.* small cake.

Gaster (**wastare*, on *vastare*,

empty, cf. *gast*), *va.* devastate, waste, use in vain.

Gaudine (on *gaut*, q.v.), *sf.* thicket, bushes, wood, woodland.

Gaudir (b. *gaudère*), *vn. & rfl.* rejoice, enjoy oneself.

Gaut (Fk. **wald*), *sm.* wood, forest.

Gehir (Germ., cf. OHG. *jĕhan*, confess), *va. & n.* confess, admit, recount. *Faire g. :* force to confess.

Geindre (var. of *giembre*, < *gemere*), *vn.* groan.

Gelde (Fk. **gelda*, band), *sf.* troops, band of soldiers. Also syn. of *geldon*, q.v.

Geldon (on *gelde*, q.v.), *sm.* foot-soldier, conscript.

Gembre, v. *geindre*. **Gementer**, v. *gaimenter*.

Gemme (*gemma*), *sf.* jewel, precious stone.

Gemmé (*gemmatum*), *adj.* set or adorned with jewels.

Gengler, v. *jangler*.

Genoill (**genuculum*, for *geniculum*), *sm.* knee.

Genoillon (on *genoill*, q.v.), *sm.* knee. *En genoillons :* kneeling, on one's knees.

Gensor (on *gent* 2, q.v.), *adj.* more beautiful, mòst beautiful, handsome.

Gent, (1) (*gentem*, clan), *sf.* people, folk, race, army ; (2) (*genitum*, born), *adj.* well-born, noble, handsome, comely.

Gentement (on *gent* 2, q.v.), *adv.* nobly, handsomely, beautifully, fairly.

Gentil (*gentilem*, belonging to a clan), *adj.* noble, high-born.

D

Gernon, v. *grenon*. **Gerrai**, 1 fut. of *gesir*, q.v.

Gesir (*jacēre*), *vn. & rfl.* lie, lie down.

Geste (*gesta*, n.pl. as fem. sing., deeds), *sf.* exploit, tale of notable deeds, family, lineage, race.

Geter, v. *jeter*. **Geu**, v. *gieu*. **Geü**, pp. of *gesir*, q.v. **Geüner**, v. *jeüner*. **Gié**, var. of **Je** (**eo* for *ego*), I. **Giembre**, v. *geindre*.

Giens (*genus*), *adv.* (with *ne*), nothing at all.

Gieu (*jocum*), *sm.* game, sport, problem. *Partir un g. :* set a problem. *G. parti :* the problem set.

Giral, 1 fut. of *gesir*, q.v.

Giron (on Fk. **gêro*), *sm.* pointed piece of cloth, panel of cloth, skirt, lap, bosom, wall (tent).

Gis, 1 pr. of *gesir*, q.v. **Giter**, v. *jeter*. **Givre**, v. *guivre*.

Glaive (*gladium*, sword), *sf.* sword, lance.

Glatir (*glattire*), *vn.* howl, yelp, cry.

Gloton (LL. *gluttōnem*, glutton), *sm. & adj.* glutton, miscreant, foul wretch.

Glous, **Gloz** (*glutto* + nom. -*s*), nom. of *gloton*, q.v. **Goie**, v. *joie*. **Goïr**, v. *joïr*.

Gole (*gula*, throat), *sf.* mouth, throat, neck ; *pl. sometimes*, collar of pieces of fur.

Golpil (on *golpille*, **vulpicula* + Germ. *wolf?*), *sm.* fox.

Gonele (on *gone*, etym. obsc.), *sf.* smock, tunic, dress.

Gonfanon (on Fk. **gundfano*),

sm. gonfalon, pennon, standard.

Gorle (Med. L. *gurla, gurrula*, for *gerula*, container), *sm*. purse, wallet, case.

Gorpil, Goupil, v. *golpil*.

Gote (*gutta*, drop), *sf*. drop. *Ne . . . g. :* not a jot.

Graaillier (*graaille* < *craticula*, small hurdle), *va. & n*. grill, char, burn.

Graanter (var. of *creanter*, q.v.), *va*. grant.

Grace (*gratia*), *sf*. favour, pardon, thanks, grace.

Gracier (on *grace*, q.v.), *va*. thank.

Graer, v. *greer*.

Graignor (*grandiōrem*), *adj*. greater, greatest.

Graile, Graisle (*gracilem*), *adj*. slender, thin; *sm*. bugle.

Grailoier, Graisloier (on *graile, graisle*, q.v.), *va*. blow (bugle); *vn*. ring out, resound.

Grain (etym. unkn.), *adj*. sad, grieved, angry.

Graindre (*grandior*), nom. of *graignor*, q.v.

Gramment (on *grant* < *grandem*, great), *adv*. greatly, much, very, for a long time, far.

Gramoier (on *graim*, v. *grain*), *vn. & rfl*. be sad, show grief, be distressed, become angry.

Graunter, v. *graanter*. **Gravance,** v. *grevance*.

Gré (*gratum*, pleasant), *sm*. permission, will, pleasure, favour, friendship. *A g. :* in welcome fashion, to one's satisfaction. *De g. :* deliberately, willingly. *Faire g. a :* oblige. *Outre*

mon g. : in spite of myself. *Venir a g. a :* please, suit.

Greer (on *gré*, q.v.), *va., n. & rfl*. grant, agree, please.

Gregeois, v. *grezois*.

Gregier (**greviare* for *gravare*, burden, oppress), *va*. harm, hurt, oppress, press hard.

Greignor, Greindre, v. *graignor, graindre*. **Greille,** v. *graile*. **Grelloier,** v. *grailoier*.

Grenon (on LL. *granum*, beard, or Gaul. **grennos*, cf. Ir. *grend*), *sm*. moustache, mustachio.

Gresil, *sm. ;* **Gresille,** *sf*. (on *gres* < Germ. **griot*, grit), hail, hailstones.

Gresle, Gresloier, v. *graile, grailoier*. **Greu,** v. *grieu*.

Grevain (on *grever*, q.v.), *adj*. heavy, painful, harmful, dangerous.

Grevance (on *grever*, q.v.), *sf*. harm, grief, misfortune, weariness.

Grever (**grevare* for *gravare*, burden), *va*. harm, hurt, vex, oppress.

Grevos (on *grever*, q.v.), *adj*. grievous, vexatious, burdensome.

Grezois (**graeciscum*, on *graecum*, Greek, + Germ. -*isk*), *adj. & sm*. Greek. *Feu g. :* Greek fire (a combustible for setting fire to ships, buildings, etc., thrown from a distance).

Grief (**grevem* for *gravem*, weighty), *adj*. mighty, heavy, hard, grievous, irksome, terrible; *sm*. (on *grever*, q.v.), wrong, worry, difficulty. *En* *g. de :* in spite of. *Also* I pr. of *grever*, q.v.

Grieu, Griex, Griu (*graecum*), *adj. & sm.* Greek.

Grifaigne (etym. obsc.), *adj.* savage, wild, cruel.

Grignor, v. *graignor*.

Griment (on *grief*, q.v.), *adv.* grievously, heavily, powerfully.

Gris (Fk. **gris*, grey), *sm.* grey fur.

Grondir (*grundire*, grunt). **Grondre** (**grunnere* for *grunnire*), *vn.* murmur, grumble, complain.

Gronir (*grunnire*, grunt), *vn.* grumble, object, murmur.

Guaires, v. *gueres*. **Guarant,** v. *garant.* **Guarde, Guarder,** v. *garde, garder.*

Guarét (**weruactum* for *vervactum*), *sm.* fallow land.

Guarir, v. *garir.* **Guarnement, Guarnir,** v. *garn-.* **Guast, Guaster,** v. *gast-.*

Gué (**wadum* for *vadum*, ford, + Germ. **wad*), *sm.* wateringplace, low-lying grassland, ditch, ford.

Gueille, v. *gorle*.

Guenchir, Guencir (Fk. **wankjan*, hesitate), *vn. & rfl.* make a detour, turn aside, go, escape ; *va.* avoid, leave. *Faire g. a :* bring to, lead to. *G. a ; G. de :* leave, abandon. *G. la resne :* let go the rein.

Gueredon, v. *guerredon*.

Gueres (Fk. **waigaro* + adv. -*s*), *adv.* much. *M'en est g. :* I do not much mind. *N'a g. :* recently. *Ne . . . g. :* not much, scarcely.

Guernon, v. *grenon.* **Gueron,** v. *giron.*

Guerpir (Fk. **werpan*, throw), *va., n. & rfl.* abandon, release, forsake, reject.

Guerredon (Fk. **widarlôn* + L. *dônum*, gift), *sm.* reward.

Gueter, v. *gaiter*.

Guiche (*vitica* + Germ. *windan*, turn), *sf.* thong or strap supporting the buckler or holding a banner, horn, etc. *Also* form of *guichet*, q.v.

Guichet, Guischet (etym. obsc.), *sm.* retreat, hiding-place, small door.

Guier (Fk. **witan*, direct), *va.* lead, guide, escort.

Guige, v. *guiche*.

Guinple (Fk. **wimpil*, streamer), *sf.* wimple.

Guionage (on *guier*, q.v.), *sm.* guide, safe-conduct, toll paid for safe-conduct.

Guisarme (etym. unkn.), *sf.* longhafted weapon.

Guise (Fk. **wisa*), *sf.* manner, wise. *En g. de :* like. *Par nule g. :* in no way. *Vestu de mainte g. :* wearing clothes with patches of different colours.

Guivre (**wipera* for *vipera*), *sf.* snake, viper, sort of javelin or arrow.

H

Ha-, try also **A-.**

Habit (on *habiter*, q.v.), *sm.* dwelling.

Habit (b. *habitum*, appearance), *sm.* condition, monk's habit.

Habitacle (LL. *habitaculum*), *sm.* dwelling.

Habiter (b. *habitare*, dwell), *va. & n.* dwell, touch, approach.

Hachiee, v. *haschies*.

Hai-, try also **Ha-**.

Hai (onom.), *excl.* ah! alas! *Also* pp. of *hair*, q.v.

Haicter, Haidier, v. *haitier*.

Haiete (dimin. of *haie*, Fk. **haga*, hedge), *sf.* small hedge, field enclosed by hedges, enclosure.

Haingre, v. *heingre*.

Hair (Fk. **hatjan*), *va.* hate; curse (*rare*).

Haire (Fk. **hârja*, hair-shirt), *sf.* hair-shirt, pain, affliction, trouble.

Hait (Fk. **hait*, pleasure), *sm.* joy, pleasure, desire, wish, courage. *A h. :* joyfully. *De h. :* willingly, freely. *A son h. :* as he wishes.

Haitier (on *hait*, q.v.), *va., n., rfl. & impers.* give pleasure to, invigorate, amuse oneself; *v. rfl.* be joyful. *Estre haitié de :* be disposed to. *Que vos en haite? :* how do you feel about it? *Se h. de :* do willingly, hasten to.

Halbere (Fk. **halsberg*, neck-protector), *sm.* hauberk, coat-of-mail.

Halçor (*altiõrem*, higher, cf. *halt*), *adj.* high, higher, highest, very high, lofty, proud.

Halt (L. *altum* + Fk. **hôh*), *adj.* high, tall, loud; *adv.* loudly, high, high up. *En h. :* loudly, aloud, on high. *Halt jor :* high day. *Halte feste :* high feast. *Paroles haltes :* proud words.

Haltaing (on *halt*, q.v.), *adj.* tall, lofty, proud.

Haltesee (on *halt*, q.v.), *sf.* height, prosperity, greatness.

Halzor, v. *halçor*.

Hanap (Fk. **hnap*), *sm.* drinking-bowl, bowl, basin, cup.

Hanste; (étym. obsc.), *sf.* shaft (spear, lance, etc.). *Pleine sa h. :* with lance outstretched.

Haole, 1 impft. of *hair*, q.v.

Haor (on *hair*, q.v.), *sf.* hatred.

Happer (Germ., cf. Flem. *happen*, bite, seize), *va.* seize, catch.

Hardement, Hardiment (on *hardir*, q.v.), *sm.* boldness, courage, daring, bravery, task to be accomplished.

Hardir (Fk. **hardjan*, harden), *va. & n.* make or become bold.

Harele (etym. obsc., perh. on *har*, onom.), *sf.* tumult, uproar, outcry, revolt.

Harier (etym. obsc., perh. on *har*, onom.), *va.* harass, annoy, torment.

Harnas (O.Sc. **hernest*, provision), *sm.* accoutrement, armour, utensils; *sometimes* harness.

Harneschier (on *harnas*, q.v.), *va. & rfl.* put on armour, arm oneself, equip.

Harnois, v. *harnas*. **Harral**, 1 fut. of *hair*, q.v.

Hart (Fk. **hard*, flax), *sm.* cord, noose, withe.

Haschiee, Hascie (on *haschiere*, LL. *hascaria*, smart, Fk. **harmskara*), *sf.* anguish, torment, pain, grief.

Haste (Germ. *harsta*, grill, infl.

by *hasta*, spear), *sm. & f.* spit, roast meat.

Haster (on *haste*, hurry, Fk. **haifst*, violence), *va. & n.* pursue, press upon, spur on, hasten, hurry.

Hastier (on *haste*, spit, q.v.), *sm.* spit, andiron.

Hastif (on *haste*, cf. *haster*), *adj.* swift, hasty, impetuous, impatient. *H. de :* quick to.

Haubergier (on *halberc*, q.v.), *va. & rfl.* put on a hauberk.

Hauberjon (on *halberc*, q.v.), *sm.* small hauberk.

Hauchier, Haucier (**altiare*, on *altum*, cf. *halt* for init. *h*), *va.* raise, lift.

Hauçor, v. *halçor.* **Hauer**, v. *hoer.* **Haultain**, v. *haltaing.* **Haür**, v. *haor.*

Haussage, Hausage (on *haucier*, q.v.), *sm.* height, arrogance, pride.

Hautece, v. *haltesce.*

Hé (on *hair*, q.v., or Fk. **hat*), *sm.* hatred. *Coillir en h. :* conceive hatred for.

Heaume, v. *helme.* **Heberge, -er,** v. *herberge, -ier.* **Hebregier,** v. *herbergier.* **Heent,** 6 pr. of *hair*, q.v.

Heingre (etym. unkn.), *adj.* thin, spare.

Helme (Fk. **helm*), *sm.* helmet.

Helt, *sm.* ; **Helte,** *sf.* (Germ., cf. OHG. *helza*, hilt), guard of a sword, hilt.

Henap, Henapt, Henat, v. *hanap.*

Herber (on *herbe* < *herba*, grass), *va., n. & rfl.* strew with grass, feed on grass, graze, flavour or

brew with herbs ; *sm.* herbbrew, potion.

Herberge (Fk. **hariberga*, camp), *sf.* encampment, resting-place, lodging, shelter. *Prendre h. :* pitch one's camp. *Syn.:* **Herbergage, Herbergement.**

Herbergier (on *herberge*, q.v., or Fk. **haribergôn*, to camp), *va., n. & rfl.* encamp, lodge, shelter, find lodging or shelter.

Hercier (**herpicare*, on *hirpicem*, harrow), *va., n. & rfl.* strike, pull.

Herege, v. *herite.* **Hereté,** v. *herité.*

Herite (for *herege*, Eccl. L. *haereticum*), *sm.* heretic.

Herité (*hērēditatem*), *sm.* heritage, possession, property.

Heritier (*hērēditarium*, inherited), *sm.* heritage, domain, kingdom.

Hermin (*Armenium*, Arminian), *sm.* ermine, fur.

Hernois, v. *harnas.* **Herupé,** v. *hurepé.* **Het,** v. *hait ;* also 3 pr. of *hair*, q.v.

Heudure (on *helde*, v. *helt*), *sf.* handle of sword.

Heur, Heuré, v. *eür, eüré.* **Heurt, Heurter,** v. *hurt, hurter.* **Heus,** form in -s of *helt*, q.v. **Hiaume,** v. *helme.*

Hide (etym. unkn.), *sf.* horror, fright, terror. *Syn. :* **Hidor.**

Hideus (on *hide*, q.v.), *adj.* hideous, horror-struck.

Hie (on *hier* < Middle Netherl. *heien*, to ram), *sm.* batteringram, blow, shock. *A h. :* with force, powerfully, repeatedly. *A une h. :* together, as one.

Hisde, Hisdeus, Hisdor, v. *hid-*.
Hochler, v. *hocier* or *oscier*.

Hocier (etym. obsc.), *va.* shake.

Hoem, Hoen, v. *huem*.

Hoer (on *hoe*, Fk. **hauwa*, hoe), *va. & n.* hoe, dig, paw the ground.

Hoese, v. *huese*. **Hoi,** v. *hui*.

Hoir (**hĕrem* for *hĕrēdem*), *sm.* heir.

Hom, v. *huem*.

Home (*hominem*), *sm.* man, vassal.

Honesté (*honestatem*), *sf.* honesty, honour.

Honir (Fk. **haunjan*, stain), *va.* shame, humiliate, disgrace.

Honison (on *honir*, q.v.), *sf.* dishonour, shame, humiliation.

Honnir, v. *honir*.

Honor (*honōrem*, honour), *sf.* honour, distinction, fief, domain, wealth.

Honoré (b. *honōratum*, or on *honor*, q.v.), *adj.* honoured; powerful, possessing lands.

Hons (*homo* + nom. -*s*), nom. sing. of *home*, q.v. *Also* used as indef. pron., " one."

Hontage (on *honte* < Fk. **haunita*, stain), *sm.* insult, shame, dishonour, shameful action.

Hoquer, var. of *hocier*, q.v.
Hordeis, Horder, v. *hourd-*.

Hore (*hōra*), *sf.* hour, time, moment. *A tel h. :* at that moment. *De male h. :* unhappily, unfortunately. *D'h. en* (*a*) *altres :* from time to time.

Horribleté (on *horrible* < *horribilem*, frightful), *sf.* horror, frightfulness, unpleasantness.

Hort (*hortum*, garden), *sm.* garden, orchard.

Hort, v. *ort* or *hourt*. **Hoschlé,** v. *oschier*. **Host,** v. *ost*. **Hostagier, Hoste, Hostel, Hosteier,** v. *ost-*. **Houdure,** v. *heudure*.

Hounir, v. *honir*. **Hourd,** v. *hourt*.

Hourdeis (on *hourd*, v. *hourt*), *sm.* palisade, retrenchment, overhanging stockade on top of a tower.

Hourder (on *hourd*, v. *hourt*), *va. & rfl.* fortify, surround with a stockade, entrench.

Hourt (Fk. **hurd*, hurdle), *sm.* palisade, fence, scaffolding, stage. *Also* has the senses of *hourdeis*, q.v.

Housel ; *pl.* **Houseaus** (on *house*, v. *huese*), *sm.* boot, hose, high-boot.

Hu (onom.), *sm.* cry, tumult, noise, war-cry, hunting-cry, hue and cry.

Huant (on *huer*, q.v.), *sm.* screech-owl, owl.

Huchie (on *huchier*, q.v.), *sf.* cry, call.

Huchier, Hucier (**hŭccare*, on Legal L. *hŭccum*, appeal), *va. & n.* call, call out, hail, publish, proclaim, summon (legal).

Huee (on *huer*, q.v.), *sf.* cry, renown.

Huem, Huen (tonic form of *homo*), nom. of *home*, q.v. *Also* serves as indef. pron., " one."

Huer (onom.), *va. & n.* call, call out, call after, decry, abuse.

Huese (Fk. **hosa*, boot, leggings), *sf.* boot, high-boot, hose.

Hui (*hodiĕ*), *adv.* to-day, that day. *Au jor d'h. :* this very day. Also var. of *hu*, q.v.

Huier, v. *huer.*

Huimais, Huimés (*hui*, q.v. + *mais*, q.v.), *adv.* now, henceforth.

Huis, v. *uis.* **Huisset,** v. *uisset.* **Huissier,** v. *uissier.* **Hum, Hume,** v. *huem, home.*

Humblesce (on *humble*, on *humilem*, low), *sf.* humility, modesty.

Humeliance (on *humele*, on *humilem*, low), *sf.* humility, courtesy, friendship.

Humeliant (on *humelier*, q.v.), *adj.* humble.

Humelier (on Eccl. L. *humiliare*, make humble), *va. & rfl.* bow before, bow, be humble, feel pity, deign, agree.

Hure (etym. unkn.), *sf.* bristling hair, head. *Faire h. :* make fun of. *Faire une h. :* look wild. *Also* var. of *hore*, q.v.

Hurepé (on *hure*, q.v.), *adj.* tousled, bristling (hair).

Hurt (perh. Fk. **hurt?*), *sm.* shock, blow, knock.

Hurter (on *hurt*, q.v.?), *va. & n.* knock against, strike, touch, spur.

Hus, v. *uis.*

Hustin (Germ., cf. Flem. *hutselen*, shake, ?), *sm.* noise, tumult, quarrel, fight.

Hy-, try **Hi-** or **He-,** e.g. **Hyde, Hydeus,** v. *hide, hideus,* and **Hyrritier,** v. *heritier.*

I

I (*ibi*), *adv.* there.

Ialz, Iaus, Iaux, var. of *eus, eux* (*illos*), *pron.* they, them. **Ialz,** v. *ueil.* **Iave, Iawe,** var. of *eave* v. *eve.*

Icest (**ĕcce istum*), *adj.* this.

Iço (**ĕcce hŏc*), *pron.* that.

Ichi, Ici (PL. *ĕcce hic*), *adv.* here.

Idle (Eccl. L. *idōlum*), *sm. & f.* idol.

Idoine (*idōneum*), *adj.* capable, suitable, appropriate.

Idone, Idonques (on *donc*, q.v.), *adv.* then.

Ie-, try also **E-.**

Ier, 1 fut. of *estre* < **essere*, be, or var. of *hier* < *heri*, yesterday. **Iere,** 1 impft. ; **Iert,** 3 impft. or fut. of *estre* < **essere*, be. **Iermin,** v. *hermin.* **Ierre,** var. of *erre*, v. *oirre.* **Ies,** 2 pr. of *estre* < **essere*, be. **Iex,** *pl.* v. *ueil.*

Igal, v. *ingal* or *ivel.*

Iglise (PL. *ēclesia* for *ecclēsia*), *sf.* church.

Ignel, v. *isnel.* **Igual, Iguel,** v. *ivel.*

Il-, try **Ill-.**

Illec, Illeques, Illeuc, Illoc, v. *illuec.*

Illuec (*illŏ locŏ*, in that place), *adv.* there.

Imagene (*imaginem*), *sf.* image, statue.

Imais, Imés, v. *huimais.*

Impression (b. *impressiōnem*, emphasis), *sf.* pressure, restraint, compulsion.

In-, try also **En-,** e.g. **Incliner,** v. *encliner.*

Inde (*Indicum*, Indian), *adj.* indigo, blue.

Ingal ; *pl.* **Ingaus** (on *aequalem*, level), *sm.* plain, flat land. *Also* var. of *ivel*, q.v.

Ingremance, Ingromance (alter. of LL. *necromantia*), *sf.* magic, necromancy.

Iraistre (*irascere*), *va.* anger ; *vn. & rfl.* become angry.

Irance (on *ire*, q.v.), *sf.* anger, sorrow.

Irasceu, pp. of *iraistre*, q.v.

Ire (*ira*), *sf.* anger, grief. *Par i. :* furiously.

Iré, v. *irié.* **Irestre**, v. *iraistre.* **Ireté, Iretier**, v. *herité, heritier.*

Irié (*iratum*, or on *ire*, q.v.), *adj.* angry, annoyed, resentful, grieved.

Iror (on *ire*, q.v.), *sf.* anger, fury, grief. *Faire i. :* fight furiously, cause slaughter.

Iros (on *ire*, q.v.), *adj.* furious, pitiless.

Irrur, v. *iror.* **Is**, 1 & 2 pr., or imper. sing. of *issir*, q.v.

Islel, Islet, *sm.*, **Islette**, *sf.* (on *isle < ĭ(n)sula*, island), small island, islet.

Isme, v. *esme.*

Isnel, Isniel (Germ., cf. OHG. *snel*), *adj.* swift, agile, nimble. *I. le pas :* at once, promptly.

Issi, v. *ensi*, or pp. of *issir*, q.v. **Issine**, v. *ensi.*

Issir (*exire*), *vn.* issue forth, leave, go out, get out (of difficulty). *Syn. :* **S'en Issir.**

Ist, 3 pr. ; **Isteral, Istral**, 1 fut. of *issir*, q.v.

Itant (on *tant*, q.v.), *adv.* as much, then, now. *A i. :* thereupon, then.

Iteil, v. *itel.*

Itel, Iteu (on *tel*, q.v.), *adj.* such, the same, similar.

Ive (*equa*), *sf.* mare.

Ivel (*aequalem*), *adj.* equal, even ; *adv.* equally, evenly.

J

Ja-, try also **Ga-.**

Ja (*jam*), *adv.* already, soon, now (*expletive*), henceforward, indeed, ever. *Ja . . . ne :* never, nevermore. *Ja jor :* never. *Ja si :* however (much). *Ja soit (ce) que :* although. *Ja tant :* however (much).

Jabois, v. *gabois.* **Jacunce**, v. *jagonce.*

Jafuer (etym. unkn.), *sm.* pleasure-seeking?

Jagonce (on *hyacinthum*), *sf.* jacinth (precious stone), ruby.

Jai, v. *ja.* **Jaillir**, v. *jalir.* **Jalole**, v. *jaole.*

Jal (*gallum*), *sm.* cock.

Jalir (on **jaculare* for *jaculari*, throw, ?), *va.* throw, throw up ; *vn. & rfl.* be thrown, rush, fly off, escape.

Jambet (on *jambe*, LL. *gamba*, ham), *sm.* blow on the leg, surprise attack, ambush, trap.

Jame, v. *gemme.*

Jangle (etym. unkn., perh. onom.), *sf.* chatter. *Syn. :* **Janglerie, Janglois.**

Jangleor (on *jangler*, q.v.), *adj. & sm.* chatterer, slanderer. *Syn. :* **Janglos.**

Jangler (etym. unkn., perh. onom.), *vn.* chatter, gossip, slander ; *sm.* chatterer, gossip, slanderer.

Jante (LL. *ganta*, Germ., cf. LG. *gante*,) *sf.* wild duck.

Jaole (LL. *caveŏla*, on *cavea*, cage), *sf.* cage, prison.

Jargon (etym. obsc.), *sm.* warbling, babbling, language.

Jargonner (on *jargon*, q.v.), *vn.* warble, babble, murmur, talk.

Jart (Fk. *gardo*), *sm.* garden, orchard.

Jasarant, Jazerant, Jazerene (orig. obsc., perh. on Arab. (*al-*) *jazaïr*, Algiers), *adj.* made of Eastern mail.

Jeofne, v. *juene*. **Jesque**, v. *jusque*.

Jeter (*jectare* for *jactare*), *va. & rfl.* throw, cast out, deliver, strike. *J. de mort :* save from death. *J. del fuerre :* draw from the scabbard. *J. la main :* stretch out one's hand. *Se j. a :* throw oneself upon.

Jeude, v. *gelde*, *sf.*

Jeûner (Eccl. L. *jējūnare*), *vn.* fast.

Joelet (on *jeu* < *jocum*, game, or on *jocalem*, pleasing), *sm.* jewel, trinket.

Joer (*jocare*), *vn.* play, make mock of.

Jogleor, v. *jongleor*. **Joglere**, nom. of *jogleor*, v. *jongleor*.

Joi, 1 pft. of *gesir*, q.v.

Joi (pp. of *joïr*, q.v.), *adj.* pleased, delighted, happy.

Joiant (pr. p. of *joïr*, q.v.), *adj.* joyful.

Joie (*gaudia* for *gaudium*), *sf.* joy.

Joint (*junctum*, well-knit, of oratory), *adj.* handsome, elegant, swift.

Jointe (pp. fem. of *joindre* < *jungere*, join), *sf.* joint (finger), pastern (horse).

Joïr (*gaudire* for *gaudēre*, rejoice), *va. & n.* welcome, caress, enjoy.

Jolif (etym. obsc., perh. on O. Sc. *jôl*, a pagan feast, or *diabolīvum*), *adj.* joyful, gay, loving, ardent, fickle.

Joliver (on *jolif*, q.v.), *vn.* philander, make love, caress.

Joliveté (on *jolif*, q.v.), *sf.* gaiety, amorous pleasure, fickleness.

Jongleor (for *jogleor* < *joculatŏrem*, joker), *sm.* minstrel, jongleur, juggler.

Jor, v. *jorn*. **Jorent**, 6 pft. of *gesir*, q.v.

Jorn (*diurnum*), *sm.* day, daylight. *Ce j. :* to-day. *Hui ce j. :* to-day, this very day. *J. que je vive :* as long as I live. *Le j. :* that day. *Nul j. :* never. *Toz jors :* always.

Jornal, Jornel (on *jorn*, q.v.), *adj.* daily ; vigorous (*rare*) ; *sm.* day, day's work.

Jornee (*diurnata*), *sf.* journey, assignment, engagement.

Jorral, 1 fut. of *joïr*, q.v. **Jos**, v. *jus*.

Joste (*juxta*), *prep.* by the side of, near to.

Joster (*juxtare*), *va., n. & rfl.* touch, join, assemble, joust, fight with. *J. une bataille :* join battle. *J. a :* joust with. *J. a terre :* bring to the ground.

Jostise, v. *justise*. **Jou-**, try **Jo-**. **Jou**, v. *gieu*. **Jouelet**, v. *joelet*. **Jougler**, v. *jongleor*. **Jouste, Jouster**, v. *joste*, *joster*. **Jovene**, v. *juene*.

Jovent (*juventum*, cf. *jovente*), *sm.* youth.

Jovente (*juventa*), *sf. & adj.*
youth, young man, young.

Juene (*juvenem*), *adj.* young.

Juerie (on *jueu*, q.v.), *sf.* Jewry.

Juesdi (*Jovis dĭem*), *sm.* Thursday.

Jueu, Juiu (*jūdaeum*), *sm.* Jew.

Jugier (*jūdicare*), *va.* judge, condemn, pass an opinion on,
appoint, assign, decree.

Jugleresse, fem. of *jugleor*, v.
jongleor.

Juignet (on *jūnium*, confused
with *juillet*), *sm.* July.

Juise (*jūdicium*), *sm.* judgment,
judgment day, trial by ordeal.

Juner, v. *jeûner*. **Jurent, 6** pft.
of *gesir*, q.v.

Jurer (*jūrare*), *va.* swear, swear
by.

Jus (*deorsum* + *sūrsum*), *adv.*
below, down, on the ground.
La j. : down below. *Sus et
j. :* here and there, from side
to side, high and low.

Jusque (**deûsque*), *prep. & conj.*
until, as far as, down to.

Juste, Juster, v. *joste, joster*.

Justiciable, Justisable (on *justicier*, q.v.), *adj.* just.

Justicier (on *justice*, v. *justise*),
va. govern, administer, pledge,
do justice.

Justise (on *jūstitia*), *sf.* justice.
Also sm. judge.

Jut, 3 pft. of *gesir*, q.v. **Juvente,**
v. *jovente*. **Juzarme,** v. *guisarme*.

K

K-. Try under **C-, Ch-,** or
Qu-.

L

Label; *pl.* **Labiaus** (Fk. **labba*,
hanging piece of cloth), *sm.*
fringe or ribbon attached to
clothes; label (*heraldic*).

Laborage (on *labor < labōrem*,
effort), *sm.* work, profession.

Lacier (*laqueare*, lace), *va.*
lace, fasten, embrace; *v. rfl.*
unite.

Laçon (on *las 2*, q.v.), *sm.* lace,
bond, net.

Ladengier, v. *laidengier*.

Ladre (Biblical *Lazarum*), *sm.*
leper.

Ladron, v. *larron*.

Laece (on *lé*, q.v.), *sf.* width.
Also var. of *leece*, q.v.

Laenz (*la < illac*, there, + *enz*,
q.v.), *adv.* therein, present.

Lagan (Germ., cf. Icel. *lögn*, net
laid in the sea, ?), *sm.* flotsam
and jetsam, right to collect
driftwood, ruin, destruction,
profusion.

Lai, (1) (Celt., cf. Ir. *laid*, poem,
song, ?), *sm.* lay; (2) (Eccl. L.
laicum), *adj. & sm.* lay, secular,
ignorant; (3) imper. of *laier*,
q.v., and var. of *La < illac*,
adv. there.

Laidangier, Laidengier (on *laid*,
v. *lait*), *va.* abuse, insult, illtreat, damage.

Laidier, Laidir (on *laid*, v. *lait*),
va. & rfl. ill-treat, harm, abuse,
dishonour.

Laidon, v. *landon*.

Laidure (on *laid*, v. *lait*), *sf.* injury, harm, wrong, shame.

Laiens, v. *laenz*.

Laier (etym. obsc.), *va.* leave,

Ne l. ne + subjve : refrain from, be slow to.

Laigne, var. of *leigne*, q.v. **Lairai**, 1 fut. of *laier*, q.v. **Lairis**, v. *laris*. **Lairon**, v. *larron*. **Lais**, 1 pr., 1 & 2 pr. subj. of *laissier*, q.v.; *also* form in *-s* of *lai* 1 & 2, q.v.

Laise, v. *laece*, width.

Laissier (*laxare*, unloosen), *va.* leave, abandon, leave undone, let. *L. a* (*de*) : leave off. *L. ester* : let be. *Ne l. ne* . . . : refrain from. 3 pr. subj.: **Laist**.

Lait (Fk. **laid*, hateful), *adj.* horrible, harmful ; *sm.* harm, wrong, affront, dishonour. *Seit bel ou seit l.* : willy-nilly. *Also* 3 pr. & pr. subj. of *laier*, q.v.

Laituaire (Late L. *ēlectuarium*, etym. obsc., perh. Gk. *ekleik-ton*), *sm.* electuary (purgative compounded with some syrup).

Lambel, Lambiaus, v. *label*.

Lambre (on *lambrois*, q.v.), *sm.* lining or panelling of wall (wood, marble, plaster, etc.) ; block of wood, marble, etc.

Lambrois, Lambruis, Lambrus (**lambrūscum*, on *labrūsca*, wild vine), *sm.* See *lambre* for senses.

Lamont (*la < illac + amont*, q.v.), *adv.* up there, on high, aloft.

Lanb-, v. **Lamb-**.

Landier (for *l'andier*, Celt. **andero-*, young bull), *sm.* and-iron, fire-dog.

Landon (etym. obsc.), *sm.* clog (for tethering animals), muzzle.

Lange (*laneum*, woollen), *adj. & sm.* woollen, woollen garment.

Lanier (on *laniare*, tear, mangle, in sense of *lament?*), *adj. & sm.* coward(ly), craven.

Laor (on *lé*, q.v.), *sf.* width.

Lapidee (on *lapider < lapidare*, throw stones at), *sf.* massacre, destruction.

Larai, Larrai, 1 fut. of *laier*, q.v.

Lardé (on *lard < lardum*, bacon fat), *sm.* fowl, etc., with strips of bacon inserted before roasting.

Larder (on *lard*. cf. *lardé*), *va.* burn, fry ; harm.

Lardier (on *lard*, cf. *lardé*), *sm.* larder, pantry ; piece of bacon (*rare*).

Largement (on *large < larga*, abundant), *adv.* a long way, greatly, plentifully. *Valeir l.* : to be worth at least. . .

Largeté (on *largitatem*, liberality), *sf.* width.

Larmier, Larmoier (on *larme*, var. of *lerme*, q.v.), *vn. & rfl.* weep, grieve ; *sm.* tears, weeping.

Larris, Laris (etym. obsc.), *sm.* fell, moor, hillside, rough ground, waste land.

Larron (*latrōnem*), acc. of *lere*, q.v.

Las, (1) (*lassum*, weary), *adj.* unfortunate, wretched. *Ha* (*Hé*) *las*(*se*) : alas ! ; (2) (*laqueum*, noose), *sm.* lace, cord, string, ribbon, snare.

Lasté (on *las* 1), *sf.* tiredness, weakness, grief, lack.

Lasus (*la < illac + sus*, q.v.), *adv.* there above.

Latimier, v. *latinier*.

Latin (*latinum*), *sm.* Latin, language, learning, speech (in general) ; ruse.

Latinier (on *latin*, q.v.), *sm.* one who speaks Latin, linguist, interpreter.

Laūr, v. *laor*.

Laūstic (for *l'aüstic*, Breton *éostik*), *sm.* nightingale.

Laz, v. *las.* **Lay-**, try under **Lai-** or **La-**.

Lé (*latum*), *adj.* wide, broad, vast ; *sm.* width. *De lonc et de lé :* on all sides.

Leal (*lēgalem*, legal), *adj.* loyal, legal.

Leans, v. *laenz.* **Leaument**, adv. on *leal*, q.v.

Lecheor (on *lecher*, Fk. *likkôn*, lick), *adj. & sm.* glutton, lecher ; *fem.* **Lecheresse**, **Legeresse**.

Lecherie (on *lecher*, cf. *lecheor*), *sf.* lechery, lewdness, licentiousness, gluttony, deceit.

Lechiere, nom. of *lecheor*, q.v. **Ledece**, v. *leece.* **Ledengier**, v. *laidengier.* **Ledir**, v. *laidir.* **Ledre**, v. *lere.*

Leece (*laetitia*), *sf.* joy, happiness, cheer.

Leens, v. *laenz.* **Leesse**, var. of *leece*, q.v.

Legerie (on *legier*, q.v.), *sf.* folly, imprudence, lightness.

Legier (*leviarium*, on *levem*, light), *adj.* light, nimble, easy. *De l. :* easily, quickly, flippantly. *L. a :* easy to, quick to.

Legne, v. *leigne*.

Lei-, try also under **Lai-** or **Loi-**.

Leigne (*ligna*), *sm. & f.* wood, firewood.

Leis, var. of *les, lez,* q.v. **Leisor**, v. *loisor.* **Len-**, try also under **Lan-**. **Lenciol**, v. *linçoel.*

Lengne, v. *leigne.* **Lenier**, v. *lanier.*

Leporin (on *leporem*, hare), *adj.* tawny, hare-like.

Lere, **Lerre** (*latro*), nom. sing. of *larron* < *latrōnem, sm.* thief, robber, knave (term of abuse).

Lerme (*lacrima*), *sf.* tear.

Lermer (*lacrimare*), *vn. & rfl.* weep, shed tears.

Lerrai, 1 fut. ; **Lerra**, 3 fut. of *laissier*, q.v. or *laier*, q.v.

Lerre, v. *lere*.

Les, Lez (*latus*), *sm.* side ; *prep.* near, by the side of.

Lesdangier, v. *laidengier.* **Lesir**, v. *loisir.* **Lessier**, v. *laissier.* **Lest**, 3 pr. subj. of *laissier*, q.v. **Let**, v. *lait* or *lé*.

Letré (*litteratum*, lettered), *adj.* written, inscribed, covered with arabesques, instructed (of persons).

Letreure, **Lettreure** (*litteratūra*, writing), *sf.* literary knowledge, instruction, learning.

Letrin (*lectrinum*, on Late L. *lectrum*), *sm.* pulpit, reading-desk.

Lettuaire, v. *laituaire.* **Leu**, var. of *lieu*, q.v., or of *lou*, q.v., or pp. of *lire* (*legere*), read. **Leüst**, 3 impft. subj. of *loisir*, q.v.

Lever (*levare*), *va. & n.* raise, exalt, wear ; rise, arise ; stand godfather to (hold over the font). *L. blasme :* bring a complaint. *L. cop :* aim a blow.

Levralte, Levrete, dimin. of **Levre** (*labra*), *sf.* lip.

Lez, v. *les.*

Liard, Liart (etym. obsc., perh. Celt., cf. Ir. *liath,* grey), *adj.* greyish, grey and white, dapple-grey; *sm.* grey horse.

Lice, Liche (perh. Fk. *listia,* edge), *sf.* barrier, palisade, field of combat, lists (tourney).

Lichiere, Licheur, v. *lechiere, lecheor.* **Lie,** var. of fem. of *lié,* q.v.

Lié (*laetum*), *adj.* happy, joyful, gay.

Liedement, Lieement, adv. on *lié,* q.v. **Lief,** 1 pr. of *lever,* q.v. **Liege,** v. *lige.*

Liepié (*lie,* from *lier,* q.v. + *pié* < *pedem,* foot), *sm.* shoe-lace.

Lier, v. *loier.*

Lieu (*locum*), *sm.* place, rank, reason, excuse. *De l. en l. :* from side to side. *El l. de ; En l. de :* in the place of, instead of, by way of.

Lieue (*leuca,* of Gaul. orig. ?), *sf.* league.

Lieuee (on *lieue,* q.v.), *sf.* a league's distance, the time taken to cover a league.

Lievent, 6 pr. of *lever,* q.v.

Ligance (on *lige,* q.v.), *sf.* allegiance (feudal).

Lige (etym. obsc., Germ., cf. OHG. *ledig,* free), *adj. & sm.* liege, feudal dependant, vassal,· lord; free; complete.

Lign, v. *lin.*

Ligne (*linea,* thread), *sf.* lineage, race, line.

Lijanee, v. *ligance.*

Lin, Ling (masc. form of *ligne,* q.v.), *sm.* lineage, race, family.

Linçoel, Linçol (*linteolum,* small linen cloth), *sm.* cloth, sheet.

Linge (*lineum*), *adj.* linen; sometimes weak. *Drap* or *Robe l. :* shirt.

Linsuel, v. *linçoel.*

Listé (on *liste,* Fk. *lista,* border), *adj.* bordered, edged, fringed, lined (rooms, tents, etc.), fortified (castles). *Var. :* **Lité.**

Liu-, try under **Leu-** or **Lieu-,** e.g. **Liue,** v. *lieue.*

Livrer (*liberare,* deliver), *va.* hand over, furnish.

Livreson, Livrison, Livroison (on *livrer,* q.v.), *sf.* gift, distribution, engagement, provision; *fig.* ill-treatment.

Lo, 1 pr. of *loer,* q.v.

Lobe (etym. obsc.), *sf.* flattery, deceit, lie.

Lobiere(s), nom. of **Lobeor** (etym. obsc.), *sm.* flatterer, liar, mocker.

Lochier (etym. obsc.), *va. & n.* shake, hang, nearly fall.

Locu (on Fk. *loc,* lock of hair, ?), *adj.* tousled (hair)?

Loé (pp. of *loer* 1, q.v.), *adj.* famous, of note.

Loee, fem. of *loé,* q.v., or var. of *lieuee,* q.v.

Loement (on *loer* 1, q.v.), *sm.* advice, opinion, consent.

Loer, (1) (*laudare,* praise), *va.* counsel, approve, praise. *L. a :* advise to. *L. que :* advise that. *Se l. de :* congratulate oneself upon; (2) (*locare,* place), *va.* reward, pay, hire, give; (3) (*lutare*), *va. & rfl.*

besmear (with mud, dirt, or blood).

Loge (Fk. *laubja*, lodge, bower), *sf.* bower (of leaves), tent, lodge, upper room.

Logier (on *loge*, q.v.), *va.*, *n.*, & *rfl.* lodge, (en)camp.

Loi (*lēgem*, set form of words), *sf.* religion, custom, rule, law. *A l. de :* as, in the manner of.

Loier, (1) (*locarium*), *sm.* salary, reward, hire ; (2) (*ligare*), *va.* bind.

Loigne (*lumbea*, on *lumbum*), *sf.* loin.

Loing (*longē*), *adv.* far, afar. *De l. :* from afar. Form in *-s :* **Loinz.**

Loisir (*licēre*), *vn.* & *impers.* be permitted ; *sm.* permission, power, leisure.

Loisor (on *loisir*, q.v.), *sf.* leisure, power, opportunity, permission, pleasure.

Loist, 3 pr. of *loisir*, q.v. **Loitier,** v. *luitier.*

Lonc (*longum*), *adj.* long ; far-carrying (sound) ; *prep.* along, beside, according to. *Also* var. of *loing*, q.v.

Long, var. of *lonc* or *loing*, q.v.

Longaigne (*longanea*, cf. Late L. *longano*, gut), *sf.* dunghill, dung, privy term applied to anything foul or contemptible.

Longes, Longues (*longa* + adv. *-s*), *adv.* for a long time.

Lorain, Lorein (Med. L. *lōranum*, bridle, on *lōrum*, thong), *sm.* ornamented leather straps attached to horse's breast-piece and crupper, saddle-straps.

Lord, Lort, v. *lourt.*

Lores, Lors (*illa hōra* + adv. *-s*), *adv.* then, at that time.

Los (*laus*), *sm.* praise, honour, reputation, fame, advice. *A mon l. :* with my consent. *Sans mon l. :* without my knowledge, or consent.

Losenge (Fk. *lausinga*, lie), *sm.* & *f.* flattery, deceit, slander.

Losengier (on *losenge*, q.v.), *adj.* & *s.* flattering, perfidious, slanderous ; *va.* flatter, deceive.

Lot, 3 pr. subj. of *loer*, q.v.

Lou-, try under **Lo-.**

Lou (*lupum*), *sm.* wolf.

Lourt (perh. *lurdum* for *lūridum*, pale, livid), *adj.* idiot, fool, stupid, dull-witted.

Lovin (*lupīnum*), *adj.* wolf-like.

Loy-, try under **Loi-.**

Loz, v. *los.* **Luer, Luier,** v. *loier* 1. **Luer,** v. *loer.*

Lues (*locō* + adv. *-s*), *adv.* then, at once, now. *L. que :* as soon as.

Lui-, try also under **Loi. Luin(z),** v. *loing.* **Luingne,** v. *loigne.*

Luisir (*lūcīre* for *lūcēre*), *vn.* shine, gleam. *Also* var. of *loisir*, q.v.

Luitier (*lūctare*), *vn.* struggle, strive, fight.

Lunges, v. *longes.* **Ly-,** try under **Li-.**

M

Macecrier, Macheclier (etym. unkn.), *sm.* butcher.

Maçue (*mattiūca*), *sf.* club. *Dimins :* **Maçuele, Maçuete,** *sf.* stick, crook.

Maderin, v. *maserin.*

Madre (OHG. *masar*), *sm.* veined wood, bowl or cup (of veined wood), mazer.

Maginols (etym. obsc.), *adj.* powerful, noble, rich, handsome.

Magrece, v. *maigrece.* **Mahaing,** v. *mehaing.*

Mahommerie (on *Mahom,* Arab. *Muhammad*), *sf.* Mohammedan temple, pagan temple, image, Islam.

Maigne, pr. subj. of *manoir,* q.v., or var. of **Magne** (b. *magnum*), great. **Maignie,** var. of *maisniee,* q.v.

Maigrece (on *maigre* < *macrum,* lean), *sf.* thinness.

Mail, Maill (*malleum*), *sm.* mallet, hammer.

Maille, Malle (**medalia* for **medialia,* on *medius,* half), *sf.* halfpenny.

Maille (*macula*), *sf.* stain; mail (armour).

Maillenter (on pr. p. of *maculare,* or on *maille* < *macula,* q.v.), *va. & rfl.* dirty, cover with blood.

Maillier (on *mail,* q.v.), *va. & n.* strike with a hammer, strike; *v. rfl.* strike one another.

Main-, try also **Man-.**

Main (*manum*), *sf.* hand; sometimes people. *De basse m. ; De pute m. :* common, of low estate. *De bonne m. :* of high degree. *Plevir en m. :* pledge, give one's hand on.

Main, Mains (*mane*), *adv.* in the morning, early; *sm.* morning. *Hui m. :* this morning. *Par m. :* in the morning.

Main, 1 pr. of *manoir,* q.v.

Mainbornir (on *main,* hand, q.v. + Germ. **muntburti,* protection), *va.* rule, govern, administer.

Mainbrunie, Mainburnie (on *mainbornir,* q.v.), *sf.* power, authority, guardianship.

Maindrai, 1 fut. of *manoir,* q.v.

Maindre, var. of **Moindre** (*minor*), less, or of *manoir,* q.v.

Maine (*magnum*), *adj.* great (cf. *magne*).

Maine, Mainent, pr. of *mener,* q.v.; **Mainent,** 6 pr. of *manoir,* q.v.

Mains, var. of *meins,* q.v., or of *main* (*mane*), q.v.; *also* 2 pr. of *manoir,* q.v.

Maint (perh. Celt. *mantî,* greatness, or on *mainz* < *magnos*), *adj.* much, many. *Also* 3 pr. of *manoir,* q.v.

Maintenant (on *maintenir,* q.v.), *adv.* at once, then, thereupon, soon. *De m. :* on end, continuously. *M. que :* as soon as.

Maintenir (**manŭtenīre* for **manŭtenēre*), *va.* maintain, protect, reign over, uphold, live with. *M. la parole :* speak, reply. *Se m.* also: behave, act (cf. *maintenement, sm.,* behaviour).

Maintien (on *maintenir,* q.v.), *sm.* manner, behaviour.

Maior, v. *majour.* **Maire,** nom. of *majour,* q.v.

Mairien (**materiamen,* on *materia,* timber), *sm.* timber (for buildings etc.), stave-wood; *fig.* material; creature (of people).

Mais (*magis*, more), *adv.* more, longer, henceforth, rather, never. *A toz jors* (*totdis*) *m.* : for ever. *M. de* : more than. *M. que* : provided that, since, except that. *Ne* . . . *m.* : no longer. *Ne m.* (*que*) : except that, no more than. *Onques* . . . *m.* : never henceforth.

Maisel (*macellum*, meat-market), *sm.* carnage, slaughter.

Maisele, Maisselle (*maxilla*, jaw-bone), *sf.* jaw, face.

Maishui (*mais*, q.v. + *hui*, q.v.), *adv.* to-day, from to-day on, now.

Maisiere (*maceria*), *sf.* wall.

Maisme, etc., v. *Meïsme, etc.*

Maisnie, Maisniede, Maisniee (**mansiōnata*, on *mansiōnem*, dwelling), *sf.* household, family ; retinue (feudal).

Maistre (*magistrum*), *sm.* master, doctor, lawyer. *M. le roy* : majordomo ; *adj.* chief, main.

Maistrie (on *maistre*, q.v.), *sf.* authority, power, learning, skill. *Par m.* : perfectly.

Maistrier, Maistroier (on *maistre*, q.v.), *va.* master, rule, overcome, educate, trouble.

Majoùr (*majōrem*), *adj.* greater, great.

Mal, (1) (*malum*), *adj.* bad, wicked, difficult. *M. aventure* : misadventure. *Metre en m. an* : overwhelm with ills. *M. goute* : disease, agony ; (2) (*malum*), *sm.* evil, harm. Used with saints' names to indicate various diseases : see Godefroy under *mal* 3, & *maladie. M. ait* : cursed be !

Par m. : with evil intent ; (3) (*male*), *adv.* ill, wrongly, badly. *M. voisié* : crafty. *Prendre m.* : go wrong. *Also* in sense of *mar*, q.v.

Malbaillir (*mal* 3, q.v. + *baillir* q.v.), *va.* ill-treat, ruin, discomfit.

Maldeçon (Eccl. L. *maledictiōnem*), *sf.* curse.

Maldehait, Maldehé (*mal*, q.v. + *dehait*, q.v.), *sm.* misfortune, harm, displeasure.

Maleiçon, v. *maldeçon.*

Maleïr (Eccl. L. *maledicere*), *va.* curse.

Malement (on *mal* 1, q.v.), *adv.* evilly, unfortunately, bitterly, extremely.

Malenter, v. *maillenter.*

Maleoit (Eccl. L. *maledictum*), *pp. adj.* cursed.

Maler (on *mal* 2, q.v.), *va.* mal-treat, abuse.

Maler (on *mail*, q.v.?), *va.* summon.

Malestru (**male astrūcum*, ill-starred), *adj.* wretched, unfortunate, in sorry state.

Maleuré (on *maleur* < *mal* 1, q.v. + *eür*, q.v.), *adj.* wretched, unfortunate.

Malfaù (*mal* 3, q.v. + **fatūtum*, on *fatum*, destiny), *adj.* ill-fated, unfortunate.

Malfé (*mal* 3, q.v. + *fatum*), *sm.* devil, demon ; (also used as a term of abuse). *Also* var. of *malfait* (*malefactum*), *sm.* misdeed, harm.

Malmetre (*mal* 3, q.v. + *metre*, q.v.), *va.* maltreat, harm, spoil, ruin ; *v. rfl.* go to the bad, foreswear oneself, break an oath.

Malostru, v. *malestru*.

Maltalent (*mal* 1, q.v. + *talent*, q.v.), *sm.* anger, temper, hatred, spite. *Par m. :* angrily.

Manage (**mansiōnaticum*, concerning the house), *sm.* house, dwelling, palace, apartment, household, family, furniture, housekeeping.

Manaide, Manaie (*main*, hand, q.v. + *aide* or *aïe*, v. *aiude*), *sf.* pity, mercy, help, power, possession.

Manant (pr. p. of *manoir*, q.v.), *sm.* owner of a dwelling, inhabitant ; *adj.* rich, powerful.

Manantie (on *manant*, q.v.), *sf.* dwelling, wealth, authority.

Manc (*mancum*), *adj. & sm.* maimed, cripple(d), lame.

Mand, v. *mant*.

Mandement (on *mander*, q.v.), *sm.* command, message, order, authority, stronghold, rallying-place, state-room.

Mander (*mandare*), *va.* command, order, summon, ask, send, announce, send to say.

Mandrai, 1 fut. of *manoir*, q.v.

Manevi (on *amanevir*, Germ., cf. Goth. *manvjan*, be willing), *adj.* agile, alert, quick, eager, willing.

Mangon (etym. unkn.), *sm.* sort of gold coin.

Mangue, Manjue, imper. & pr. of **Mangier** (*mandūcare*), eat.

Manicle (on *manicula*, little hand), *sm. & f.* part of armour covering the hand, manacle.

E

Manier, Manoier (on *main*, hand, q.v.), *va.* caress, strike, handle, finger, treat, maltreat, govern ; *vn. & rfl.* conduct oneself, deal with, attack each other ; *adj.* manual, hand-, supple. *M. de* (*a*) *:* skilled in. . . .

Maniere (on *manier*, *adj.*, q.v.), *sf.* appearance, bearing, moderation, intention, custom. *A sa m. :* to one's liking.

Manke, v. *manc*.

Manoir (*manēre*, pass the night), *vn.* dwell, stay, remain. *M. en :* persist in, continue in.

Manovrer (PL. *manŭoperare*, work with the hands), *va.* make, manufacture, prepare, mount (gems) *vn.* act ; *sm.* fabrication, manufacture.

Manrai, 1 fut. of *manoir*, q.v.

Mant (on *mander*, q.v.), *sm.* command, proclamation.

Maor, Maür, v. *majour*.

Mar (*mala hŏra*), *adv.* unfortunately, to one's misfortune. *M. portai :* it was unfortunate for me that I bore. . . . *M. + fut.*, often : one should not.

Marage, Maraige (on *mare*, sea), *adj.* sea-, river-, maritime ; *fig.* wild, dangerous ; *sm.* place by the sea or river, dangerous place.

Marage, *sm.* ; **Marance,** *sf.* (on *marrir*, q.v.), affliction, grief.

Marbré, Marbrin (on *marbre* < *marmor*, marble), *adj.* of marble.

Marce, Marche (Fk. **marka*), *sf.* march, border country, country.

Marcheant (**mercatantem*, on *mercatum*, market), *adj. & sm.* merchant; in good condition, well-stocked.

Marchir (on Fk. **markôn*, stamp), *va. & n.* tread underfoot.

Mare, Marement, v. *mar, marrement.*

Mareschal (Fk. **marhskalk*, stable-hand), *sm.* servant in charge of the horses, farrier; marshal (title).

Mari, var. of *marri*, pp. of *marrir*, q.v.

Mariement (on *marier* < *maritare*, marry), *sm.* marriage.

Marin, *sm.*; **Marine,** *sf.* (*marinum, -am*, adj., sea-), sea, sea-shore, beach.

Marir, v. *marrir.* **Marmorin,** var. of *marbrin*, q.v.

Marois (Fk. **marisk*), *sm.* bog, marsh.

Marreglier (LL. *matricularium*, keeper of a register), *sm.* churchwarden, beadle.

Marrement (on *marrir*, q.v.), *sm.* grief, affliction, displeasure.

Marrir (Fk. **marrjan*, anger), *va.* afflict, grieve, offend, anger, maltreat, lose (way); *vn. & rfl.* lament, be sad, be resentful. *M. le sens :* go mad (with grief). *Marri,* pp. adj.: troubled, vexed, sorrowful.

Marruglier, v. *marreglier.*

Marteleis (on *martel* < **martellum*, on *marcum*, hammer), *sm.* hammer-blow, clash of arms.

Martirer (on *martir*, b. Eccl. L. *martyr*, martyr), *va.* persecute, torture, slaughter.

Martirie (b. Eccl. L. *martyrium,*

martyrdom), *sm. & f.* martyrdom, torture, suffering, slaughter.

Martrin (on *martre*, Fk. **marthor*), *adj.* of marten (fur); *fem.* **Martrine ;** *also sf.,* the fur itself.

Marvoier (on *mar*, q.v. + *voie* < *via*, way), *vn.* stray (physical and moral), go mad.

Masdre, v. *madre.*

Maserin (on *masdre*, q.v.), *adj.* of veined wood; *sm.* veined wood, bowl or cup of veined wood.

Masseis, Massis (on *masse* < *massa*, lump), *adj.* massive, solid, firm.

Mat (from Pers. (*châh*) *mât*, the king is dead, cf. Eng. *checkmate*), *adj.* conquered, overcome, downcast, sad, afflicted, humbled. *Mate chiere :* sad cheer, sorrowful countenance.

Mater (on *mat*, q.v.), *va.* conquer, mate (chess). *Maté*, adj. & sm., conquered, downcast, weakling.

Mau-, try also under **Mal-.**

Maubailli, v. *baillir.* **Maudehait, -hé,** v. *maldehait, -hé.*

Maugré (*mal* 1, q.v. + *gré*, q.v.), *sm.* pain, grief, ill-will; *prep.* in spite of.

Maugreer (on *maugré*, q.v.), *va.* curse, bear ill-will towards.

Maus, form in *-s* of *mal* 1 & 2, q.v. or of *mail*, q.v.

Mecine (*medicīna*, art of healing), *sf.* remedy.

Meciner (on *mecine*, q.v.), *va.* cure, care for, dress (wounds).

Medler, v. *mesler.*

Mehaignier (LL. *mahamiare*, Germ. *man* + *hamjan*, maim, ?), *va.* wound, mutilate, harm, ruin, maltreat; *v. rfl.* hurt oneself, wound oneself.

Mehaing (on *mehaignier*, q.v.), *sm.* wound, mutilation, harm, illness.

Meins (*minus*), *adv.* less. *Also* var. of *main*(*s*), q.v.

Meir, v. *mier*. **Meis**, v. *mois*.

Meïsme (**metipsimum*, on **metipse*, on *egomet ipse*, I myself), *adj. & adv.* self, same, even, also. *A m. de* : very near to. *A m. une fontaine* : at the spring itself. *De m.* : again, similar.

Meïsmement (on *meïsme*, q.v.), *adv.* above all, especially.

Mel, var. of *mal* 2, q.v.

Melancolie (b. LL. *melancholia*, black bile), *sf.* bile, ill-disposition, anger, annoyance.

Meller, v. *mesler*. **Mels, Melz**, v. *miels*.

Membré, (1) (on *membre* < *membrum*, limb), *adj.* stout-limbed, strong, mighty, handsome; (2) (pp. of *membrer*, q.v.), *adj.* famous, clever, sensible, skilful.

Membrer (*memorare*), *va., rfl. & impers.*, remember.

Membru, cf. *membré* 1.

Men-, try also under **Man-**, e.g. **Menage**, v. *manage*.

Mendi (*mendicum*), *adj.* needy, destitute, in want, exhausted (land). *M. de* : deprived of, bereft of ; *sm.* beggar.

Menee (pp. of *mener*, q.v.), *sf.* blast of the horn, cry (hounds), pursuit, noise.

Mener (PL. *minare*, drive animals forward, on *minari*, threaten), *va.* lead, take, display (emotions) ; *v. rfl.* behave. *Se m. de* : provide oneself with.

Menestrel (LL. *ministerialem*, on *ministerium*), *sm.* servant, workman, minstrel ; *fig.* worthless wretch.

Mengler, var. of *mangier* (*manducare*), eat.

Menor (*minōrem*), *adj.* less, smaller, less valuable, lower (rank).

Menouvrer, v. *manovrer*. **Menral**, 1 fut. of *mener*, q.v.

Mentevoir (*mentē habēre*), *va.* recall, mention.

Mentir (PL. *mentīre* for *mentīrī*, lie), *va.* lie, fail to fulfil ; *vn.* fail. *Dieu qui ne menti* (cheville): by the God of truth. *Foi m.* : break one's promise.

Menu (*minūtum*), *adj.* small, unimportant (people). *Chevels m.* : thick curly hair ; *adv.* quickly, delicately. *M. et sovent* : again and again.

Menuement (on *menu*, q.v.), *adv.* delicately, often, closely.

Menuier (on *menu*, q.v.), *adj.* slender, thin, shrill ; *sm.* shrill horn.

Meorc, Meort, 1 & 3 pr. of *morir*, q.v.

Merc, *sm. ;* **Merche**, *sf.* (Fk. **merka*), mark, trace, boundary-stone.

Merchié (*mercatum*), *sm.* market.

Merci (*mercēdem*, salary ; in PL. prize, favour), *sf.* pity, mercy. *En la m. de* : at the mercy of. *La m. Dieu* : thanks to God, by God's grace. *Vostre m. :* thanks to you, thank you.

Mercier (on *merci*, q.v.), *va.* reward, thank.

Merel, *sm. ;* Merelle, *sf.* (etym. unkn.), token (coinage), luck, plight, blow. *Mestraire le (la) m. :* suffer a reverse, be unfortunate.

Merencolie, v. *melancolie.*

Meriaine, Meriane, Meriene (*meridiana* (*hōra*)), *sf.* midday, midday siesta.

Merir (**merire* for *merēre*, earn), *va. & n.* merit, obtain, reward, repay ; *sm.* reward. *Deus vos le mire :* God reward you ! *M. qqch. a qq'un :* give him something as reward or compensation.

Merit (*merītum*, deserts), *sm.*, reward, punishment, worth, value. *Syn. :* **Merite,** *sf.*

Merr-, try under **Mair-, Mare-,** or **Mer-.** **Merrai,** 1 fut. of *mener*, q.v. **Merrien,** v. *mairien.*

Merveille (**miribilia* for PL. *mirabilia*, fem. sing. for n. pl.), *sf.* marvel, wonder. *Avoir m. :* be astonished, wonder. *Tenir a m. :* be astonished at. *Venir a m. :* astonish.

Merveillos (on *merveille*, q.v.), *adj.* amazed, marvellous, prodigious, dreadful, terrible.

Mes, pp. of *manoir*, q.v., or var. of *mais*, q.v.

Mes (*ma(n)sum*, pp. of *manēre*), *sm. & f.* country house, farm, garden, dwelling.

Mes (*missum*, pp. of *mittere*, send, place), *sm.* messenger, envoy, good target ; dish.

Mes-. For verbs and nouns, try also under the simple form, and add the necessary negative or pejorative value of **Mes-** (Germ. *miss-*, cf. OHG. *missa-*, Goth. *miss-* & L. *minus*), e.g. **Mesaisié** (on *mesaise < mes- + aise,* q.v.), *adj.* unfortunate, uncomfortable, ill at ease, poor. **Mesaler** (*mes- + aler*), stray, fail. **Mesamer** (*mes + amer,* love), hate.

Mesavenir (*mes- + avenir,* q.v.), *v. impers.* turn out badly. *Mesavenant,* pr. p. adj. : unbecoming, displeasing.

Mescheoir (*mes- + cheoir,* q.v.), *v. impers.* turn out badly.

Meschief (*mes- + chief,* q.v.), *sm.* misfortune, harm. *Estre a m. :* be unfortunate.

Meschin (on Arab. *miskîn*, poor), *adj. & sm.* young, youth ; *fem.* **Meschine,** girl, lady, servant. *Dimin. :* **Meschinete,** *sf.*

Mescler, v. *mesler.*

Mescreire (*mes- + creire < crēdere*, believe), *va.* disbelieve, doubt, suspect. **Mescreu,** *pp. adj.* : miscreant, unbeliever, renegade.

Mesdit (*mes- + dit*, pp. of *dire < dīcere*, say), *sm.* calumny, slander, lie.

Mesel (LL. *misellum*, leper), *adj. & sm.* leprous, leper ; *fig.* foul.

Mesentendant (*mes- + entendant*, pr. p. of *entendre*, q.v.), *adj.* hard of understanding, perverse, evil-minded.

Mesese, v. *mesaise* under *mesaisié.*

Mesestance (*mes- + estance*, q.v.), *sf.* sorry plight, difficulty, misfortune, affliction.

Mesgresce, v. *maigrece.* **Meshaing, Meshaigner,** v. *meh-.* **Mesiaus,** nom. of *mesel,* q.v.

Mesire (*meus* + **seior* for *senior*), nom. of *monseigneur* (on *seignor,* q.v.).

Mesler (PL. *misculare,* on *miscēre*), *va.* mingle, embroil; *vn.* quarrel; *v. rfl.* become embroiled, quarrel, combat, faint. *Barbe meslee :* greying beard. *Estre meslé a :* lose favour with, be embroiled with. *M. le poing en :* seize by. *Se m. de :* deal with.

Mesme, v. *meīsme.* **Mesnage,** v. *manage.* **Mesnie(e),** v. *maisnie(e).*

Mespenser (*mes-* + *penser,* q.v.), *vn.* doubt, indulge in cowardly thoughts.

Mesprendre (*mes-* + *prendre,* q.v.), *va.* commit (error, crime); *vn.* act wrongly, commit a crime, break a law or custom, make a mistake, misbehave.

Mesprison (on *mespris,* on *mesprendre,* q.v.), *sm. & f.* wrongful act, fault, misdeed, treason, outrage, unseemly behaviour, ill-treatment. *Torner a m. :* regard as a fault.

Mesquerrai, 1 fut. of *mescreire,* q.v. **Mesrien,** v. *mairien.*

Message (on *mes* < *missum*), *sm.* messenger, message, mission.

Mest, Mestrent, 3 & 6 pft. of *manoir,* q.v.

Mestier (*ministerium,* perh. become *mi(n)sterium*), *sm.* service, work, help, need, utensil. *Avoir m. a :* be of use to, help. *Avoir m. de :* need. *De m. :* by profession. *Estre m. :* be necessary.

Mestraire (*mes-* + *traire,* q.v.), *vn.* act wrongly, trick, misbehave; *va.* lose by an unlucky throw, win by trickery. *Merel m.,* v. *merel.*

Mestre, Mestrie, Mestroier, v. *maistr-.*

Metre (*mittere,* in PL. place), *va.* use, spend, put, impute, portray; *vn.* strike blows, wager, delay, rush. *Metre a raison :* address. *M. avant :* bring forward. *M. des coups :* lay on blows. *M. en ni :* deny. *M. en oubli :* forget. *M. peine :* take trouble. *M. son gage :* wager. *M. sur :* accuse. *M. sus :* establish, build, accuse. *Se m. de :* quit, depart from. *Se m. en (sur) :* leave the decision to.

Meü, pp., **Meüsse,** impft. subj. of *moveir,* q.v.

Meürer (*matūrare*), *va., n., & rfl.* ripen.

Mi (*medium*), *adj. & sm.* (in the) middle; *fem.* **Mie** or **Mige.** *A mi ; En mi ; Emmi :* in the middle of. *Par mi :* amid, across, in half. *Par mi tot ceo que :* although.

Mie, var. of *mire,* q.v.

Mie (*mica,* crumb), *sf.* crumb, bit. *N'avoir m. de :* be without, lack. *Ne . . . mie :* not one bit, not at all. *Also* with adv. *-s,* **Mies.**

Miege, v. *mire.*

Mieldre, Mieudre (*melior*), nom. of *meillor* (*meliōrem*), *adj.* better.

Miels, Mielz (*melius*), *adv.* better, rather; *sm. & adj.* (the) better, the better part.

Mier (*merum*), *adj.* pure, whole.

Mignot (etym. obsc.), *adj.* pretty, gracious, affectionate.

Millor, var. of *meillor* (*meliōrem*), *adj.* better.

Milsoldor (*mille solidōrum*, 1,000 " solidi "), *adj.* precious; *sm.* valuable war-horse.

Mirable (*mirabilem*), *adj.* wonderful, astonishing; *fig.* great, strong, powerful.

Mire (*medicum*), *sm.* doctor (*fem.* **Miresse, Mirgesse**). *Also* 3 pr. subj. of *merir*, q.v.

Mirer (PL. *mirare*, stare at, for *mirari*, be surprised), *va.* look, look at, look in the mirror; *v. rfl.* fix one's attention upon.

Mis-, try also under **Mes-** or **Meis-.**

Miserele (alter. of *miserēre*, have mercy), *sf.* penitential litany, *miserere.*

Misoudor, Missodor, v. *milsoldor.*

Moe (perh. Fk. *mauwa), *sf.* mouth, lip.

Moel, Moiel (*modiolum*, little vase), *sm.* nave of wheel; *fig.* centre. *Also* (*mĕdiolum*), egg-yolk.

Moie (*mĕa*), *pron. & adj. fem.* my, mine.

Moien (LL. *medianum*, mid-), *adj.* mid-, medium, middle-class; *sm.* middle, means.

Moigne (on *mŏnicum for Eccl. L. *mŏnachum*), *sm.* monk.

Moillier (*mulierem*), *sf.* wife.

Moillier (*molliare, on *mollem*, soft), *va.* wet, dip (sop).

Moine, pr. of *mener*, q.v. & var. of *moigne*, q.v.

Moinet (dimin. of *moine*, v. *moigne*), *sm.* sparrow.

Mois (*mē(n)sem*), *sm.* month. *Des m. :* for a long time.

Moler, Moller (on *modle* < *modulum*, measure), *v. rfl.* take the shape of, press against, succeed in. *Molé*, pp. adj. : well-shaped (limbs), proved (courage).

Moleste (*molestum*), *adj.* disagreeable, troublesome, troubled, furious; *sf.* (*molesta*) wrong, harm, tiredness, confusion.

Mollier, v. *moillier.* **Molt,** v. *moult.*

Molu (pp. of *moldre* < *molere*, grind away), *adj.* sharpened, sharp (weapon).

Mon (etym. obsc.), *adv.* certainly, surely, right.

Mondain (Eccl. L. *mundanum*, secular), *adj.* worldly, noble, perfect.

Monde (b. *mundum*), *adj.* pure. *Also* var. of *mont* 1, q.v. or of *monte*, q.v.

Monder (*mundare*), *va.* cleanse, purify.

Moniage (on *monie*, v. *moigne*), *sm.* monasticism, entry into a monastery, monk's orders, monastery.

Monie, v. *moigne.*

Monjoie (*mont* 2, q.v. + *joie*, q.v.), *sf.* summit, height, pile, abundance, joy. *Also* war-cry of the French.

Mont, (1) (*mundum*), *sm.* world;

(2) (*mõntem*), *sm.* mountain, hill, mound ; *fig.* pile. *A m. :* aloft. *A m. e a val :* high and low ; (3) Syn. of *moult*, q.v.

Montanee (on *monter*, q.v.), *sf.* value, cost, total, duration. *Ne vaut la m. de :* it is not worth. . . .

Monte (on *monter*, q.v.), *sf.* mountain ; value, cost, number. *A une m. :* at once, together.

Monteplier, v. *mouteplier*.

Monter (*mõntare, on *mõntem*), *va.* help to mount, increase, equal, be of use to, matter. *A vos que monte? :* what is it to you? ; *vn.* equal ; arise ; *v. rfl.* arise. *Montant*, pr. p. adj. : on horseback ; *sm.* value, worth.

Mordrir (Fk. *morthrjan), *va.* kill.

More (etym. unkn.), *sf.* point (weapon).

More (PL. *mõra*, fem. sing. for n. pl.), *sf.* mulberry.

Moré (on *More < Maurum*, Moor), *adj.* dark brown.

Morel (*maurellum, Moorish), *adj.* dark brown, black ; *sm.* brown or black horse.

Morir (*morire for *mori*, die), *va.* kill ; *vn.* die ; *v. rfl.* be dying. *Vos a mort :* he has killed you.

Mors (*morsum*), *sm.* bite, biting, piece.

Mortrisor (on *mortre <* Fk. *morthor, murder), *sm.* murderer.

Mostier (*monisterium for Eccl. L. *monastērium*), *sm.* monastery, convent, church.

Mostrer (*mo(n)strare*, show), *va.* show, declare, reveal ; *vn.* reveal the truth ; *v. rfl.* expound one's knowledge.

Mot (*mottum for LL. *muttum*, murmur), *sm.* word. *Dire mal m. de :* insult. *Ne soner m. :* remain silent.

Moult (*multum*), *adj.* numerous, many ; *adv.* (*multum*), many, very.

Moüs, 2 pft. of *movoir*, q.v.

Moustier, v. *mostier*.

Moustrance (on *mostrer*, q.v.), *sf.* proof, demonstration.

Mouteplier (*multiplicare*), *va.*, *n.* & *rfl.* multiply, increase.

Moutier, v. *mostier*.

Moveir, **Movoir** (*movēre*), *va.* move, cause, stir up ; *vn.* & *rfl.* move, stir, depart, originate. *M. guerre :* make war.

Moy-, try under **Moi-** or **Mei-**.

Mu-, try also under **Mo-**.

Mu (*mütum*), *adj.* dumb, speechless.

Muable (*mütabilem*, variable), *adj.* that will moult, changeable.

Mucier, **Muchier** (etym. obsc.), *va.* & *rfl.* hide, cover.

Mue (on *muer*, q.v.), *sf.* hiding-place, retreat, prison, mew (hawks, etc.), cage (birds, usually for fattening).

Muel (dimin. of *mu*, q.v.), *adj.* dumb. *Also* var. of *moel*, q.v.

Muer (*mütare*), *va.*, *n.*, & *rfl.* change, move, moult. *M. que :* prevent. *Ne puet m. ne plort :* he cannot help weeping. *M. le sanc :* change colour. *Also* var. of *muier*, q.v.

Muerc, 1 pr.; **Muerge,** pr. subj. of *morir*, q.v. **Muet,** 3 pr. of *movoir*, q.v.

Muete (LL. *movita*, pp. fem., moved), *sf.* uprising, riot, expedition, departure.

Mui, 1 pft. of *movoir*, q.v.

Muier (on *muer*, q.v.), *adj.* moulted (term of praise applied to falcons).

Muillier, v. *moillier.* **Muir,** 1 pr.; **Muire,** pr. subj. of *morir*, q.v.

Muire, alter. of *muïr* (*mūgīre*, bellow), *vn.* roar, howl, bray, cry.

Mult, v. *moult.* **Mun-,** try under **Mon-.** **Munie,** v. *moigne.* **Mur-,** try under **Mor-.** **Murdrissor, Murtrissor,** v. *mortrisor.*

Musart (on *muser*, q.v.), *adj. & sm.* fool, dreamer, wanton.

Muscler, v. *mucier.*

Muser (on Old Fr. **mus*, snout, Late L. *mūsum*, orig. unkn.), *va.* think, muse; *vn.* amuse oneself, waste one's time, play the fool.

Musdrir, v. *mordrir.* **Musser,** v. *mucier.* **Mustier,** v. *mostier.*

Mustrance, v. *moustrance.* **My-,** try also under **Mi-.**

N

Nace, Nache, v. *nage* 1.

Nacion (on *natiōnem*), *sf.* birth, extraction, rank; descendants (*rare*).

Nadel (*natalem* (*dïem*)), *sm.* Christmas.

Nafrer, v. *navrer.*

Nage, (1) (**natica*, on *natis*), *sf.* buttock; (2) (on *nagier*, q.v.), *sf.* sailing, (sea-)voyage.

Nageor (*navigatōrem*, or on *nagier*, q.v.), *sm.* sailor.

Nagier (*navigare*), *vn. & rfl.* sail, row; *va.* take by boat or ship, cross the water.

Naï (var. of *naïf*, q.v.), *adj.* bare, natural (rock), virgin (forest).

Naie, v. *naje.* **Naif,** v. *nef.*

Naïf (*natïvum*), *adj. & sm.* native, natural, foolish.

Nais, form in -s of *naïf*, q.v. or of *naï*, q.v.

Naissement (on root *nasc-*, cf. PL. *nascere* for *nascï*, be born), *sm.* birth, dawn.

Naje (*na + je*, not I), *adv.* no.

Narille (**narïcula*, on *naris*, nostril), *sf.* nostril.

Nasal (on *nés < nasum*, nose), *sm.* nose-piece (of helmet).

Nasaus, form in -s of *nasal*, q.v. **Nasel,** cf. *nasal.*

Nasquir (for *naistre*, PL. *nascere*, by analogy with pft. *nasqui*), *vn.* be born.

Nastre (*natrïcem*, serpent, scourge), *adj.* wicked, deceitful.

Nataus, form in -s of **Natal** (from *natalem*, birthday), *sm.* Christmas day; any high feast (Easter, Ascension, etc.).

Nation, v. *nacion.*

Natural, Naturel (*natūralem*, natural), *adj.* natural, by birth, proper, pure, knightly.

Naturé (pp. of *naturer*, on *nature*, *< natūra*, nature, qualities), *adj.* noble, mighty.

Navee (on *nave*, b. *navis*, ship), *sf.* shipload, boatload.

Navie, v. *navire*.

Navire (alter. of *navilie* < **navilium* for *navigium*, ship), *sm.* ship, fleet. *Var.*: **Navie, Navilie, Navoi.**

Navrer (on Old Fr. **navre*, Fk. **narwa*, scar), *va.* wound.

Navreure (on *navrer*, q.v.), *sf.* wound.

Ne (*nec*), *conj.* neither, nor; or, and (separating two distinct elements in a proposition). *Ne ce ne quoi :* not at all; in any way.

Ne (atonic develt. of *nōn*), *adv.* not. *Ne que :* any more than; no more than.

Neant, v. *neïent.* **Nectelet,** v. *netelet.* **Ned,** form of *ne* < *nec*, q.v., used before a vowel. **Neel,** v. *neiel.*

Nef (*navem*), *sf.* ship, nave (of church).

Negun (*nec ūnum*), *adj. & pron.* no, no one.

Neiel (*nigellum*), *sm.* black enamel, engraved pattern filled with enamel. *Also used for* buckle.

Neielé (on *neiel,* q.v.), *adj.* enamelled, patterned.

Neient, 6 pr. of *neier*, q.v.

Neïent (*nec entem*, not a being), *sm. & adv.* nothing, not at all, in no way. *De n. :* in anything. *Ne . . . n. :* in no way. *N'i a n. de + infin. :* there is no means of. . . . *Pour n. :* in no way, in vain, nearly.

Neier, v. *noier* 1 or 2. **Neif,** v. *noif.*

Neis (*nec ipsum*), *adv.* not even, even; again (*rare*). *N. que ; N. com :* no more than.

Neïs, var. of *nés*, q.v. or of *neïs*, q.v. **Nek-,** v. **Nequ-.** **Nen,** var. of *ne* (*nōn*), q.v.

Nenil, Nennil (*ne* < *nōn* + **illi* for *ille*), *adv.* not, no.

Neporoc, Neporoec (*ne* < *nōn* + *poroc*, q.v.), *conj.* none the less.

Neporquant (on *porquant*, q.v.), *adv.* none the less.

Nequedent, Nequendent (*nōn cōgito inde?*), *conj. & adv.* nevertheless, none the less.

Nercir, v. *noircir.*

Nes, contr. of *ne les* or *ne se*, or var. of *neïs*, q.v.

Nés (*nasum*), *sm.* nose. *Also* form in *-s* of *nef*, q.v.

Nessement, v. *naissement.*

Nesun (*nec ipsum ūnum*), *adj.* none, not (even) one.

Neteé (on *net* < *nitidum*, gleaming), *sf.* cleanness, purity.

Netelet (dimin. of *net* < *nitidum*, gleaming), *adj.* beautiful, handsome.

Neu (*nōdum*), *sm.* knot. *Also* for *nel = ne le.*

Neü, pp. of *nuire*, q.v.

Neül (*nec ullum*), *adj.* no, not one.

Nevot, Nevuld (*nepōtem*), *sm.* nephew.

Nez (*natus*, pp. of *naistre*), born, a native of. . . . *Also* var. of *nés*, q.v.

Ni (*nidum*), *sm.* nest. *Also* var. of **Ne** (*nec*), q.v., & 1 pr. and pr. subj. of *noier* 1 & 2, q.v.

Niant, v. *neïent.*

Nice (*nescium*, ignorant), *adj.* ignorant, foolish, stupid, clumsy.

Nicet, dimin. of *nice*, q.v. **Nielle,** var. of *niule*, q.v. **Nient,** v. *neïent.* **Nier,** v. *noier.* **Niés** (*nepos*), nom. of *nevot*, q.v.

Niquier (Germ., cf. MHG & Netherl. *nicken*), *vn.* nod ; *va.* strike.

Nis, v. *neïs.* **Nisun,** v. *nesun.*

Niule (*nebula*), *sf.* cloud, mist.

No (on *noer*, v. *nouer*), *sm.* swimming. *Passer a no :* swim across.

Noal(z) (on Late L. *nõgalem* for *nũgalem*, trifle), *adv.* worse ; *sm.* the worst, disadvantage.

Noaudre, nom. of *noelor*, q.v.

Noceler, Nocier (on *noces* < *noptias for *nũptias*, marriage), *va.* & *n.* marry. *Femme noceiee :* lawful wife.

Noche, Nosche (Fk. *nusca), *sf.* necklace, bracelet, brooch, buckle.

Nod-, v. **No-,** e.g. **Nodrir,** v. *norrir.* **Noefme,** v. *nuefme.*

Noel (*nõdellum), *sm.* knot, buckle. *Also* var. of *nadel*, q.v.

Noelor (compar. of *noalz*, on model of *meliõrem*, etc.), *adj.* less, worse ; *sm.* the worst, the lesser people.

Noer (*nõdare*), *va.* knot, tie. *Also* var. of *nouer*, q.v.

Noiel, -é, v. *neiel, -é.* **Noient** v. *neïent.*

Noier, (1) (*negare*), *va.* deny, refuse ; (2) (*necare*, kill), *va.* & *n.* kill, drown.

Noif (*nivem*), *sf.* snow.

Noircir (*nigricïre for *nigrescere*), *va.* & *n.* blacken, de-

prive of colour, turn pale ; *pp. adj.* & *sm.* perverse, distressed ; devil.

Noiron (*Nerõnem*), Nero. *Le pré N. :* the Vatican, Rome. *La geste N. ; Le lignaige N. :* the pagans (by confusion with *noir* < *nigrem*, black,?).

Noise (*nausea*, sea-sickness), *sf.* noise, rumour, commotion, painful situation, quarrel.

Noisier (*nauseare*, be sea-sick ; talk nonsense), *vn.* make a noise, shout, quarrel ; *sm.* noise, commotion, quarrel.

Noisos, Noisous (on *noise*, q.v.), *adj.* turbulent, strife-seeking, quarrelsome.

Nom, v. *non* (*nõmen*).

Nomeement (*nomee*, pp. fem. of *nomer*, q.v. + *-ment*), *adv.* exactly, namely, especially ; in person.

Nomer (*nõminare*), *va.* name, fix, appoint. *Nomé*, pp. adj. : renowned.

Non (stressed form of *nõn*), *adv.* not. *Ge non ! :* not I !

Non (*nõmen*), *sm.* name. *Avoir* (a) *n. :* be called. *Par n. de :* as one named to . . ., by right of, in virtue of.

Nonain (Eccl. L. *nonna* + *-ain* < *-anem*), *sf. acc.* nun.

Nonchaleir (*non* < *nõn* + *chaleir*, q.v.), *sm.* heedlessness. *Metre en n. :* pay small heed to.

Noncier (*nuntiare*), *va.* announce, tell.

None, Nonne (Eccl. L. *nõna* (*hõra*)), *sf.* nones (3 p.m.).

Nonne (Eccl. L. *ncnna*), *sf.* nun.

Nonporquant, v. *neporquant.*

Nonsachant (*non* + *sachant*, analog. pr. p. of *saveir*, q.v.) ;
Nonsavant (*non* + *savant*, pr. p. of *saveir*, q.v.), *adj.* ignorant, foolish.

Noreture (*nutritūra*), *sf.* food, education, training.

Norreçon (*nutritiōnem*, food), *sf.* food, upbringing, education, family, behaviour.

Norri (pp. of *norrir*, q.v.), *sm.* fellow-guest, dependant, retainer.

Norrir (*nutrīre*), *va.* feed, bring up, rear, retain in one's service.

Norrois (Fk. **norrisk*), *adj.* Norwegian ; *fig.* fierce, strong.

Nou-, try also under **No-**.

Nouer (**nōtare* for *natare*, swim, infl. by *nauta*, sailor), *vn.* swim ; *sm.* swimming. *Also* var. of *noer*, q.v.

Nourreçon, v. *norreçon*. **Nourriture**, v. *noreture*.

Noveler (*novellare*), *va.* renew, tell ; *vn.* revive, renew.

Novelier (on *novel* < *novellum*, new, or on *novele* < PL. *novella*, news), *adj.* fickle, gossiping, cowardly.

Nu-, try also under **No-** or **Nou-**.

Nu (*nūdum*), *adj.* bare, devoid. *N. a n. :* without hindrance, unopposed.

Nubler (on *nūbilem*, cloud), *va.* cover with cloud, obscure.

Nuef, (1) (*novum*), *adj.* new ; (2) (*novem*), *num.* nine.

Nuefme (**novimum* for *nōnum*), *ordin. num.* ninth.

Nuire (**nocere* for *nocēre*), *va.* harm.

Nuisance (on *nuisir*, q.v.), *sf.* harm, trouble.

Nuisir (*nocēre*), *va.* harm.

Nuitie (on *nuit* < *noctem*), *sf.* night.

Nul (*nūllum*), *adj. & pron.* none, no one, no. *May also mean* some, someone, anyone.

Nullui, Nului, oblique case of *nul*, q.v. **Nun,** var. of *non* (*nōn* or *nōmen*), q.v. **Nunein,** v. *nonain.* **Nurir,** v. *norrir.* **Nus,** form in *-s* of *nul*, q.v., or var. of *nos* (*nōs*), *pron.* we, us.

O

O, (1) (*hōc*), *adv.* yes ; *pron.* that ; (2) (*apud*), *prep.* with. *Ensemble o. :* together with. *O. tot :* together with ; (3) (*aut*), *conj.* or.

Oan, v. *ouan.*

Obliance (on *oblier*, q.v.), *sf.* forgetfulness, omission.

Oblier (**oblītare*, on pp. of *obliviscī*), *va.* forget, neglect ; *vn. & rfl.* fail in one's duty, be neglectful.

Obs-, try under **Os-.**

Obvier (LL. *obviare*, go to meet), *vn.* approach, oppose, reproach.

Occire, v. *ocire.* **Occolson,** v. *ochoison.*

Ocholson (*occasiōnem*, opportunity), *sf.* occasion, chance, reason, cause, accusation ; *sometimes* calamity. *Par nulle o. :* in no way. *Sans o. :* without opposition, without cause.

Ocire (*auccidere). *va.* kill, bring about the death of.

Ocise (pp. fem. of *ocire*, q.v.), *sf.* murder, slaughter.

Ocision (*occisiōnem*), *sf.* slaughter, murder.

Ocisis, 2 pft. of *ocire*, q.v. **Octroyer**, v. *otroyer*. **Od,** form of *o* 2, q.v. **Odi-,** try also under **Oi-**.

Odide (*audita*, pp. fem. of *audire*, hear), *sf.* hearing, ear, sound, echo.

Odrai, 1 fut. of *oïr*, q.v.

Oe (*auca for *avica, on *avis*, bird), *sf.* goose.

Oeil, v. *ueil*.

Oeille (LL. *ovicula*, on *ovis*), *sf.* sheep.

Oeilliere (on *oeil*, v. *ueil*), *sf.* vizor, eye-piece.

Oel, var. of *ivel*, q.v. **Oelent,** 6 pr. of *oloir*, q.v. **Oënt,** 6 pr. of *oïr*, q.v. **Oes,** v. *ues*. **Oeseuse,** v. *oiseuse*.

Oevre (*opera*), *sf.* work, deed, act, feat. *A l'o. de* : made in the style of. *En o.* : in deed.

Oëz, 5 pr. & imper. pl. of *oïr*, q.v.

Offendre (*offendere*, strike, offend), *va.* attack, offend, strike against ; *vn.* attack.

Offrois, v. *orfreis*. **Oi,** 1 pr. of *oïr*, q.v., 1 pft. of *avoir*, or var. of *hui*, q.v. **Oï,** 1 pft. & pp. of *oïr*, q.v. *Also excl.,* ah !

Oiance (on *oïr*, q.v.), *sf.* hearing. *En o.* : publicly, aloud.

Oiant, pr. p. of *oïr*, q.v. *En o. ; O. toz* : openly, in everyone's hearing, publicly.

Oidme, v. *uidme*.

Oie (for *oje*, q.v.), *adv.* yes (I do, will, etc.). *Also* pr. subj. of *oïr*, q.v., and var. of *odide*, q.v.

Oignement (*unguentum*, salve, unguent), *sm.* unguent, perfume, ointment.

Oil (*o* < *hŏc*, + *il* < *illi for *ille*), *adv.* yes. *O. voir* : yes indeed. *Also* var. of *ueil*, q.v.

Oindre (*ungere*), *va.* anoint, consecrate ; *fig.* flatter (*rare*).

Oint (on pp. of *oindre*, q.v.), *sm.* grease, oil.

Oiole, 1 & 3 impft. of *oïr*, q.v.

Oir, var. of *hoir*, q.v.

Oïr (*audire*), *va.* hear. *See also oiant.*

Oire, Oirre, pr. & pr. subj. of *errer* (*iterare*), q.v. *Also* var. of *orie*, q.v.

Oirre (*iter*, or on *errer* < *iterare*), *sm. & f.* journey, way, speed. *Adresser son o. vers* : travel towards. (*A*) *Grand o.* : at great speed, rapidly. *A plein o.* : at full speed. *En o.* : at once.

Oisdif (connected with *oisos*, q.v., but suffix obsc.), *adj.* idle, vain.

Oisdive (on *oisdif*, q.v.), *sf.* idleness, futility.

Oiseaus, form in -*s* of **Oisel** (*aucellum for *avicellum, dimin. of *avis*), *sm.* bird.

Oiseler (on *oisel*, v. *oiseaus*), *vn.* hunt (birds) ; *fig.* rejoice ; *va.* catch (birds) ; *fig.* capture. *Aveir bien oiselé* : to have been successful. *Aveir mal oiselé* : to have failed.

Oiseuse (on *oiseus*, v. *oisos*), *sf.* idleness, cowardice, relaxation, foolish speech.

Oisos (*ōtiōsum*, at leisure), *adj.* idle, leisured ; cowardly.

Oissor (*uxōrem*), *sf.* wife.

Oiste (*hostia*, sacrificial victim), *sf.* the Host (*Eccl.*).

Oit, 3 pr. ; **Oit,** 3 pft. of *oīr*, q.v. **Oixur,** var. of *oissor*, q.v.

Oje (*o* < *hōc*, + *je*, *eo* for *ego*), *adv.* yes (I do).

Okeson, Okison, v. *ochoison*.

Olent (*olentem*), *adj.* perfumed, fragrant ; *sometimes* stinking.

Olif (*olīvum*, on *olīva*), *sm.* olive-tree, olive.

Olifant (*elephantum*, elephant), *sm.* ivory, horn, elephant.

Oloir (*olēre*), *vn.* smell.

Olor, Olur (*olōrem* for *odōrem*, infl. by *olēre*, smell), *sf.* odour, scent, smell.

Olt-, try under **Out-,** e.g. **Oltre,** v. *outre*.

Om, atonic form of *huem*, q.v.

Ombrage (on *ombre* < *umbra*, shadow), *sm.* shadow, shade ; *adj.* shady, obscure ; (of people) taciturn, suspicious.

Ombroier (on *ombre* < *umbra*, shadow), *va.* shade ; *vn. & rfl.* take shelter in the shade, rest in the shade ; take fright (horses) ; *vn.* give shade.

Ome, v. *home.* **Onb-,** try under **Omb-. Onc, Onkes,** v. *onques.*

Oni, Onni (pp. of *onir* for *unir* < *ūnīre*), *adj.* equal, uniform.

Onniement (on *onni*, q.v.), *adv.* equally, together, without ceasing.

Onnir, v. *honir.*

Onques (*unquam* + adv. *-s*), *adv.* ever, never, not, nowhere. *O. ainz . . . ne :* never before. *O. jor :* never hereafter, never thereafter. *O. mais :* never thereafter. *Qui c'o. :* who-ever.

Ont (*unde*), *adv.* whence, where, wherefore. *Par o. :* whence, by which way.

Or, Ore ((*ad*) *hōram*), *adv. & conj.* now, then, soon. *Des or :* right now, at once. *D'or en avant :* henceforward. *Also,* with adv. *-s,* **Ores.**

Oral, I fut. of *oīr*, q.v., & I pft. of *orer*, q.v.

Oraille (on *ōra*, edge), *sf.* edge, border.

Orains (*or, ore*, q.v. + *ainz*, q.v.), *adv.* recently, previously.

Orb (*orbum*, bereft), *adj.* blind, obscure, dark.

Orcel (dimin. of *orca*, wide earth-enware jar), *sm.* jar, holy-water basin. *Syn. :* **Orcele,** *sf.*

Orde, fem. of *ort*, q.v.

Ordene (*ordinem*), *sm. & f.* order, rank, priest's orders.

Ordené (pp. of *ordener*, q.v.), *sm.* ordained priest.

Ordenement (on *ordene* or *ordener*, q.v.), *sm.* rule, order, arrangement.

Ordener (on *ordinare*, put in order), *va.* order, arrange ; (*eccl.*) consecrate, ordain.

Ordiere (*orbitaria*, on *orbita*, rut), *sf.* rut, track.

Ordoier (on *ord*, v. *ort*), *va.* dirty, sully, dishonour ; *vn. & rfl.* be sullied.

Ordonner, var. of *ordener*, q.v. (perh. infl. by *donner?*). **Ordre,** later form of *ordene*, q.v.

Ore (*hŏra*), *sf.* hour. *D'o. a* (*es*) *altres :* from time to time. *Also* var. of *or*, q.v.

Ore (*aura*), *sf.* wind.

Oré, (1) (on *ore < aura*, q.v.), *sm.* wind, storm, tempest ; (2) (on *or < aurum*, gold), *adj.* golden, gilded ; (3) (cf. *oree* 1), *sm.* edge, border ; (4) pp. of *orer*, q.v.

Oree, (1) (on *or < *ŏrum* for *ŏra*), *sf.* edge ; (2) (on *ore < aura*, q.v.), *sf.* wind, shower, storm.

Oreillier (on *oreille < auricula*, ear), *va. & n.* listen (to), attend to.

Orendreit (= *or endreit*), *v. endreit.* **Orent,** 6 pft. of *avoir* or 6 pr. of *orer*, q.v.

Orer (*ŏrare*, speak), *va., n., & rfl.* pray, worship.

Ores, v. *or, ore. Also* form in *-s* of *ore*, *sf.*, q.v.

Orfe (Eccl. L. *orphqnum*), *sm. & adj.* orphan ; *adj. sometimes =* bereft.

Orfenin (Eccl. L. **orphaninum*, or on *orfene*, form of *orfe*, q.v.), *sm.* orphan.

Orfreis (perh. **aurum phrygium*, Phrygian gold), *sm.* orphrey, cloth embroidered with gold threads.

Orgoil (Fk. **urgôli*, pride), *sm.* pride, proud words, outrageous behaviour ; *sometimes* valiant warrior.

Orgoillos (on *orgoil*, q.v.), *adj.* wonderful, valiant, mighty, proud.

Orguener (on *organum*, organ), *va. & n.* play the organ, sing to organ accompaniment, sing clearly, charm by singing.

Orguil-, v. *orgoil-*.

Orie (*aureum*), *adj.* golden, gilt.

Ori(e)flambe (*orie*, q.v. + *flambe*, q.v.), *sf.* oriflamme.

Orine (*originem*), *sf.* origin, lineage, birth, race.

Oriol (*aureolum*, golden), *sm.* oriole.

Orle (**ŏrulum*, on *ŏra*), *sm.* edge, hem.

Orlé (pp. of *orler*, on *orle*, q.v.), *pp. adj.* hemmed, edged.

Orne (form of *ordene*, q.v.), *sm. & f.* order. *A o. :* in order, in succession.

Orral, 1 fut. of *oïr*, q.v. **Orribleté,** v. *horribleté*.

Ort (*horridum*, horrible), *adj.* dirty, filthy, horrible, repugnant. *Also* var. of *hort*, sm., q.v.

Ortell (alter. of *articulum*, joint), *sm.* toe. Form in *-s* usually **Ortaus.**

Os (*ausum*), *adj.* daring, bold.

Os, 2 pr. of *oïr*, q.v., or 1 pr. and 1 & 2 pr. subj. of *oser*, q.v. *Also* form in *-s* of *ost*, q.v.

Osberc (on O. Pr. *ausberc*, Southern equiv. of *halberc*, q.v.), *sm.* hauberk.

Oschier (etym. unkn.), *va.* notch, break.

Oseur (*obscūrum*), *adj.* obscure, dark, hidden.

Oseque (LL. *obsequia* for *exsequiae*, infl. by *obsequium*, deference, compliance), *sm.* funeral rites.

Oser (*ausare*, on *ausus*, pp. of *audēre*, dare), *va. & n.* dare. *Osé*, pp. adj.: bold, daring.

Osiere (Late L. *auseria*, orig. obsc.), *sf.* osier, withy, wicker.

Ost (*hostem*, enemy), *sm. & f.* army, enemy, camp. *Also* 3 pr. subj. of *oser*, q.v.

Ostage (on *oste*, q.v.), *sm.* lodging, hostage, pledge.

Ostagier (on *ostage*, q.v.), *va.* give as hostage, provide a guarantee ; *sm.* hostage.

Ostal, v. *ostel*.

Oste (*hospitem*), *sm.* host, landlord.

Osteier (on *ost*, q.v.), *vn.* campaign, wage war.

Ostel (LL. *hospitalem*, guestroom), *sm.* lodging, dwelling, hall. *Prester h. :* provide hospitality, lodge.

Osteler (on *ostel*, q.v.), *va. & n.* lodge, shelter, stay, provide hospitality.

Oster (*obstare*, in LL. prevent, retain), *va.* remove, take away, exempt, ban, exile ; *v. rfl.* avoid, refrain from.

Osterin (on *ostrinum*, purple), *adj.* purple, blue, red ; cloth dyed some shade of blue, purple or red.

Osteus, form in -*s* of *ostel*, q.v. **Ostier**, v. *osteier*.

Ostor (LL. *auceptōrem* for *accipiter*), *sm.* hawk.

Ostorin, v. *osterin*. **Ot**, 3 pr. of *oïr*, q.v., 3 pft. of *avoir*, or var. of *o* 2, q.v. **Otot** (= *o tot*), v. *o* 2. **Otrier**, v. *otroier*.

Otroier (*auctōrizare*, on LL. *auctōrare*, guarantee), *va. &*

rfl. grant, agree to, admit, approve ; *v. rfl. also* surrender.

Ou (*ubi*), *adv.* where, wherever, seeing that ; *rel.* in whom. *Also* var. of *el* (= *en le*), q.v.

Oü, pp. of *avoir* (*habēre*).

Ouan (*hōc annō*, this year), *adv.* this year, now, to-day, ever.

Oublee (Eccl. L. *oblata*, oblation, fem. pp. of *offerre*, offer), *sf.* offering, victim ; (*Eccl.*) unconsecrated wafer ; wafer (thin biscuit).

Oue, v. *oë*. **Ouir**, v. *oïr*. **Oulant**, v. *olent*.

Ouquel (*ou* = *en le* + *quel*, q.v.), *pron.* in which.

Ourent, 6 pft., **Out**, 3 pft. of *avoir* (*habēre*).

Outrage (on *outre*, q.v.), *sm.* abuse, insult, excess. *A o. :* extremely, unnecessarily. *Parler d'o. :* speak insultingly, abusively.

Outrance (on *outrer*, q.v.), *sf.* violence. *Mener a o. :* vanquish, defeat.

Outre (*ultra*), *prep. & adv.* beyond, past, through, forward. *Aler o. :* pass on. *Faire o. :* complete. *Metre o. :* thrust right through. *O. cuivert:* thorough scoundrel or coward. *O. ma volenté :* against my will. *O. mon gré :* against my will or wishes. *Passer o. :* go past. *Tout o. :* completely, out and out.

Outreement (on pp. of *outrer*, q.v.), *adv.* entirely, thoroughly, violently, excessively.

Outrepasser (*outre*, q.v. + *passer*, q.v.), *vn. & rfl.* pass beyond.

Outrer (on *outre*, q.v.), *va.*, *n.*, *&
rfl.* go beyond, pass, surpass,
finish, vanquish.

Ouverrai, 1 fut. of *ovrer*, q.v. or
of *ovrir*, q.v. **Ouvrer**, v. *ovrer*.
Ovre, v. *oevre*.

Ovraigne, Ovrainne (on *ovre*, v.
oevre), *sf.* work.

Ovrer (LL. *operare* for *operari*),
va. & n. work, take pains,
make, do, act, embroider.

Ovrir (**operīre* for *aperīre*, infl. by
cooperīre, cover), *va. & n.* open,
expose, disclose. *O. un conseil :* dissolve a meeting, ter-
minate a session.

Oz, 2 pr. & imper. sing. of *oïr*,
q.v., & form in *-s* of *ost*, q.v.

P

Pae-, try under **Pai-** or **Pao-**.

Paienie, *sf.*, **Paienisme**, *sm.* (on
paien < Eccl. L. *paganum*,
heathen ; CL. peasant), pagan
or Saracen land.

Paienor (*paganōrum*, gen. pl.),
adj. of the pagans, pagan.

Paier (*pacare*, pacify), *va.* appease, satisfy, make peace with,
reconcile, pay ; *vn. & rfl.*
secure peace, grow calm. *P.
un colp :* strike a blow. *Paié*,
pp. adj. : satisfied.

Paile, v. *paille*.

Paillart (on *paille*, straw < *palea*,
stalk), *sm. & adj.* wretch,
good-for-nothing.

Paille (*pallium*, sort of cloak),
sm. cloth of silk ; *sometimes*
covering, tent. For **Paille**, *sf.*,
cf. *paillart*.

Paine, v. *peine*. **Pair**, v. *per*.
Pair, 1 pr., **Paire**, 1 pr. subj. of
paroir, q.v.

Pais (*pacem*), *sf.* peace, satisfaction. *Also* var. of *pas*,
q.v.

Pais (LL. *pagĕ(n)sem*, country-
dweller), *sm.* country, land.
Tenir un p. : rule, govern.

Paisier (on *pais*, q.v.), *v. rfl.* be
appeased, reconciled, grow
calm.

Paisson (on root of *paissel*
< **paxellum* for *paxillum*), *sm.*
stake, pole, prop.

Paistre (*pascere*), *va.* feed ; *vn.*
graze.

Pal, v. *pel*, *sm.*

Palacre, Palagre (on *pelagus*, sea,
with new suffix), *sm.* sea,
ocean-swell.

Palasin = *palazin*, v. *palatin*.

Palasinos (on *palasy* for *paralisie*,
on Medic. L. *paralysis*), *adj.*
paralytic, palsied.

Palatin (Med. L. *palatīnum*, adj.,
court-), *adj.* of the court ; *sm.*
paladin. *Also spelt* **Palazin** under infl. of *palais* (*palatium*).

Palefroi (LL. *paraverēdum*, on
Gk. *para*, near, + Gaul. *uor-
ēdd*, charger), *sm.* palfrey.

Palie, v. *paille*, *sm.*

Palis, Paliz (on *pal*, v. *pel*, *sm.*),
sm. stake, palisade, hedge.

Palmier (on *palme* < *palma*, palm),
sm. pilgrim (bearing branch of
palm).

Palmoier, v. *paumoier*. **Pal-
tonier**, v. *pautonier*.

Palu (*palûdem*), *sf.* marsh, mud.

Pan-, try under **Pen-**, e.g. **Pandant**,
v. *pendant*.

Pan (*pannum*, piece of cloth), *sm.* skirt (hauberk, etc.), streamer (gonfalon), portion (territory), pannel, flap (tent); net (*rare*). *Tenir son p.* : stand firm.

Pancer (var. of *penser*, q.v.), *va.* care for, treat (wounds), curry (horse).

Panel (******panellum*, on *pannum*), *sm.* piece of cloth, rag or cushion beneath saddle. *Trosser son p.* : flee.

Panre, var. of *penre*, q.v. **Panser**, v. *pancer* or *penser*.

Paor (*pavŏrem*), *sf.* fear.

Par-. Sometimes, for infinitives, nouns or adjectives beginning *par-*, add the idea of completeness to the simple form; e.g. **Parfaire**, to finish completely, complete.

Par-, try also under **Per-**.

Par (*per*), *prep.* through, during, after, by. *De p.* (for *De part*) : on behalf of, supporting. *P. desroi* : in unseemly fashion. *P. honor* : loyally. *P. lui* : he alone, on his own. *P. nom de* : at the risk of. *P. pechié* : wrongfully. *P. quei* : therefore, why. *P. semblant* : feignedly. *P. som* : at the top of. *P. voir* : in truth, truly. Also used before *avoir & estre* to intensify a following adjective : very, completely.

Parage (on *par < parem*, equal), *sm.* extraction, lineage, family, high degree.

Parc (8th c. L. *parricum, parcum*, etym. obsc.), *sm.* lists (chivalry), enclosure. *Faire p.* : slaughter.

F

Parcenier, Parçonier (on *parçon < partiliōnem*, share), *sm.* partner, fellow sharer, associate; *adj.* common.

Pardoins, 1 pr., **Pardoinse**, 1 & 3 pr. subj. of **Pardoner** (on *doner*, < *dōnare*, give), forgive, give.

Pardon (on *pardoner*, v. supra), *sm.* gift, pardon. *En p.* : in vain.

Paredis, v. *pareïs.* **Pareir**, v. *paroir.*

Pareïs (Eccl. L. *paradīsum*), *sm.* paradise, parvis, close.

Parement (on *parer*, q.v.), *sm.* adornment, apparel, mantle.

Parenté (******parentatum*, on *parentem*), *sm.* family, lineage.

Parer (*parare*, arrange), *va.* prepare, arrange, adorn ; expiate ; pare, peel.

Pareü, pp. of *paroir*, q.v.

Parfin (*par*, q.v. + *fin < finem*, end), *sf.* very end, end.

Parfit (*perfectum*), *adj.* perfect. perfected.

Parfont (*profundum*, with change of prefix), *adj.* deep ; *odv.* deeply ; *sm. & f.* depths.

Parlement (on *parler*, q.v.), *sm.* conversation, speech, council, meeting, conference.

Parler (******paraulare* for Eccl. L. *parabolare*), *va. & n.* speak.

Parleure (on *parler*, q.v.), *sf.* speech, language.

Parlier (on *parler*, q.v.), *sm.* speaker ; *adj.* fluent, gossipy, slanderous.

Parmain, on *main* (*mane*), q.v.

Parmenable (on *parmanoir*, v. *permanoir*), *adj.* eternal, unchanging.

Parmi (*par*, q.v. + *mi*, q.v.), *adv.* & *prep.* through the middle (of), amid, by means of. *Tres p. :* across, through.

Paroir (*parēre*), *va.* & *n.* appear, show.

Paroir = *par* + *oïr*, q.v.

Paroistre (LL. *parēscere*, inchoat. of *parēre*), *vn.* appear, show.

Parol, 1 pr. & pr. subj. of *parler*, q.v.

Parole (**paraula* for Eccl. L. *parabola*, parable), *sf.* word, speech. *Metre en p. :* address. *Tenir p. de :* speak of.

Parons, 4 pr. of *parer*, q.v., or of *paroir*, q.v. **Parrai,** 1 fut. of *paroir*, q.v.

Parsome (*par*, q.v. + *some*, *sf.*, q.v.), *sf.* utmost end, very end.

Part (*partem*), *sf.* part, side, direction, faction. *A p. mei :* on my own. *Celle p. :* on that side, in that direction. *De l'altre p. :* on the other hand, in addition. *De male p. :* wicked. *De meie p. :* from me. *De p. :* on behalf of, in —'s name.

Partir (**partire* for *partīrī*, divide), *va.*, *n.* & *rfl.* divide, part, share in, break up, depart. *En p. :* depart, escape. *P. un jeu*, v. *gieu. Se p. de :* depart from, abandon.

Pas (*passum*), *sm.* step, pace, passage, pass, ford. *Le p. :* slowly. *Ne p. ne trot :* in no wise. *Trestot le p. :* quite slowly.

Pasmoison (on *pasmer* < **pasmare* for *spasmare*, on Medic. L. *spasmus*, convulsion), *sf.* swoon.

Fasser (**passare*, on *passum*, step), *va.* pass, traverse, experience, transgress ; *vn.* & *rfl.* cross, make one's way, go beyond.

Passet, *sm.*, dimin. of *pas*, q.v.

Pastorel (on *pastor* < *pastōrem*), *sm.* shepherd ; *fig.* dullard. Form in *-s* often **Pastoriaus.**

Pastoure (fem. of *pastour* < *pastōrem*), *sf.* shepherdess.

Pastre (*pastor*), nom. of **Pastor, -our** (*pastōrem*), *sm.* shepherd (*lit.* & *metaph.*).

Paterne (*paterna*, fatherly, *adj. f.* as *sf.*), *sf.* God the Father, fatherly love.

Patrenostre (*Pater noster*), *sf.* Lord's Prayer, prayer. *Les p——s, often :* the Rosary.

Pau, v. *pou.*

Paumoier (on *paume* < *palma*, palm of the hand), *va.* twirl, flourish, strike ; *vn.* & *rfl.* wring one's hands.

Pautonier (on **palitōnem*, from LL. *palitari*, wander), *sm.* vagabond, wretch, beggar ; *adj.* wicked.

Pavellon, v. *pavillon.*

Pavement (*pavimentum*), *sm.* stone-flagged floor, floor, ground, paved entrance.

Pavillon (*papiliōnem*, butterfly ; in LL., tent), *sm.* tent, pavilion.

Peage (**pedaticum*, right of passage, on *pedem*, foot), *sm.* toll.

Pecché, v. *pechié.* **Peceole,** 1 & 3 impft. of *peçoier*, q.v.

Pechable (on *pecher* < *peccare*, sin), *adj.* & *s.* sinning, sinner, unfortunate, wretched.

Pecheor (Eccl. L. *peccatõrem*, on *peccare*, sin), *sm.* sinner. *Nom. sing. :* **Pechiere** (*peccator*).

Pechié (*peccatum*, error ; in Eccl. L., sin), *sm.* sin, misfortune. *Par p. :* wrongfully, to one's disadvantage. *Pechiez est de :* pity.

Peçoler (on *piece*, q.v.), *va.* shatter; *vn. & rfl.* be shattered.

Pecol (*pedicullum*, leaf-stalk), *sm.* bedpost, leg of bed or chair, etc.

Pedron, v. *perron*.

Peignier (*pectinare*), *va.* comb.

Peil (*pilum*), *sm.* hair.

Peine (*poena*), *sf.* grief, work, fatigue, difficulty. *A p. :* with difficulty, scarcely. *Also* 3 pr. of *pener*, q.v.

Peior (*pējõrem*), *adj.* worse, worst ; *sm.* the worst. *Avoir le p. :* be beaten, come off worst.

Peis, v. *pois*. **Peisson**, var. of *poisson*, fish, or v. *paisson*.

Peiz, v. *pois* (*picem*). **Pejur**, v. *peior*.

Pel (*palum*), *sm.* stake, palisade.

Pel (*pellem*, animal skin), *sf.* skin (*human & animal*), parchment.

Peler (*pilare*), *va.* remove the skin or hair from, peel.

Pelice (LL. *pellīcia*, on *pellīcius*, of fur, skin), *sf.* mantle of fur.

Peliçon (on *pelice*, q.v.), *sm.* mantle of fur, mantle.

Pelisse, v. *pelice*.

Pendant (pr. p. of *pendre*, q.v.), *sm.* slope.

Pendre (**pendere* for -*ēre*, weigh), *va. & n.* hang. *P. a l'ueil :* threaten.

Pene, (1) (*penna*), *sf.* feather, wing, pen. *Also* (by extension), cloth, fur, leather covering of the buckler ; (2) (*pinna*, battlement), *sf.* top, apex. *P. halte :* very top.

Peneance (*poenitentia*, in Eccl. L. penance), *sf.* penance, repentance.

Péneant (*poenitentem*, repentant), *sm.* penitent.

Peneïr (**penitīre* for *poenitēre*), *v. rfl.* repent. Cf. *pentir*.

Pener (on *peine*, q.v.), *va.* torment, torture, harass, pain ; *v. rfl.* exert oneself. *Se p. de :* work to obtain, try hard for.

Penitence, learned form of *peneance*, q.v.

Penoncel (dimin. of *penon*, pennon, on *pene* 1, q.v.), *sm.* pennon, coat-of-arms.

Penos (on *peine*, q.v.), *adj.* painful. *La p——e semaine :* Holy Week.

Penre, var. of *prendre*, q.v., or of *pendre*, q.v.

Penser (*pēnsare*, weigh [via the written form]), *va. & n.* think, plan. [In sense of *panser*, v. *pancer*.] *P. de :* think of, see to, remember; *sm.* thought, opinion. 3 pr. *subj.* **Penst.**

Pentir (**penitīre* for *poenitēre*), *v. rfl.* repent. Cf. *peneïr*.

Peon (LL. *pedõnem*, walker, ?), *sm.* foot-soldier, pawn (chess).

Per-, try also under **Par-.**

Per (*parem*), *adj. & s.* equal, peer, companion, husband, wife. *Also* var. of *par*, q.v.

Percevance (on *percevoir*, q.v.), *sf.* recognition, discovery. *Por* *p. de :* fearing recognition by. *Sans p. (de) :* unseen (by).

Percevoir, remodelling of *perçoivre,* q.v.

Perche (*pertica,* rod), *sf.* rod, antler.

Perçoivre (*percipere,* understand), *va. & rfl.* perceive, understand.

Perdre (*perdere,* lose), *va. & rfl.* lose, die, kill, harm, bring about the downfall of ; *vn.* perish. *Jugier a p.:* doom to be destroyed, condemn to death. *P. a :* fail to. *P. son aé :* lose one's life.

Pere, 1 & 3 pr. subj. of *paroir,* q.v., or 3 pr. of *parer,* q.v.

Perece (*pigritia*), *sf.* idleness.

Perent, 6 pr. & pr. subj. of *paroir,* q.v., or of *parer,* q.v. **Peresse,** v. *perece.*

Periller (on *peril < periculum,* test, danger), *va.* kill, put in danger ; *vn.* shipwreck, perish.

Perir (*perire*), *va.* kill, destroy ; *vn.* perish.

Permanoir (*permanēre*), *vn.* endure. *En permanent :* constantly, eternally.

Pern-, try **Pren-,** e.g. **Pernez** = *prenez.*

Perrin (on *pierre < petra,* stone), *adj.* of stone.

Perron (on *pierre < petra,* stone), *sm.* stone, rock, block of stone, pillar, staircase.

Pers (LL. *persum,* etym. obsc.), *adj.* dark blue, purple, livid (face). *Also* 1 & 2 pr. of *perdre,* q.v., 2 pr. of *paroir,* q.v., & form in -s of *per,* q.v.

Pert, 1 & 3 pr. of *perdre,* q.v., or 3 pr. of *paroir,* q.v.

Pertuis (on *pertuisier,* on tonic forms of **pertŭsiare,* on pp. of *pertundere,* pierce), *sm.* hole, opening, refuge, narrow passage.

Pes, var. of *pais,* q.v.

Pesance (on *peser,* q.v.), *sf.* grief, worry, heaviness.

Pesant (pr. p. of *peser,* q.v.), *adj.* heavy, grievous, bitter, bad, powerful.

Peser (*pē(n)sare,* weigh), *va., n. & impers.* weigh, grieve, trouble. *Ce poise mei :* it grieves me, I regret.

Pesme (*pessimum*), *adj.* very bad, terrible, fierce.

Pesoier, v. *peçoier.*

Pestor (*pistōrem*), *sm.* baker.

Pestre, v. *paistre.*

Petit (**pettittum,* prob. connected with Gaul. **pett,* cf. *piece*), *adj., adv., & sm.* little. *A bien p. que,* (*Par*) *Por un p. que :* very nearly. . . .

Peu, v. *pou.* **Peü,** pp. of *paistre,* q.v., or of *pooir,* q.v. **Peut,** sometimes 3 pft. of *pooir,* q.v.

Pevree (on *peivre < piper,* pepper), *sf.* pepper, spiced dish.

Pi (*pium*), *adj.* pious, merciful.

Picois (on *pic,* perh. fig. use of **piccum* for *picum,* woodpecker), *sm.* javelin, pick, spade, hoe.

Pieça (*piece,* q.v. + *a < habet ; lit.* it is a time (since)), *adv.* recently, some time before. *Des p., P. que :* for some time now. *Grant p. :* long ago.

Piece (**pettia,* on Gaul. **pett,* cf. W. *peth,* thing, & Ir. *cuit,* part), *sf.* (space of) time, piece.

A chief de p. : again, after a time. *Ne . . . a p. :* never.

Pied (*pedem*), *sm.* foot; person.

Piedre (*petra*), *sf.* stone, rock.

Pietaille (on *piet*, v. *pied*), *sf.* foot-soldiers, infantry; the people, the poor.

Pieur, v. *peior.*

Pigne (*pectinem*), *sm.* comb.

Pigner (remodelling of *peignier*, q.v., infl. by *pigne*, q.v.), *va.* comb.

Pignoncel, v. *penoncel.*

Piler (**pilare*, on *pila*, column), *sm.* pillar.

Piment (*pigmentum*, pigment; in LL., spice), *sm.* spiced wine.

Piquois, v. *picois.* **Pire** (*pejor* for *pējor*), nom. of *peior*, q.v.

Pis (*pejus* for *pējus*), *adv. & adj. n.* worse; *sm.* the worst, misfortune. *Also* var. of *piz,* q.v.

Pitance (on *pitié*, q.v.), *sf.* piety, pity, pittance (monastic).

Piteus (LL. *pietōsum*, on *pietas*, in Eccl. L., pity), *adj.* compassionate, full of pity; pious.

Pitié (*pietatem*, piety; in Eccl. L., pity), *sf.* pity, piety.

Piu, v. *pi.* **Pive,** fem. of *pif*, var. of *pi*, q.v.

Piz (*pectus*), *sm.* chest, breast, breast-piece (harness).

Place (**plattea* for *platea*, wide street), *sf.* place, spot. *En la p. :* here, there, in this (that) spot. *Also* pr. subj. of *plaire,* q.v.

Plaid, v. *plait.*

Plaideis (on *plaid*, v. *plait*), *sm.* plea, pleading, law-suit; advocate, defender.

Plaidier (on *plaid*, v. *plait*), *va.* plead; *vn.* hold a court of justice, plead.

Plaier (on *plaie < plaga*, wound), *va.* wound, cover with wounds.

Plaigne (**planea*), *sf.* plain. *Also* pr. subj. of *plaindre*, q.v.

Plain (*planum*), *adj.* level, smooth, clear. *Plains chans :* open fields. *sm.* plain; flat part of shield. *Also* var. of *plaint*, q.v., or of *plein* (*plēnum*), *adj.* full.

Plaindre (*plangere*), *va., n., & rfl.* complain, lament, pity, regret.

Plaingnier, var. of *plenier*, q.v.

Plains, 2 pr. & 1 pft. of *plaindre*, q.v.; *also* form in -s of *plain*, q.v., or for *plainz*, v. *plaint.* **Plainsis,** 2 pft. of *plaindre*, q.v.

Plaint (on pp. of *plaindre*, q.v.), *sm.* complaint, lament, moan.

Plaire (remodelled form of *plaisir*, q.v.), *va. & n.* please.

Plaisié, v. *pleissié.*

Plaisir (*placēre*), *va. & n.* please; *sm.* pleasure, will. *Venir a p. :* please.

Plaisseis, cf. *pleissié.* **Plaissier,** v. *pleissier.*

Plait (*placitum*, pleasing; in LL., court), *sm.* judicial tribunal, assize; lawsuit, trial, judgment, agreement, speech. *Aveir bon p. :* be in a good position. *Prendre p. :* make peace. *Semondre al p. :* summon before the court. *Tenir p. de :* pay attention to. *Tenir p. sur :* discuss. *Tenir tel p. :* argue thus. . . . *Also* var. of *pleit*, q.v.

Plançon (**plantiōnem*, on *planta*, plant), *sm.* young plant, shoot, branch, trunk, stake.

Planer (LL. *planare*, on *planum*, level), *va.* level, destroy; *v. rfl.* flow smoothly. *Plané*, pp. adj. : smooth, polished.

Planson, v. *plançon*. **Planté**, v. *plenté*.

Planteis (on *plante* < *planta*, plant), *sm.* wooded land, vine-yard.

Plantureux (*plentiveus*, q.v. + infl. of *eureux*, cf. *eür*), *adj.* plentiful, abundant.

Plasmer (Med. L. *plasmare*, on Late L. *plasma* from Gk. *plassein*, mould), *va.* create, fashion, form.

Plate (on *plat* < **plattum*, flat; etym. obsc.), *sf.* sheet or bar of metal, silver.

Pleg(g)e, v. *pleige*. **Pleier** (*plicare*), orig. form of *plier*, q.v.

Pleige (etym. obsc.), *sm.* pledge, guarantee.

Pleindre, v. *plaindre*.

Pleissié (var. of *plaissié*, on **plaxillum* for *paxellum*, infl. by *pleissier*, q.v.), *sm.* park, enclosure.

Pleissier (**plexare*, on *plexum*, pp. of *plectere*, plait), *va.* weave, bend, cast down, abase; *vn.* fall, yield; *v. rfl.* bend, humble oneself, rush; *sm.* cf. *pleissié*.

Pleit (*plicitum*, pp., folded), *sm.* knot, pleat, fold. *Also* var. of *plait*, q.v.

Plenier (LL. *plēnarium*), *adj.* complete, thorough, great, princely, plentiful.

Plenté (LL. *plēnitatem*), *sf.* abundance. *A p.* : abundantly. *Adv.* much.

Plenteif, Plentif (on *plenté*, q.v.), *adj.* abundant, wealthy.

Plentiveus (on *plentif*, on *plenté*, q.v.), *adj.* plentiful, abundant, wealthy.

Plet, v. *plait*. **Pleürent,** 6 pft. of *plaire*, q.v. **Pleurer,** v. *plorer*. **Pleüsse,** 1 impft. subj. of *plaire*, q.v.

Plevir (etym. obsc.), *va., n., & rfl.* pledge, stand surety for, promise.

Plier (var. of *pleier* < *plicare*, by analogy with *prier*, etc.), *va.* fold, bend, knot; *vn.* bend, yield. *Guant pleié :* folded glove given as a gage.

Ploi (on *ploier*, q.v.), *sm.* line, order, bond, state. *Also* 1 pft. of *plaire*, q.v., or 1 pr. of *ploier*, v. *plier*.

Ploier, var. of *pleier*, v. *plier*.

Ploreis (on *plorer*, q.v.), *sm.* weeping, lamentation.

Plorent, 6 pft. of *plaire*, q.v., or 6 pr. of *plorer*, q.v.

Plorer (*plōrare*), *va. & n.* weep, lament.

Plot, 3 pft. of *plaire*, q.v. **Plourer,** v. *plorer*.

Plusors (**plūsiōres* for LL. *plūriōres*, infl. by *plūs*), *adj. & pron.* several. *Li plusor :* most, the greater part.

Poant (pr. p. of *pooir*, q.v.), *adj.* powerful.

Poc, 1 pft. of *pooir*, q.v. **Pod-.** Try without the intervocalic *-d-*, e.g. **Podeir,** v. *poeir.*

Podrai, 1 fut. of *pooir*, q.v.

Podriere (on *podre*, v. *poldre*), *sf.* dust.

Poe (etym. obsc., perh. Germ., cf. Dut. *poot*), *sf.* paw, claw.

Poeir, v. *pooir*.

Poeste (**potesta* for *potestas*, *-atem*), *sf.* power, force. *A p. :* vigorously, rapidly.

Poesté (*potestatem*), *sf.* power, force. *Par p. :* forcibly.

Poestelf (on *poeste*, q.v.), *adj.* powerful. *P. de :* master of, ruler of.

Poet, 3 pr., **Poez,** 2 pr., **Poëz,** 5 pr., **Poi,** 1 pft. of *pooir*, q.v.

Poi (*paucum*, with vocalization of yod), *adj.* little, small, a few; *adv.* little. *En p. d'ore :* rapidly, in a short time. *A p. ne :* nearly. See also *pou*.

Poignant, pr. p. of *poindre*, q.v.

Poigne, pr. subj. of *pondre*, q.v. or of *poindre*, q.v.

Poigneis (on *poignier < pugnare*, fight), *sm.* battle, struggle.

Poignel (on *poing*, q.v.), *adj.* in the hand, for use in the hand.

Poigneor (*pugnatōrem*), *sm.* great fighter, warrior. *Nom. sing. :* **Poignierre** (*pugnator*).

Poin, v. *poing*.

Poindre (*pungere*, prick), *va.* spur ; *vn.* spur on, gallop, hurry ; sprout, project ; *sm.* battle, attack.

Poing (*pugnum*), *sm.* fist, wrist, hand, pommel.

Pois, (1) (*pē(n)sum*), *sm.* weight. *Desus le p. de, Encontre le p. de, Sor le p. de :* against the will of ; (2) (*pisum*), *sm.* pea ; (3) (*picem*), *sf.* pitch.

Pois, 1 pr. and 1 & 2 pr. subj. of *peser*, q.v., or 1 pr. of *pooir*, q.v. ; *also* var. of *puis*, q.v.

Poise, 3 pr. of *peser*, q.v.

Poison (*pōtiōnem*), *sf.* drink, potion, philtre, medicine.

Poissance (on *poissant*, q.v.), *sf.* power, strength, valour.

Poissant (on *poiss-* root of *pooir*, q.v.), *adj.* powerful, strong, valiant.

Poitral, Poitrel (*pectorale*, breast-plate), *sm.* breast-piece of harness, breast-plate (for horse).

Poldre (*pulverem*), *sf.* dust, ashes. Cf. *podriere*.

Pom (*pōmum*, fruit ; later, apple), *sm.* pommel.

Pomeaus, form in *-s* of **Pomel** (on *pom*, q.v.), *sm.* pommel ; *sometimes*, top.

Pomelé (on *pomel*, q.v.), *adj.* dappled.

Poncel (dimin. of *pont* 2, q.v.), *sm.* small bridge, drawbridge.

Pondre (*pōnere*, put), *va. & n.* put, place, lay (eggs).

Pone, pr. subj. of *pondre*, q.v. **Ponee,** v. *posnee*. **Pong,** v. *poing*. **Ponre,** v. *pondre*.

Pont, (1) (etym. obsc.), *sm.* pommel ; (2) (*pontem*), *sm.* landing-bridge, gangway. *P. torneis :* swing-bridge.

Ponu, pp., **Ponul,** 1 pft. of *pondre*, q.v.

Pooir (**potēre* for *posse*), *v.* be able, have cause ; *sm.* power, capacity. *A mon p. :* according to my power, to the best of my ability. *Il ne poet en avant :* he can go no further.

Qui le poet amer : who finds him worthy of love. *Qui plus puissent :* who can do no more.

Poon (var. of *paon < pavŏnem*), *sm.* peacock.

Poor, v. *paor.*

Por (*prŏ*, in front of), *prep.* for, on behalf of, because of, in return for, to the point of. *Ne fust p. :* were it not for the fear of. *P. ceo :* because of this. *Por ceo que :* so that. *P.* (*ceo*) *que :* provided that. *P. les ueilz perdre :* even at the cost of losing his eyes. *P. poi que . . . ne :* nearly, almost. *P. quei :* wherefore. *Tenir p. :* regard as.

Por-. For some infinitives, add the idea of completeness or thoroughness to the simple infinitive.

Porchacier (*por*, q.v., + *chacier*, q.v.), *va., n., & rfl.* pursue, seek, try to obtain, take steps (to), achieve.

Porchas (on *porchacier*, q.v.), *sm.* expedition, pursuit, provision, resource, instigation.

Porent, 6 pft. of *pooir*, q.v.

Porfit (*prŏfectum*), *sm.* profit, use.

Porloignier (on *loing*, q.v.), *va., n., & rfl.* delay ; *va.* prolong.

Poroc, Poroec (*por*, q.v., + *hoc*), *conj.* for that, therefore.

Porparler (*por*, q.v., + *parler*, q.v.), *va.* discuss thoroughly, plot.

Porpens (on *porpenser*, q.v.), *sm.* thought, idea, intention. *Metre en p. :* think about.

Porpenser (*por*, q.v., + *penser*, q.v.), *va.* plan, intend ; *vn. & rfl.* think, reflect, decide, bethink oneself. *Estre porpensez de :* take care to, determine to. *Se p. de :* remember.

Porpre (*purpura*, purple), *sm. & f.* silken fabric, dark-coloured material, inferior fur ; *adj.* scarlet, purple.

Porprendre (*por*, q.v., + *prendre*, q.v.), *va.* enclose, surround, occupy, seize ; *vn.* spread.

Porprin (on *porpre*, q.v.), *adj.* purple, red ; *sm.* cloth of " porpre," q.v.

Porquant (*por*, q.v., + *quant*, q.v.), *conj.* yet, however.

Porquerre (*por*, q.v., + *querre*, q.v.), *va.* seek, obtain, furnish ; *v. rfl.* make efforts. *Se p. de :* provide oneself with, make efforts to.

Porseurre (*por*, q.v., + *seurre*, form of *sivre*, q.v.), *va.* pursue, seek, continue.

Port (*portum*, port), *sm.* pass, defile, port. *Prendre p. :* land, make port.

Portaster (*por*, q.v., + *taster < *tastare*, etym. obsc.), *va.* feel, sound or examine thoroughly.

Porteure (on *porter < portare*, carry), *sf.* offspring, child, children.

Portraire (*por*, q.v., + *traire*, q.v.), *va.* depict, engrave ; achieve ; accuse, convict ; *vn.* resemble.

Porveance (on *porveoir*, q.v.), *sf.* provision, forethought, wisdom, providence.

Porveoir (*por*, q.v., + *veoir*, q.v.), *va. & n.* provide, see to, examine, govern. *Porveu*, pp., *also* = determined, ready.

Pose (*pausa*), *sf.* pause, time, leisure, rest ; *adv.* for a time.

Posnee (etym. obsc.), *sf.* pride, arrogant behaviour or speech, bravado.

Post (*positum*), pp. of *pondre*, q.v. & *sm.* post.

Poste (fem. pp. of *pondre*, q.v.), *sf.* post, position.

Posteïf, v. *poesteïf.*

Postic, Postiz (**posticium* for *posticum*, back-door), *sm.* small door, gate, wicket, leaf of a door.

Pot, 3 pft. of *pooir*, q.v.

Pou (PL. *paucum*, adv.), *adv.* little. *A p. n'enrage :* he nearly goes mad. *Por p. (que) :* nearly. *P. m'est de :* I care little for.

Poü, pp. of *pooir*, q.v. **Poudre,** v. *poldre.* **Pour,** v. *por.* **Poür,** var. of *paor*, q.v. **Pour-,** try also under **Por-.**

Pourpos (on *prōpositum*), *sm.* speech, intention.

Pourpris (pp. of *porprendre*, q.v.), *sm.* enclosure, garden.

Poüsse, impft. subj. of *pooir*, q.v.

Poutrel, -iel (dimin. of *poutre* < **pullitra*, on *pullum*, young animal), *sm.* foal.

Poverte (**pauperta*, on *pauper*, poor), *sf.* poverty, distress. *Syn :* **Poverté** (*paupertatem*).

Prael, *sm.*, **Praele,** *sf.* (dimins. of *pré* < *pratum*), field, meadow.

Praer, v. *preer.*

Praerie (on *pré* < *pratum*), *sf.* field, meadow.

Prametre, var. of *prometre* (*prōmittere*), *va.* promise.

Preder, v. *preer.*

Pree (PL. *prata*, n. pl. as fem. sing), *sf.* meadow.

Preer (*praedare*), *va. & n.* ravage, devastate, take booty, go on a foray ; carry off (people).

Pregniez, 5 pr. subj. of *prendre*, q.v. **Preier, Preiere,** v. *proier*, *proiere.* **Preigne,** pr. subj. of *prendre*, q.v. **Preisier,** v. *proisier.*

Premerain (*premier*, q.v., + *-ain*, < *-anum*), *adj.* first ; *adv.* (also written **Premerains**), at first.

Premier (*primarium*), *adj.* first ; *adv.* (also written **Premiers**), at first, first.

Prendent, 6 pr. of *prendre*, q.v.

Prendre (*prēndere* for *prehendere*, seize), *va.*, *n. & rfl.* take, seize, take away ; hold, receive ; *v. rfl. also* compare, engage oneself, promise. *En p. a :* begin to. *Lui prent a :* he begins to. . . . *Mal p. :* go wrong. *P. conseil a :* seek advice from. *P. conseil que :* decide to. *P. cops :* receive blows. *P. fin :* end, cease talking. *P. havre :* make port. *P. un jor :* fix a day. *(Se) p. a :* begin to, take hold of. *Talent lui prent :* he desires.

Prenge, pr. subj. of *prendre*, q.v.

Pres (*pressum* or *pressē*), *adv. & prep.* nearly, near.

Preseignier (*pre-* < *prae* + *seignier*, q.v., cf. *praesignis*, distinguished), *va.* make the sign of the cross over, baptize, bless.

Present (*praesentem*), *sm.* presence; present, gift. *En p. :* here (there) present, straightway. *En p. a :* present before. *En p. de :* in the presence of. *Metre en p. :* bring forward, present.

Presignier, v. *preseignier.*

Presse (on *presser*, q.v.), *sf.* crowd, throng, thick of the battle, serried ranks.

Presser (*pressare*, frequentative of *premere*), *va.* press.

Prest, 3 pr. subj. of **Prester** (*praestare*, provide), lend. **Prestre** (Eccl. L. *presbyter*), nom. of *prevoire*, q.v. **Preu,** v. *prou.* **Preuvent,** 6 pr. of *prover*, q.v.

Prevoire (Eccl. L. *presbyterum*), *sm.* priest.

Pri (on *preier*, v. *proier*), *sm.* prayer, pleading. *Also* 1 pr. of *proier*, q.v.

Priembre (*premere*), *va.* press, crush.

Prient, 3 pr. of *priembre*, q.v., or 6 pr. & pr. subj. of *proier*, q.v. **Prier, Priere,** v. *proier, proiere.*

Prime (Eccl. L. *prima* (*hŏra*)), *sf.* prime, 6 a.m. *Halte p. :* nearing 9 a.m. *Also* fem. of *prin*, q.v.

Primes (on *primŏ* + adv. -s), *adv.* at first, for the first time.

Prin (*primum*), *adj.* first, early. *De p. saut :* at the first onset, at first.

Princier (on *prince* < *principem*, first, ruler), *sm.* prince, leader.

Prinsautier (on *prin*, q.v., + *saut*, v. *sait*), *adj.* lively, agile, quick; presumptuous.

Prinsome (*prin*, q.v., + *some* 2, q.v.), *sm.* beginning of the night, first sleep.

Prinst, Print, 3 pft. of *prendre*, q.v.

Pris (*pretium*), *sm.* price, prize, esteem, worth, fame. *De p. :* valiant, noble, worthy. *Metre en p. :* enhance the value of.

Pris, 1 & 2 pr. subj. of *proier*, q.v., 1 pr. and 1 & 2 pr. subj. of *proisier*, q.v., and pp. & 1 pft. of *prendre*, q.v. **Prisent,** 6 pr. of *proisier*, q.v., or 6 pft. of *prendre*, q.v. **Prisier,** v. *proisier.*

Prison (*prē(n)siōnem*, arrest), *sf.* capture, imprisonment, prison; *sm.* prisoner. *Fiancer p. :* give one's parole. *Mener en la p. de :* take away as the prisoner of. *N'avoir p. :* give or receive no quarter.

Prist, 3 pft. of *prendre*, q.v., 3 pr. subj. of *proier* or *proisier*, q.v.

Privé (*privatum*), *sm.* & *adj.* friend, intimate, privy, of one's personal household, private, personal.

Priveement (on *privé*, q.v.), *adv.* secretly, privately, especially.

Pro, Prod, v. *prou.*

Prodhome (*prod*, v. *prou*, + *de* + *home*, q.v.), *sm.* wise man, noble man, worthy man.

Proece (on *pro*, v. *prou*), *sf.* prowess, noble qualities.

Profit, v. *porfit.* **Prol,** var. of *pri*, verbal form.

Prole (*praeda*, plunder), *sf.* booty, plunder; flock (sheep, etc.).

Proier (PL. *precare* for *precari*), *va. & n.* pray, implore, request. *Also* var. of *preer*, q.v.

Proiere (*precaria, fem. adj. as sf.), *sf.* prayer, request.

Prois, var. of *pris* (*proier* & *proisier*), q.v.

Proisier (LL. *pretiare*, on *pretium*, price), *va.* value, esteem. *Faire a p. :* act in a worthy manner, be noble. *P. a :* regard as, esteem no more than.

Proisme (*proximum*), *adj.* near by, near, nearest; *sm.* near relative, neighbour.

Proposement (on *propos*, v. *pourpos*), *sm.* intention, decision.

Prosme, v. *proisme*. **Prot,** v. *prou*.

Prou (PL. *prōde*, on the *prōd-* of *prōdesse*), *sm.* profit, quantity; *adj.* noble, valiant, wise, good, advantageous, helpful; *adv.* much, enough, profitably. *Avoir p. a :* gain by. *De son p. :* to his advantage.

Prouver, v. *prover*.

Provance (on *prover*, q.v.), *sf.* proof.

Provende (Eccl. L. *praebenda* + infl. of *prō-*), *sf.* provision, prebend, prebendaryship.

Provendier (on *provende*, q.v.), *sm.* pensioner, dependant, provider.

Prover (*probare*, put to the test), *va.* put to the test, prove; *v. rfl.* show oneself. *P. a :* prove . . . to be. . . . *P. de :* taste of.

Provoire, v. *prevoire*. **Proz,** case in *-s* of *prot*, v. *prou*. **Prozdom,** nom. of *prodhome*, q.v. **Pru,** v. *prou*.

Pruef (*prope*), *adv.* near, nearly. *A bien p. :* nearly. *A p. ne* . . . nearly. *Also* 1 pr. & pr. subj. of *prover*, q.v.

Pruet, 3 pr. subj., **Prueve,** pr. & pr. subj. of *prover*, q.v.

Pu-, try also under **Po-** or **Pou-. Pueent,** 6 pr. of *pooir*, q.v.

Puet, 3 pr. of *pooir*, q.v. *Puet cel estre :* perhaps.

Pui-, try also **Poi-.**

Pui (*podium*, pedestal), *sm.* mountain, hill, height.

Puier (*podiare, on *podium*, in sense of " height "), *va.* climb, increase; *vn.* climb, (*fig.*) grow in honour; *v. rfl.* lean.

Puindre, v. *poindre*.

Puir (*pūtire for *-ēre*), *vn.* stink. *Faire son jeu p. a :* cause to repent, make . . . sorry.

Puis (*postius, on *post*, infl. by *melius*), *adv. & prep.* after, since, then. *P. que :* since, after.

Puissance, Puissant, v. *poissance, -ant.*

Puissedi (*puis*, q.v., + *ce*, this, + *di*, q.v.), *adv.* since then, later. *P. que :* since, after.

Pullent (Late L. *pūtulentem*), *adj.* stinking, foul.

Pun (var. of *pon* < *pōmum*), *sm.* apple.

Punais (*pūtinasum), *adj.* stinking, foul.

Put (*pūtidum*), *adj.* stinking, vile. *De p. aire :* of vile birth. *Also* 3 pr. of *puïr*, q.v.

Puterie (on *put*, q.v.), *sf.* shameful conduct, vice, debauchery.

Q

Q-, try under **Qu-. Qu-,** try also
under **C-.**

Quanque (for *quant que*, v. *quant*
1), *adj.* whatsoever, all that.
Q. il poet : with all his
might.

Quant, (1) (*quantum*, how much),
adj. how much, how big, how
many, so much ; *adv.* as. *A
q. que :* as much as, to the
utmost. *En q. :* as. *Ne por
q. :* nevertheless. *Ne tant ne
q. :* in no way, nothing at all.
Q. que : as much as, all that ;
(2) (*quando*), *conj.* when, since,
even if. *Q. et :* with.

Quanz, form in -*s* of *quant* 1,
q.v. **Quar,** v. *car.*

Quarré (*quadratum*, squared), *pp.
adj.* divided into four, four-
sided.

Quarrel (******quadrellum*, on *quadrus*,
square), *sm.* arrow, bolt from
a cross-bow, flagstone, piece.
Form in -*s* often **Quarriaus.**

Quart (*quartum*), *adj.* fourth.

Quartain (on *quart*, q.v.), *sm.*
quarter, bit, morsel, place of
safety, mercy. *Escu de q. :*
quartered shield.

Quas (on *quasser*, q.v.), *adj.*
broken.

Quasser (*quassare*, shake violently), *va.* break, smash, hurt,
destroy.

Quatir (******quatire* for -*ere*), *va.* strike,
thrust, hide ; *v. rfl.* hide oneself.

Que (*quid* for *quod*), *conj.* that,
since, so that. *D'ici q. :* as
far as. *Que . . . que :* as
many . . . as, both . . . and.

Quel (tonic form of *quid*), *neut.
pron.* what. *Also* var. of *coi*,
q.v.

Queïsse, impft. subj. of *querre*,
q.v. **Queit,** early form of *coi*,
q.v. **Queit =** *quei*, q.v. + *te.*

Quel (*qualem*), *adj. & pron.*
which, what.

Quen-, try under **Con-.**

Quene, Quenne (O. Sc. *kinn*,
cheek), *sf.* jaw, tooth.

Quenoistre, v. *conoistre.* **Quens,**
v. *cuens.* **Queor, Quer,** v. *cuer.*
Quer, v. also *car.*

Querele (Legal L. *querēla*), *sf.*
dispute, lawsuit, litigation.

Querge, 3 pr. subj. of *querre*, q.v.

Querir, remodelled form of
querre, q.v.

Quernu (var. of *crenu* < ******crīnū-
tum*, on *crinem*, hair). *adj.*
maned, long-haired.

Querre (*quaerere*), *va. & n.* seek,
ask, wish, call upon. *A celer
nel vos quier :* I tell you
frankly; I admit.

Querrons, 4 pr. of *querre*, q.v., or
= *crerrons*, 4 fut. of *croire*
(*crēdere*), believe.

Quesis, 2 pft., **Quesisse,** impft.
subj. of *querre*, q.v. **Queu,** v.
cou. **Queurent,** 6 pr., **Queurt,**
3 pr. of *corre*, q.v. **Queus,** form
in -*s* of *queu*, q.v., or *quel*, q.v.
Queuvre, 3 pr. of *covrir* (*cooperire*), cover. **Quex,** var. of
queus, q.v.

Qui (*quī & cuī*), *rel. pron.* which,
who; to whom, whose. *Qui
donc veïst . . . :* if only you
(one) had seen. . . . !

Qui-, try also under **Coi-. Quidier,**
v. *cuidier.*

Quiement (*quiēta* + *-ment* < *mentē*), *adv.* quietly.

Quier, 1 pr., **Quiere, 1** & 3 pr. subj. of *querre*, q.v. **Quin** = *qui en*.

Quint (*quintum*), *adj.* fifth.

Quintaine (*quintana*, fem. adj. as noun ; sense-devel. obsc.), *sf.* tilting-block.

Quir = *cuir* (*corium*), *sm.* hide, skin.

Quirent, 6 pft. of *querre*, q.v. **Quis, 1** pft. & pp. of *querre*, q.v. (also contraction of *qui les* or *qui se*). **Quist, 3** pft., **Quistrent, 6** pft. of *querre*, q.v., **Quit, 1** pr. of *quidier*, q.v.

Quitance (on *quiter*, q.v.), *sf.* release from obligation or duty, tranquillity.

Quite (b. Legal L. *quiētum*, pron. *quitum*), *adj.* relieved of (legal obligation), bereft, absolved, freed. *Clamer q. :* renounce all rights over, free.

Quitedé, Quiteé (on *quite*, q.v.), *sf.* quiet.

Quiter (b. Legal L. *quiētare*, pron. *quitare*), *va.* quit, give up, leave, forgive, release.

Quoisier (on *quoi* = *coi*, q.v.), *vn.* be silent.

Quoite, v. *coite.* **Quor, v.** *cuer.* **Quos** = *que vos.*

R

Ra-, try also under **Re-**, and see note to **Re-**.

Raconsivir (on *aconsivir*, q.v.), *va.* attain, overtake.

Racorder (on *acorder*, q.v.), *va.* reconcile ; *vn.* & *rfl.* make peace.

Rade (*rapidum*), *adj.* rapid, vigorous.

Radoté, cf. *redoter.*

Raembre (*redimere*, buy back), *va.* redeem, free, pay ransom for.

Rai, 1 pr. of *ravoir* (on *avoir* < *habēre*), have again, have for my part.

Rai (*radium*), *sm.* ray (sun), beam, spoke (wheel), stream.

Raie (Gaul. *rica*, cf. W. *rhych*, Ir. *rech*), *sf.* line, ridge, furrow. Cf. *roié.*

Raier (on *rai* < *radium*, q.v.), *vn.* beam, streak, stream.

Raim, Rain (*ramum*), *sm.* branch, branches ; *fig.*, small streak. *Par r.*, formula which = for ever.

Raire, v. *rere.*

Raisnable (on *raisnier*, q.v.), *adj.* reasonable, just.

Raisnier (*rationare*, on *ratiōnem*), *va.* reason, address ; *vn.* speak, declare.

Raison (*ratiōnem*, calculation), *sf.* speech, discourse, statement, reason, deliberation, right. *A peler de fiere r. :* speak proudly. *Aprendre* (*Dire*) *r. a :* speak to, point out to. *Dreite r. rendre :* reply satisfactorily, give good advice. *Metre a r. :* address. *Parler par fiere r. :* speak proudly. *Par r. :* reasonably, fairly.

Raisoner (on *raison*, q.v.), *va.* Cf. *raisnier* for sense.

Raiz (*radicem*), *sf.* root, source. *Par r. :* thoroughly, from top to bottom.

Raler (on *aler* < **allare*, etym. obsc.), *vn.* go, go again, return, depart. *S'en r.* : return.

Ralier (on *alier*, q.v.), *va. & n.* rally.

Ralier (on *lié*, q.v.), *va.* cheer up.

Ramage (on *raim*, q.v.), *adj.* branchy; *fig.*, wild; *sm.* forest, bird-song, twitter.

Ramé (on *raim*, q.v.), *adj.* branchy, leafy, wooded, full of trees.

Ramee (on *raim*, q.v.), *sf.* bower.

Rameint, 3 pr. subj. of *ramener*, cf. *mener.*

Ramembrer (LL. *rememorare*), *va., n., & rfl.* remember. (*Il*) *me ramembre de* : I remember, I recall.

Ramentevoir (on *amentevoir*, q.v.), *va.* recall, remember, relate, mention.

Ramier (on *raim*, q.v.), *adj.* full of trees, wild; *sm.* branch, wood, forest.

Ramper (etym. obsc.), *va. & n.* climb; crawl (*rare*). *Rampant,* pr. p. adj.: erect, rampant (*heraldic*).

Ramposne (etym. obsc.), *sf.* insult, mockery. Cf. *ramprosner.*

Ramprosner (etym. obsc.), *va.* make jest of, jeer at, scoff at; *vn.* jest, jeer.

Ramu, cf. *ramé.* **Ranc,** v. *renc.*

Rancor (LL. *rancōrem*, in Eccl. L., rancour), *sf.* rancour, ill-will.

Rancure (alter. of *rancor*, q.v., infl. by *cure* < *cūra*, care), *sf.* rancour, ill-will, dislike.

Randir (Fk. **randjan?*), *vn.* gallop, rush, run.

Randon (Fk. **rando*), *sm.* violence, impetuosity, confusion. *A r., De r.* : rapidly, violently. *En un r.* : on end, without pause.

Randonee (on *randoner*, on *randon*, q.v.), *sf.* rush, onrush, onslaught. *A r., De r.* : vigorously, rapidly, speedily.

Randoner (on *randon*, q.v.), *vn.* dash, run quickly.

Rapaier (on *apaier*), v. *paier* for sense.

Raplegier (on *pleige*, q.v.), *va.* guarantee, stand security for.

Raser (**rasare*, on *rasum*, pp. of *radere*, scrape, smooth), *va.* fill to the edge or top, polish.

Rasoagier (on *asoagier* < **assuaviare*, on *suavis*, sweet), *va.* comfort, console; *vn. & rfl.* grow calm, be reassured.

Rasor (PL. *rasōrium*), *sm.* razor.

Ravine (*rapina*), *sf.* plunder; rushing water, landslide, impetus. *De r.* : violently, rapidly. *Par r.* : by force.

Raviner (on *ravine*, q.v.), *vn.* rush along (water); *va.* carry off by force.

Raviser, cf. *aviser.*

Ravissable (on *raviss-* forms of *ravir* < **rapire* for *-ere*), *adj.* ravishing, ravisher.

Ravolier, cf. *avoiier.*

Re-. For infinitives beginning **Re-** or **R-,** add to the simple infinitive the idea of " again," " back," or, in some cases, of " for his part," " also." Sometimes it adds little or nothing to the sense of the simple infinitive.

Ré (Fk. *rât*), sm. & f. pyre.

Rebors (LL. *reburrus*), adj. with hair standing on end; *fig.* turned upside down, rebellious, unpleasant, hostile. *A r. :* against one's wishes, upside down.

Rebourser (on *rebours*, v. *rebors*), va. turn up, lift up, go up.

Rebouter, cf. *boter.*

Rebrasser (on *bras < brachium*, arm), va. turn up, fold back; v. rfl. turn back one's sleeves, lift one's skirts.

Receivre, v. *reçoivre.*

Receler (on *celer < cēlare*, hide), sf. secret, ambush. *A r., En r. :* secretly, in hiding.

Recercelé (on *cerce*, form of *cercle < circulum*), adj. curly.

Recet (*receptum*, pp. of *recipere*), sm. house, dwelling, castle, shelter, hiding-place.

Receter (on *recet*, q.v.), va. shelter, give refuge to, hide; vn. hide, take refuge.

Rechignier, v. *reschignier.*

Reching (on *rechignier*, q.v.), sm. rebuff, refusal, kick.

Rechoite, v. *reçoite.*

Reclaim (on *reclamer*, q.v.), sm. claim, request, appeal, lament; saying, proverb. *Also* 1 pr. & pr. subj. of *reclamer*, q.v.

Reclamer (on *clamer*, q.v.), va. call, call upon, name, pray, desire. *R. sa colpe,* cf. *clamer.*

Reclore, cf. *clore.* **Reclost,** 3 pft. of *reclore*, q.v. **Recoi,** v. *requoi.*

Recoillir (on *coillir*, q.v.), va. collect, gather, welcome.

Reçoite (fem. pp. of *reçoivre*, q.v.), sf. quiet spot. *En r. :* secretly.

Reçoivre (*recipere*), va. receive, recover, seize, welcome.

Reconoistre (*recognōscere*), va. disclose, recognize, do homage for, confess to (fault, crime).

Recorde (on *recorder*, q.v.), sf. reconciliation.

Recorder (LL. *recordare* for *recordari*, remember), va. recall, remember, indicate, relate; vn. & rfl. remember. *Also,* va. (infl. by *acorder*, q.v.), reconcile.

Recorre (on *corre*, q.v.), vn. run back, run again, have recourse to. *Also* var. of *rescorre*, q.v.

Recort (on *recorder*, q.v.), sm. memory, word, testimony, verdict. *Also* 1 pr. and 1 & 3 pr. subj. of *recorre*, q.v.

Recovrance (on *recovrer*, q.v.), sf. recovery, delivery, help.

Recovrer (*recuperare*), v. recover, regain, obtain, receive, gain ground, attack again; vn. & rfl. be restored, recover oneself. *Sans recovrier (sm.) :* without fail, without recovery, without hope of help.

Recreant (pr. p. of *recroire*, q.v.), adj. & sm. ready to confess oneself defeated, cowardly, renegade, weak.

Recreu, pp., v. *recroire.*

Recreüe (fem. pp. of *recroire*, q.v.), sf. confession of defeat or submission. *Corner la r. :* sound the retreat

Recroire (on *croire < crēdere*, entrust), *va.* trust, release on parole, conquer; *vn. & rfl.* give up, give in, take back a request. *Se r. :* yield, hand oneself over to the mercy of, tire oneself, retract, forswear oneself.

Recueil (on *recueillir*, v. *recoillir*), *sm.* welcome.

Recuit (*recoctum*, pp. of *recoquere*, perh. infl. by *coquere* in sense of " contrive "), *adj.* astute, cunning, wicked.

Rede, v. *roide.*

Redire (on *dire < dīcere*), *va.* say again, speak in one's turn, answer.

Redoter, cf. *doter. Redoté,* pp. *adj.* : redoubtable; timorous, doddering.

Referir, cf. *ferir.*

Refraindre (on *fraindre*, q.v.), *va.* break, lessen, moderate, temper; *vn.* sound, resound; *v. rfl.* restrain oneself.

Refu, 3 pft. of *restre* (on *estre < *essere*), was also.

Reful (on *refugium*), *sm.* refuge, aid. *Also* 1 pft. of *restre*, cf. *refu.*

Regart (on *regarder*, cf. *garder*), *sm.* look, sight, consideration, preoccupation, care, fear. *Au r. de :* compared with, concerning.

Regehir, cf. *gehir.*

Regne (*rēgnum*), *sm.* kingdom.

Regné (on *regne*, q.v.), *sm.* kingdom.

Regort, Regot (cf. Med. L. *gordus,* connected with *gurges?*), *sm.* deep water, bay, current; defile.

Regreter (perh. on O. Sc. *grâta,* weep), *va. & n.* recall, lament the memory of, call upon; *v. impers.* cause grief to, grieve.

Reguart, v. *regart.*

Rehaitier (on *haitier*, q.v.), *va.* comfort, gladden; *v. rfl.* be glad, take comfort.

Rehorder, cf. *hourder.*

Reial (*rēgalem*), *adj.* royal; *sm.* king's man, soldier in the king's army.

Reialme (*regimen*, government, infl. by *reial*, q.v.), *sm.* kingdom.

Reigne (var. of *resne*, q.v., cf. O. Pr. *renha*), *sf.* rein. *Also sm.,* var. of *regne*, q.v.

Reille (*rēgula*), *sf.* bar, beam, grill, chain.

Reis, v. *rois* (*rētes*). **Reisne,** v. *resne.*

Relevee (fem. pp. of *relever < relevare*, lift again), *sf.* raising, uprising; afternoon.

Remaindre, var. of *remanoir*, q.v.

Remanant (pr. p. of *remanoir,* q.v.), *sm.* the rest, the others.

Remanoir (*remanēre*, cf. *manoir*), *vn.* remain, survive; cease, come to an end. *Ne remaindra que . . . 'ne :* (I, He, *etc.*) will not fail to. . . . *R. en estant :* remain where one is, stand still.

Remansist, 3 impft. subj. of *remanoir*, q.v. **Rembatre,** cf. *embatre.*

Remerir (on *merir*, q.v.), *va.* reward.

Remés (*remansum*), pp., **Remest,** 3 pft., **Remestrent,** 6 pft. of *remanoir*, q.v.

Remire (on *remedium*), *sm.* remedy, comfort.

Remirer (on *mirer*, q.v.), *va.* look at again, examine, admire; *v. rfl.* examine oneself.

Remuer (on *muer*, q.v.), *va. & n.* change, exchange, depart; *v. rfl.* stir, change. *Li sans li remue :* he is much agitated, he trembles with anger, fear, etc. *Remuant*, pr. p. adj. : lively, changeable.

Renc (Fk. **hring*, ring), *sm.* rank, line.

Rencliner (on *encliner*, q.v.), *vn.* bow again, bend again; *va.* bow (to).

Renclos, Renclus (pp. of *renclore*, on *enclore < *includaere* for *inclūdere*), *adj.* enclosed; *sm.* recluse, hermit, enclosure, place of safety.

Rendre (**rendere* for *reddere*, infl. by *prendere*), *va.* give up, return, render, lay down, requite; *v. rfl.* become a monk or nun.

Rendu (pp. of *rendre*, q.v.), *sm.* monk.

René, v. *regné.* **Reneer, Reneier,** v. *renoier.*

Renge (Fk. **hringa*), *sf.* girdle, buckle, strap attached to the shield.

Renoer (on *noer*, q.v.), *va.* knot, tie, attach.

Renoier (**renegare*), *va.* refuse, renounce, disown; *v. rfl.* forswear oneself, break one's oath or vow, become a renegade. *Renoié*, adj. : renegade, traitor, faithless.

G

Rentercier, cf. *entercier.* **Reoignier,** v. *roegnier.*

Reont (**retundum* for *rotundum*), *adj.* round.

Repaidrier, v. *repairier.*

Repaire (on *repairier*, q.v.), *sm.* return home, dwelling, place.

Repairier (LL. *repatriare*, on *patria*), *vn. & rfl.* return, retire. *R. arriere :* return. *S'en r. :* return. *sm.* return.

Repentaille (on *repentir*, q.v.), *sf.* repentance, penance-money, forfeit.

Repentir (on *pentir*, q.v.), *vn. & rfl.* repent.

Reperier, v. *repairier.*

Repost (*repositum*, pp., put behind, hidden), *adj.* hidden, secret. *En r :* in secret.

Reproche, Reproece (on *reprocher*, blame, *< *repropiare*, bring forward, put near), *sf.* reproach, shame, defect.

Reprover (Eccl. L. *reprobare*), *va.* reproach, reprove.

Reprovier (on *reprover*, q.v.), *sm.* reproach, exhortation, advice, proverb; shameful conduct.

Requeillit, 3 pft. of *recoillir*, q.v. **Requeit,** v. *requoi.*

Requerre (**requaerere* for *requirere*), *va., n. & rfl.* seek, ask, call upon, attack. *Le r. de :* ask him for. *Pp. & 1 pft. :* **Requis.**

Requoi (on *quoi*, v. *coi*), *adj.* quiet, serene ; *sm.* rest, calm, quiet, retreat, shelter. *En r. :* secretly, out of sight, hiding.

Rere (*radere*), *va.* cut down, mow, remove, shave.

Res (*rasum*), pp. of *rere*, q.v., or form in *-s* of *ré*, q.v., or var. of *rez*, q.v.

Resachier (on *sachier*, q.v.), *va.* draw off, pull again; *sm.* withdrawal.

Resbaldir, cf. *esbaldir*.

Reschignier (perh. on Fk. **kīnan*, grimace), *vn.* grimace, refuse, display disgust or disapproval. *Chiere reschigniee* : disagreeable or hideous countenance. *R. les* (*des*) *denz* : show one's teeth, snarl, gnash one's teeth.

Rescorre (on *escorre*, shake, q.v.), *va.* recover, get possession of, save, rescue; *v. rfl.* free oneself; *sm.* help.

Rescos (pp. of *rescorre*, q.v.), *sm.* help.

Rescosse (fem. pp. of *rescorre*, q.v.), *sf.* help, relief, liberation, rescue; recapture.

Resembler (on *sembler* < LL. *similare*, resemble), *vn.* seem, look like.

Resleecier (on *leece*, q.v.), *va.* please, make happy; *v. rfl.* rejoice.

Resne (**retina*), *sf.* rein.

Reso-, try also **Resso-**.

Resort (on *resortir*, q.v.), *sm.* reservation, help, remedy.

Resortir (on *sortir*, q.v.), *vn.* rebound; *vn. & rfl.* retire, withdraw; *va.* overthrow, pursue.

Respasser (on *ex + passum*), *va.* cure; *vn. & rfl.* recover, be cured.

Respit (*respectum*, backward look, refuge), *sm.* delay, respite; saying. *Metre en r.* : consider.

Respitier (on *respit*, q.v.), *va.* grant respite, delay, prevent, spare, save; *vn.* grant respite.

Respondié, 3 pft. of **Respondre** (**respondere* for *-ēre*), *va. & n.* reply, answer for.

Respons (*respōnsum*), *sm.* response, reply.

Ressoignier (on *soignier*, perh. on Fk. **sunnja*, worry), *va.* fear; *Ressoigné*, pp. adj. : redoubtable, feared. *Faire a r.* : be redoubtable.

Ressourdre (on *sourdre*, v. *sordre*), *vn.* spring up, rebound, resurrect, rise again; *v. rfl.* rise again, re-establish oneself.

Rest, 3 pr. of *restre* (on *estre* < **essere*), is again, is also. (If auxil., take the *Re-* with the past part. for sense.)

Restif (**restīvum*, on *restare*, stop), *adj.* stationary, mettlesome.

Restorer (on *estorer*, q.v.), *va.* repair, replace, substitute, avenge. *Restoré*, pp. adj. : new, substitute.

Restut, 3 pft. of *restoveir*, v. *estoveir*, or of *rester* (*restare*), remain, stop. **Resui**, 1 pr. of *restre*, I am again, I am also, I too am.

Resver (etym. obsc.), *vn.* wander, seek pleasure, be delirious.

Retenir (**retinīre* for *-ēre*), *va.* keep, detain, retain, take prisoner, hold, uphold; *v. rfl.* stand firm.

Retenue (fem. pp. of *retenir*, q.v.), *sf.* restraint, delay, holding back; memory; retainers, retinue.

Reter (*reputare*, appraise), *va.* accuse, blame.

Retoldre, Retolir (on *toldre, tolir*, q.v.), *va.* take back, take away.

Retor (on *retorner*, q.v.), *sm.* return, refuge, means of safety.

Retorner (on *torner*, q.v.), *va.* turn back, bring back, change; *vn.* return, retreat.

Retraçon (*retractiōnem for *re-tractatiōnem*, denial), *sf.* reproach.

Retraire (*retragere for *retrahere*, cf. *traire*), *va. & n.* draw back, retire, remove; relate. *R. a mal :* interpret badly. *Sans r. :* without delay, without recovery. *Se r. de :* withdraw from.

Retrait (*retractum*, pp. of *retrahere*, v. *retraire*), *sm.* retreat, dwelling, refuge, return; account.

Retter, v. *reter*. **Returner,** v. *retorner*.

Reüser (*recūsare*, refuse), *va.* put to flight, repel, ward off; *vn. & rfl.* draw back.

Reva, 3 pr. of *raler*, go again, go also.

Revel (on *reveler*, q.v.), *sm.* rebellion, pride, violence, joy, pleasure.

Reveler (*rebellare*, renew war), *vn. & rfl.* rebel; rejoice.

Reveler (b. *revēlare*, uncover), *va.* reveal.

Revenchier, var. of *revengier*, q.v. **Revendrai,** v. *revenrai*.

Revengier (on *vengier* < *vindicare*), *va.* avenge.

Revenrai, 1 fut. of **Revenir** (*re-venīre*), return, come back.

Reverser (on *verser*, q.v.), *va. & n.* overthrow, overturn, turn up, tuck up.

Revertir (*revertire for -*ere*), *vn.* return, turn to, turn out.

Revestir (on *vestir*, q.v.), *va.* put on, don, put in charge of.

Revisder (on *visder*, q.v.), *va.* visit, see again, recognize.

Revoit (*revictum*, convicted), *adj.* convinced, assured; treacherous, wicked. *Felon r. :* thoroughly disloyal. *Traitre r. :* thorough traitor.

Rez (*rasum*, pp. of *radere*), *adv. & prep.* near. (*A*) *R. de :* up against, level with. *R. a r. :* close, level. *Also* var. of *res*, q.v.

Ribaut (on *riber*, q.v.), *sm.* lecher, wretch; porter (*rare*).

Riber (Germ., cf. MHG. *riben*, be in rut), *vn.* go a-whoring, behave lecherously, amuse oneself; *va.* flirt with, debauch.

Riche, Rice (Fk. *rîki, powerful), *adj.* powerful, mighty, magnificent, rich, precious.

Richeté (on *riche*, q.v.), *sf.* power, wealth. *Faire ses r——s :* enjoy one's wealth.

Rien (*rem*), *sf.* thing, anything, person. (From 15th c. may be *sm.*, nothing.) *N'a r. del + infin. :* there is no chance of. . . . *Ne . . . r. :* nothing. *Por r. :* for anything, in any way. *R. nee :* anything, anyone.

Rieule (*rēgula*), *sf.* rule, order, precept.

Rimor, var. of *rumor*, q.v.

Ris (*risum*), *sm.* laugh. *Jeter un r. :* give a laugh, laugh.

Riviere (PL. *riparia*, fem. adj. as sf., bank), *sf.* shore, bank, district by the shore, river, the hunting of waterfowl.

Rivoier (on *rive < ripa*, river-bank), *vn.* hunt waterfowl.

Roaiment (pop. form of *raemant*, pr. p. of *raembre*, q.v.), *sm.* redeemer.

Robe (Fk. **rauba*, booty), *sf.* booty, dress, tunic, costume.

Rober (Fk. **raubôn*, steal), *va.* steal, rob, pillage, despoil, ravish.

Roe (*rota*, infl. by atonic *o* in *roer < rotare*, etc.), *sf.* wheel.

Roé (on *roe*, q.v.), *adj.* patterned (with wheels or rings).

Roegnier (**rotundiare*, on *rotundum*, round), *va.* cut round, tonsure, cut the hair of, behead, cut, clip.

Roeiller (**roticulare*, on *rotare*), *va. & n.* roll (eyes) ; *va. also* = beat, burnish.

Roele (LL. *rotella*, on *rota*, wheel), *sf.* small wheel, round buckler, coin.

Roide, fem. of *roit*, q.v.

Roié (on *roier*, v. *raie*), *adj.* streaked.

Roignier, v. *roegnier*.

Roïne (*rēgina*, infl. by *roi < rēgem*), *sf.* queen.

Roion (*regiōnem*, region), *sm.* country, district.

Rois (*rētes*, pl. of *rētis*, net), *sf.* net. *Also* form in *-s* of *roi* (*rēgem*), king, or of *roit*, q.v.

Roit (*rigidum*), *adj.* straight, firm, unyielding, harsh, dire.

Roiz, v. *rois*.

Rolleis (on *roeler*, on *roele*, q.v.), *sm.* slaughter ; fortification, barricade (of tree-trunks).

Romant, Romanz (**rōmanice*, in Latin), *sm.* the vernacular, French, work written in French.

Ronci(n) (orig. obsc., perh. on LL. *ruccinum*, on Germ. *rukki*, back), *sm.* packhorse.

Ront, 3 pr. of *rompre* (*rumpere*), break. *Also* may be var. of *reont*, q.v.

Roont (*rotundum*), *adj.* round.

Ros, (1) (*russum*), *adj.* tawny, red ; *sm.* horse ; (2) (Germ. **raus*), *sm.* reed, thatch.

Rosee (**rōsata*, on *rōs*, *rōrem*), *sf.* dew.

Rosel (on *ros* 2, q.v.), *sm.* reed.

Rot, 3 pft. of *ravoir*, have again, also to have ; *or* var. of *rout*, q.v.

Rote (Celt., form uncertain), *sf.* stringed instrument, sort of harp. *Also* var. of *route*, q.v.

Rou-, try also under **Ro-.**

Rout (*ruptum*), *pp.* broken. Form in *-s :* **Rous.**

Route (*rupta*, fem. pp. of *rumpere*, break), *sf.* road, way ; band of men, crowd, troops, rout.

Routure (*ruptūra*, fracture ; in PL., freshly turned soil), *sf.* fracture, feudal due, tenure.

Rover (*rogare*, with special devel. of *-g-*), *va.* ask, seek to, desire, order. *En r., S'en r. :* desire to, care about.

Rovir (*rubīre* for -*ēre*), vn. red-
den, blush.

Rovoisons (Eccl. L. *rogatiōnes*,
cf. *rover*), sf. Rogation pro-
cession or prayers.

Ru-, try also under **Ro-** or **Rou-**.

Ru (*rīvum*), sm. stream, edge.
A r. : in streams.

Rubeste (etym. unkn.), adj. harsh,
wild, violent.

Ruer (LL. *rūtare*, on *rutum*, pp.
of *ruere*), va. hurl ; v. rfl. rush.

Rueve, 3 pr., **Ruis,** 1 pr. of *rover*,
q.v.

Ruiste (*rūsticum*, of the country),
adj. vigorous, violent, terrible.

Rumor (*rūmōrem*),· sf. noise,
quarrel, dissension, revolt.

Rusee, var. of *rosee*, q.v. **Ruste,**
v. *ruiste*.

S

S' for (1) *se*, refl. pron ; (2) *se*,
if ; (3) *sa*, fem. poss. adj. ;
(4) *si*, thus (*rare*).

Sabelin, v. *sebelin*.

Sablon (*sabulōnem*, gravel), sm.
sand, sandy ground. *Syn. :*
Sablonier, sm.

Sace, v. *sache*.

Sachant (pr. p. of *saveir*, q.v.)
adj. clever, experienced.

Sache, pr. subj. of *saveir*, q.v., or
pr. of *sachier*, q.v.

Sachel, Sachet (dimins. of *sac* <
saccum), sm. satchel, bag.

Sachiee (on *sac* < *saccum*), sf.
sack, sackful.

Sachier (etym. obsc.), va. draw,
pull, drag, pull aside, remove.

Sade (*sapidum*), adj. pleasant,
agreeable.

Saeller, v. *seeler*. **Saete,** v. *saiete*.

Safré (connected with Med. L.
safranum < Arabo-Pers. *za-
'faran*), adj. yellow-burnished.

Saichier, v. *sachier*. **Saier,** v.
seier.

Saiete (*sagitta*), sf. arrow.

Saillir (*salīre*, infl. by forms ·in
l mouillé), vn. jump, rush, leap
forth, gush out.

Sain, v. *sein*, bell.

Saïn (*sagīmen* for *sagīna*, fattening), sm. fat, grease.

Sainteé (*sanctitatem*), sf. holiness.

Sairement, v. *serement*.

Saisine (on *saisir*, q.v.), sf. possession. *Par s. :* in token of
possession.

Saisir (perh. Fk. *sakjan*, claim,
or Fk. *satjan*, put, or fusion
of the two), va. seize, rule, put
in possession of ; vn. be seised
of. *Estre saisi de :* possess
legally, be seised of.

Saive, var. of **Sage** (*sapicum*,
sapium, or *sabiēs* for *sa-
piē(n)s*), adj. wise, learned.

Sal-, try also under **Sau-**. **Sal-
drai,** 1 fut. of *saillir*, q.v.

Salir, orig. form of *saillir*, q.v.

Sals, 2 pr. of *saillir*, q.v., or
2 pr. subj. of *sauver*, q.v., or
form in -*s* of *salf*, v. *sauf*.

Salt (*saltum*), sm. leap. *De prin
s.*, v. *prin*. *Les salz :* with
leaps, leaping. *Prendre un mal
s. :* come to a sorry plight.
Venir a son s. : come to one's
doom. Cf. *saut*.

Salteler (on *salter*, q.v.), vn.
jump, beat (heart).

Salter (*saltare*), vn. jump, leap,
dance.

Salvement (on *salve*, v. *sauf*), *adv.* safely. *Also* var. of *sauvement*, *sm.*, q.v.

Salverre (Eccl. L. *salvator*), nom. of **Salveör** (Eccl. L. *salvatōrem*), *sm.* saviour.

Samit (Med. L. *samītum*, ult. on Gk. *hexamiton*, six threads), *sm.* samite (rich silk fabric).

San, v. *sen.*

Sanc (*sanguen*, neuter), *sm.* blood. *Muer le s. :* change colour, grow pale.

Saner (*sanare*), *va.* cure, heal, care for; *vn.* get well, heal.

Sangle (var. of *sengle* < *singulum*), *adj.* single, simple, plain.

Sangler (for *sengler* < PL. *singularem* (*porcum*)), *sm.* boar.

Saol (PL. *satullum* for *saturum*), *adj.* satiated, full.

Saoler (PL. *satullare* for *saturare*), *va.* satiate, fill.

Sap (on *sapin* < *sappinum*), *sm.* pine-tree, fir.

Saral, 1 fut. of *saveir*, q.v.

Sarcel (**sarcellum* for *sarculum*), *sm.* hoe, pruning-hook.

Sarcou (LL. *sarcophagum*, adj. as noun), *sm.* coffin.

Sas, form in -*s* of *sac* (*saccum*), *sm.* sack, bag, sackcloth.

Sau-, try also under **Sal-.**

Sauf (*salvum*); *fem.* **Sauve** (*salvam*), *adj.* safe; efficacious to save souls. *Also* 1 pr. & pr. subj. of *sauver*, q.v.

Saul-, try under **Sau-** or **Sal-.**

Saur, v. *sor*, adj. **Saurral,** 1 fut. of *saillir*, q.v.

Saus, *sm.*; **Sausse,** *sf.* (*salicem*), willow.

Sause (PL. *salsa*, *fem. adj.*, salty, as noun), *sf.* sauce, seasoning.

Saut, v. *salt ;* also 3 pr. of *saillir*, q.v., 3 pr. subj. of *sauver*, q.v., or var. of *sot* (*sapuit*), knew.

Sauvement (on *sauver*, q.v.), *sm.* salvation, safety. *Also* var. of *salvement*, adv., q.v.

Sauver (LL. *salvare*), *va.* save ; *v. rfl.* save oneself, get out of a difficulty.

Sauveté (on *sauf*, *sauve*, q.v.), *sf.* safety, salvation.

Saveir (**sapēre* for *sapere*, taste), *va. & n.* know, be able, discover ; *vn.* taste of ; *sm.* knowledge, wisdom. *Ne s. mot de :* know nothing about. *S. de :* know the art of, be well versed in. *Tort a folie o a s. :* whether it turn out well or ill, whatever the result.

Savie, v. *saive.* **Savoir,** v. *saveir.*

Savral, 1 fut. of *saveir*, q.v.

Sceüst, var. of *seüst*, 3 impft. subj. of *saveir*, q.v.

Se (*si*), *conj.* if, although, whether. *Se . . . ne :* unless. *Se . . . non :* except, but, unless. *Also* occasionally for *si* (*sic*).

Sëant (pr. p. of *sēoir*, q.v.), *adj.* fitting, suitable, becoming. *Bien s. :* well situated (castles, etc.); handsome (people)?. *En s. :* seated.

Sebelin (var. of *sabelin*, on *sable*, sable < Med. L. *sabellum*, of Slav. orig.), *adj. & sm.* sable.

Secorre (*succurrere*), *va.* help, succour.

Secourre (*succutere*), *va.* shake.

Secrol, v. *segroi.* **Sedeir,** v. *sēoir.*

Sedme (*septimum*), *adj.* seventh.

Seel (*sigellum* for *sigillum*), *sm.* seal, wax.

Seeler (*sigellare* for *sigillare*), *va.* seal, seal up.

Seete, v. *saiete.*

Seeur (on *seier,* q.v.), *sm.* one who cuts, harvester.

Seez, 5 pr. & imper. pl. of *sēoir,* q.v.

Segrol (*sēcrētum,* separated), *adj.* secret; *sm.* secret, "Secreta" (secret prayers at Mass). *En s. :* secretly.

Segur, v. *seür.*

Sei, v. *soi.*

Seie (for *soue,* q.v., infl. by *meie* < *mēa*), *poss. adj. fem.* his, her. *Also* pr. subj. of *estre* (**essere*), be, & var. of *soie,* silk, q.v.

Seier (*secare,* cut), *va.* cut, saw, mow, harvest.

Seiez, 5 pr. of *seier,* q.v., and 5 pr. subj. & imper. pl. of *estre* (**essere*), be.

Seignier (*signare,* place a mark), *va.* mark, sign, make the sign of the cross over, bless; *v. rfl.* cross oneself. *Also* common var. of *saignier* (**sanginare* for *sanguinare*), *va. & n.* bleed; *v. rfl.* be bled.

Seignor (*seniōrem*), *sm.* lord. (N.B. this form is also the nom. pl., and, used as a vocative, = "My Lords.")

Seignori (on *seignor,* q.v.), *adj.* chief, princely, noble.

Seignorie (on *seignor,* q.v.), *sf.* power, rule, baronial jurisdiction. *Par s. :* by right of rank.

Seignorier (on *seignor,* q.v.), *va.*

& *n.* rule, govern. *Syn. :* **Seignourir.**

Sein, (1) (*signum,* sign; in LL., bell), *sm.* mark, sign, bell; (2) (*sinum,* fold), *sm.* breast, heart.

Seint, var. of *saint* (*sanctum*), or of *sein* 1, q.v. **Seit,** v. *soi* 1; *also* 3 pr. subj. of *estre,* be, or var. of *set,* 3 pr. of *saveir,* q.v.

Seiz, form in -*s* of *seit,* thirst, v. *soi* 1.

Sejor (on *sejorner,* q.v.), *sm.* leisure, rest, stay, delay, lodging. *A s. :* at rest, quietly. *Estre a s. :* sojourn.

Sejorner (alter. of *sojorner* < **subdiurnare,* last for a time), *vn.* stay, dwell, rest, delay; *va.* cause to rest, hold back. *Sejorné,* pp. adj. : rested, fresh, mettlesome.

Selon(c) (**sublongum,* along), *prep.* along, alongside, the length of, near, according to; *adv.* near, alongside.

Selt, v. *suelt.*

Semblant (pr. p. of *sembler,* resemble, appear < *similare,* resemble), *sm.* appearance, bearing, mien, opinion, sign. *Bel s. :* friendly mien. *Faire s. de :* make a show of, pretend. *Faire s. que :* seem to. *Par s. :* feignedly, on the surface.

Semme, v. *sedme.* **Semonant,** pr. p. of *semondre,* q.v.

Semondre (alter. of *somondre* < **submonere* for -*ēre,* warn), *va.* warn, urge, summon.

Semons, pp., **Semont,** 3 pr. of *semondre,* q.v.

Sempres (*semper*, always, + adv. -*s*), *adv.* straightway, soon, always. *S . . . s . . . :* now . . . now. *S. + fut. :* to be going to. . .

Sen (Fk. **sin*, sense), *sm.* sense, reason, opinion, way, direction. *Also* var. of *son* (*suum*), his, her.

Sené (on *sen*, q.v.), *adj.* wise, sensible. *Mal s. :* foolish, mad.

Senestre (*sinistrum*), *adj.* left.

Sengler, v. *sangler*.

Sens (*sēnsum* + infl. of *sen*, q.v.), *sm.* sense, direction. *Changier de s. :* go mad.

Sente (*sēmita*), *sf.* path. *Dimins.:* **Sentele, Sentelete.**

Sëoir (*sedēre*), *vn.* sit, be seated, be situated, suit, please ; *v. rfl.* sit ; *va.* besiege.

Serain (on *seir*, evening, *sērō*, late), *sm.* evening, dusk.

Sercher, v. *cerchier*.

Serement (*sacramentum*, gage), *sm.* oath.

Sereur = *seror*, v. *soror*.

Serf (*servum*, slave), *sm.* servant, serf, slave. *Also* 1 pr. & imper. sing. of *servir*, q.v.

Sergent, v. *serjant*.

Seri (*serēnum*, with change of suffix), *adj.* gentle, calm, serene ; *adv.* quietly, gently, sweetly. *A (En) s. :* quietly.

Serjant (*servientem*, pr. p. of *servire*), *sm.* servant, man-at-arms, retainer.

Sermon (*sermōnem*, conversation ; in Eccl. L., sermon), *sf.* speech, discourse, sermon.

Seror, Serorge, v. *soror, sororge*.

Serre (on *serrer* < **serrare*, on *sera*, bar, bolt), *sf.* lock, prison, bit (horse's).

Sers, form in -*s* of *serf*, q.v., or 2 pr. of *servir*, q.v.

Servir (*servire*, be a slave), *va. & n.* serve ; *vn.* be useful, behave. *S. de :* follow the profession of, use, help oneself to.

Ses = *si les* or *si se ; also* 2 pr. of *saveir*, q.v., or nom. (*suus*) of *son* (*suum*), his, her, etc.

Ses (*satis*), *sm.* fill, sufficiency, pleasure, will.

Set (*septem*), *num.* seven. *Also* 3 pr. of *saveir*, q.v.

Seü, pp. of *sivre*, q.v., or of *saveir*, q.v. **Seue,** v. *soue*.

Seür (*sēcūrum*), *adj.* sure, assured, safe. *A s. :* in safety, with assurance. *Estre a s. :* be sure, be safe. *Metre a s. :* safeguard, put in safety.

Seure, var. of *sivre*, q.v.

Seürté (*sēcūritatem*, freedom from care), *sf.* promise, undertaking, oath.

Seüsse, impft. subj. of *saveir*, q.v.

Seut, 3 pr. of *sivre*, q.v., or 3 pft. of *saveir*, q.v.

Sevals, Sevels (*seu vel* + adv. -*s*), *adv.* at least.

Sevrer (PL. *sēperare* for *sēparare*), *va.* separate, put aside ; *vn. & rfl.* separate, take one's leave.

Sez (*satis*), *adv.* enough, much. *Also* var. of *ses* (*sapes, suus*, or *satis*).

Si (*sīc*), *adv.* and, thus, so, greatly ; *conj.* yet, until. *De si que :* v. *deci*. *Par si que :* so that, provided that. *Also*

nom. pl. (*suī*) of *son*, his, her, their, & *may sometimes* = *se*, if, q.v.

Sié, v. *siet.*

Siecle (on *saeculum*), *sm.* century, world ; this life, pleasure ; the people.

Siet (on *sēoir*, q.v.), *sm.* seat, stronghold, capital, see (Eccl.). *Also* 3 pr. of *sēoir* q.v.·

Sievir, Sievre, v. *sivir*, *sivre.*

Sifaitement, cf. *faitement.*

Siglaton, v. *ciclaton.*

Sigler (on *sigle* < Germ., cf. *segel*, sail), *va.* & *n.* sail.

Simle, Simbre (on *simila*, finest wheat flour), *sm.* wheat flour, bread or cake of wheat flour.

Sin = *si en.* **Singlaton,** v. *ciclaton.* **Singler,** v. *sigler.* **Sire** (**seior* for *senior*), nom. sing. of *seignor*, q.v. **Sis,** v. *ses* < *suus: also* pp. & 1 pft. of *sēoir*, q.v.

Siste (*sextum*), *adj.* sixth.

Siu, 1 pr. of *sivre*, q.v. **Sivir,** remodelled form of *sivre*, q.v.

Sivre (PL. *sequere* for *sequī*), *va.* follow, pursue, secure.

Socorre, v. *secorre.*

Sodant (on Arab. *sultan*), *sm.* sultan, Mohammedan prince.

Soe, v. *soue.*

Soef (*suavem*), *adj.* & *adv.* sweet-(ly), gentle(-ly), tender(ly).

Soen, v. *suen.* **Soentre,** v. *soventre.* **Soer,** v. *suer.*

Soffrance (on *soffrir*, q.v.), *sf.* permission, delay, tolerance, patience.

Soffrete, v. *sofraite.*

Soffrir (**sufferire* for *sufferre*), *va.* & *n.* suffer, endure, have

patience, allow, await ; *v. rfl.* contain oneself, have patience, do without.

Sofraite (*suffracta*, noun from fem. pp. of *suffringere*, break in pieces), *sf.* want, distress, privation. *Avoir s. de :* lack.

Sofraitos, Sofretos (on *sofraite*, q.v.), *adj.* in want.

Sol, (1) *sf.* (*sitim*), thirst ; (2) 1 pft. of *saveir*, q.v. ; (3) 1 pr. of *estre*, be ; (4) *refl. pron.* (*se*), himself, herself, etc.

Sole (*sēta*, bristle, hair), *sf.* silk.

Soler, v. *seier* or *sēoir.*

Soif (*sēpem*), *sm.* & *f.* hedge, fence. *Also* var. of *soi* 1, q.v.

Soing (perh. on Fk. **sunnja*), *sm.* care. *N'àveir s. de :* not to care about, scorn.

Soivre (on stressed root, *sei-*, *soi-*, of *sevrer*, q.v.), *adj.* separate, deprived.

Sojor, v. *sejor.* **Sojorner,** early form of *sejorner*, q.v.

Sol, (1) (*sōlum*), *adj.* alone ; *adv.* only ; (2) (*solidum*), *sm.* coin (of varying value), penny.

Solas (*sōlacium*, consolation), *sm.* pleasure, satisfaction, comfort.

Soldee (on *sold*, first form of *sol* 2, q.v.), *sf.* sou's worth, payment, reward ; *pl.* paid services as a soldier.

Soldoier (on *sold*, first form of *sol* 2, q.v.), *sm.* mercenary, paid soldier ; *vn.* take service with a lord.

Soldre (*solvere*, untie), *va.* pay for, settle, solve.

Soleir, v. *soloir.*

Solier (*sōlarium*, balcony), *sm.* top room, room, apartment.

Soller (LL. *subtēlarem*, adj. as noun), *sm.* slipper, shoe.

Soloir (*solēre*), *vn.* be wont to, be accustomed to.

Solt, Solu, pp. of *soldre,* q.v. **Solt-,** v. **Sout-.**

Som (*summum*, highest), *sm.* top. *En* (*Par*) *s. :* at the top of, on high, above. *Par s. l'aube :* at dawn.

Some, (1) (*summa*, fem. adj. as noun), *sf.* quantity, summary, completion. *A pou de s. :* briefly; (2) (*somnum*), *sm.* sleep.

Some (LL. *sagma*, pack-saddle), *sf.* load, pack, beast of burden.

Somier (LL. *sagmarium*), *sm.* packhorse, beast of burden.

Somondre, v. *semondre.* **Son,** v. *som.* *Also poss. adj.* (*suum*), his, her, etc.

Soneïs (on *soner,* q.v.), *sm.* noise, blowing of horns, peal or toll of bells.

Soner (*sonare*), *va.* sound, play (instruments); *vn.* sound, resound. *S. mot :* speak, talk, utter a word.

Sons, 2 pr. subj. of *soner,* q.v. **Sont,** 6 pr. of *estre* or 3 pr. subj. of *soner,* q.v.

Sor (Fk. **saur*, dried (of leaves), yellow), *adj.* yellow, sorrel, auburn.

Sor, Sore (*super* or *supra*), *adv.* above; *prep.* on, over, by, in the name of, for the sake of, in addition to. *Metre s. :* accuse of.

Sordois (*sordidius*), *sm.* the worst, worse; *adj.* bad, dire; *adv.* worse.

Sordre (*surgere*), *vn.* arise, spring.

Sore, v. *sor,* on. **Sorent,** 6 pft. of *saveir,* q.v.

Sormonter (*sor,* over, + *monter,* q.v.), *va.* surpass, exalt.

Soror (*sorōrem*), *sf.* sister, dear friend (endearment).

Sororge (*sorōrium,* -*iam,* adj. as noun), *sm. & f.* brother-in-law, sister-in-law.

Sorquidié (*sor,* over, + pp. of *quidier,* q.v.), *adj.* overwhelming, arrogant.

Sort, (1) (*sortem*), *sm. & f.* fate, prediction; (2) (*surdem*), *adj.* deaf; (3) 3 pr. of *sordre,* q.v. or of *sortir,* q.v.

Sortir (perh. PL. *sortīre* for -*īri*), *va.* have as one's lot, predict, provide, decree; *vn.* prophecy.

Sos-, try under **Sous-.**

Sot (etym. obsc.), *adj. & sm.* foolish, fool. *Also* 3 pft. of *saveir,* q.v.

Sotain, v. *soutain.* **Sou-,** try also under **Sol-** or **So-.** **Soü,** pp. of *saveir,* q.v. **Soudee, Soudeier,** v. *soldee, soldoier.*

Soudement (on fem. adj. *soude* < *subita*), *adv.* rapidly, suddenly.

Souduiant (pr. p. of *souduire,* seduce, deceive < *subdūcere,* withdraw secretly), *adj.* false, treacherous.

Soue (tonic form of *sua*), *adj. & pron.* his, her, hers, their, theirs.

Soué, v. *soef.* **Soufrete,** v. *sofraite.*

Souhaidier, Souhaitier (*sou-,* v. *soz,* + *haitier,* q.v.), *va.* wish, desire.

Souler, v. *soller.*

Souploier (sou-, v. soz, + ploier, q.v.), va. lower, abase; vn. & rfl. bend, bow, submit.

Sourdre, v. sordre. **Sous,** v. soz, or form in -s of sol, q.v., or of solt, q.v.

Sousprendre (sous, v. soz, + prendre, q.v.), va. take by surprise, deceive, afflict, oppress, press upon, vanquish.

Soüsse, impft. subj. of saveir, q.v.

Soutain (*sōlitanum, solitary), adj. lonely, hidden, secret.

Soutement, v. soudement. **Soutif,** alter. of soutil, q.v., or of soutain, q.v.

Soutil (subtilem, slender, acute), adj. subtle, fine, clever, secret.

Souvin (supinum, lying on the back), adj. flat on the back, on one's back.

Souz, v. soz.

Soventre (on LL. sequenter, on PL. sequere, cf. sivre), adv. & prep. after, afterwards, as a result, according to.

Soz (subtus), prep. below, under. Also form in -s of sol, q.v.

Sozceinte (soz, q.v., + ceinte < cincta, fem. pp. as noun), sf. girdle, belt.

Sozterrin (soz, q.v., + terrin < *terrinum, on terra, earth; on model of subterraneus), sm. cellar.

Su-, try also under **So-** or **Sou-**. **Suffre,** 1 & 3 pr. & pr subj. of soffrir, q.v. **Suelt,** 3 pr. of soloir, q.v.

Suen (tonic form of suum), adj. & pron. his, her, hers, their.

Suer (soror), nom. of soror, q.v.

Sui, 1 pr. of estre or of sivre, q.v. May also be nom. pl. (suî) of son (suum), his, her. **Suivir,** v. sivir. **Sul,** var. of sol 1, q.v. **Sur(e),** v. sor, sore.

Sus (PL. sūsum, for sūrsum, upwards), adv. & prep. above, up, on high, on, upwards. En s. : aloft, afar, away. La s. : up there, aloft. Metre s. : install, raise. Metre s. a : accuse of. Par s. : over. S. en : up into. S. et jus : up and down, everywhere.

T

Tables (tabulas), sf. pl. a game played with board and counters.

Tafur (etym. obsc.), adj. & s. heathen, vagabond, wretch.

Tai (Germ., cf. OHG. zâhi, sticky), sm. mud, mire, bog.

Taillier (*taliare, on talea, a cutting), va. cut, cut off, carve, inlay.

Tainer, v. taner. **Taint,** v. teint.

Taion (on LL. thium, Gk. theios), sm. great uncle, ancestor.

Taire, remodelling of taisir, q.v.

Taisant (tacentem, pr. p.), adj. silent; sometimes, cowardly.

Taisir (tacēre), vn. & rfl. be silent.

Talent (talentum; sense devel. from New Test. parable), sm. desire, ardour. A mon t. : to my satisfaction, according to my wishes. Avoir t. : intend, desire. T. me vient : I desire.

Talentif (on talent, q.v.), adj. desirous, swift.

Tamaint (on *tam magnum*), *adj.*
many.

Tan-, try also under **Ten-.**

Tandis (*tamdiŭ*, so long, + adv.
-*s*), *adv.* meanwhile. *T. que :*
whilst.

Taner (etym. obsc.), *va.* weary,
harass ; *v. rfl.* tire oneself.

Tans, v. *tens*, or form in -*s* of
tant, q.v.

Tant (*tantum*), *adj.* so many, so
much, so long, many a ; *adv.*
so much, so, only ; *pron.* so
many, so much. *A t. :* then,
thereupon, now. *En t. que :*
so that. *Faire t. que :* act so
that. . . . *Fors t. que :* except
in so far as. *Ne t. ne quant :*
in no way, nothing at all.
Par t. : therefore, nevertheless. *Tant . . . et :* both . . .
and. *Tant . . . ne :* however (much) . . . not. *Tant
. . . tant :* partly . . . partly.
T. com : as long as, whilst,
until. *T. que :* until.

Tantost (*tant*, q.v., + *tost*, q.v.),
adv. at once, straightway, just
now. *T. com, T. que :* as
soon as.

Targe (Fk. **targa*), *sf.* targe,
shield, buckler.

Targer (on *targe*, q.v.), *va.* protect ; *v. rfl.* protect or cover
oneself.

Targier (**tardiare* for *tardare*),
va. delay ; *vn. & rfl.* delay,
tarry. *Me targe :* I long to
(for) . . . *Sans t. :* at once.
Se t. de : be slow to.

Tarier (Fk. **targen?*), *va.* pro-
voke, incite, vex.

Tart (*tardē*, slowly), *adv.* late,

too late. *A t. :* with difficulty, too late. *Estre t. a :* be
a matter of regret or impatience
to.

Tasel, v. *tassel*. **Tasner,** v. *taner*.

Tassel (etym. obsc.), *sm.* tassel,
fringe.

Tastoner (on *taster*, touch < **tastare*, orig. obsc.), *va.* massage,
stroke, caress.

Tavel (on *tavelle* < *tabella*, board,
tablet), *sm.* square (on cloth
or chessboard).

Teche (Germ., cf. G. *Zeichen*,
form. obsc.), *sf.* characteristic,
quality (good or bad).

Teie, alter., infl. by *meie* < *mēa*,
of *toue*, q.v. **Teigne,** 1 & 3
pr. subj. of *tenir*, q.v. **Teil,** v.
til.

Teindre (*tingere*), *va.* dye, cause
to change colour ; *vn.* change
colour, blench.

Teint (*tinctum*, pp. of *tingere*), *adj.*
pale ; cloudy, dark.

Teisant, v. *taisant*.

Tel (*talem*), *adj. m. & f.* such ;
sometimes, this ; *sf.* **Tele,** such
a blow.

Tempier (**temperium*, weather,
on *tempus?*), *sm.* storm, noise,
quarrel.

Tempre (*tempori*), *adv.* early,
soon.

Temprer (*temperare*, keep within
limits, mix liquids), *va.* soak,
moderate, tune (harp), heat
(water).

Tenant (pr. p. of *tenir*, q.v.), *sm.*
dependant, vassal, supporter ;
adj. clinging, firm. *En un t. :*
on end, one after the other.

Tencier (prob. **tentiare*, on *tentus*,

pp. of *tendere*, strive), *va.* rail at ; *vn.* fight, struggle, discuss. *T. a. :* quarrel with, chide, insult. *Also* var. of *tenser*, q.v.

Tençon (**tentiōnem*), *sf.* quarrel, dispute, strife.

Tendrai, 1 fut. of *tendre*, q.v., or of *tenir*, q.v.

Tendre (*tendere*), *va.* stretch, extend, pitch (tent). *T. de :* concentrate upon.

Tendror (on *tendre* < *tenerum*, tender), *sf.* tenderness.

Tenir (**tenire* for *-ēre*), *va. & n.* hold, retain, restrain, be faithful to (a feudal lord), keep, observe (custom). *Se t. a :* keep to, behave as, regard oneself as. *Se t. de :* refrain from. *T. a :* regard as, cling to. *T. cure de :* care about. *T. de :* be a vassal of. *T. en :* regard as. *T. la crestienté :* be a Christian. *T. por :* regard as. *T. que :* intend, wish. *T. qq'un a qq'un :* reconcile . . . with . . . *T. un païs :* govern a land, be master of a land. *T. un païs de :* hold a land as a vassal of.

Tenis, 2 pft. of *tenir*, q.v. **Tenner**, v. *taner*. **Tenrai**, 1 fut. of *tenir*, q.v.

Tens (*tempus*), *sm.* time, life, weather, tempest. *De son t. n'i a plus :* he is near death. *Par t. :* in time, soon, early. *Tot* (*Toz*) *t. :* always.

Tensement (on *tenser*, q.v.), *sm.* protection, help.

Tenser (**tensare*, on *tensum*, pp. of *tendere*, stretch out), *va.*

protect. *Also* var. of *tencier*, q.v.

Tentir (**tinnitire*, on *tinnitus*, pp. of *tinnire*), *va.* ring, sound, utter (word) ; *vn.* resound, ring out.

Tenve (*tenuem*), *adj.* fine, slender, light.

Terdre (*tergere*), *va.* wipe, clean, rub.

Terme, Termine (*terminum*), *sm.* time, appointed time, period of grace, delay, boundary. *A t. :* at the appointed time.

Terral (on *terre* < *terra*, earth), *sm.* land, territory, earthwork.

Terremoete, Terremote (*terra *movita*), *sf.* earthquake.

Terrier (on *terre* < *terra*, earth), *sm.* lord holding territory ; ground, earthwork.

Terrin (**terrinum*, on *terra*, earth), *adj.* of earth, earthly.

Ters, pp., **Terst**, 3 pft. of *terdre*, q.v. **Tesant**, v. *taisant*.

Teser (**tē(n)sare*, on *tēnsus*, pp. of *tendere*), *vn.* tend, contend.

Testee (on *teste* < *testa*, in PL., head), *sf.* blow on the head, idea, project, whim.

Teü, pp. of *taire*, q.v. **Teue**, v. *toue*. **Teüsse**, impft. subj. of *taire*, q.v. **Teus, Tex** (for *tels*), form in *-s* of *tel*, q.v. **Th-**, try under **T-**. **Tiegne**, 1 & 3 pr. subj. of *tenir*, q.v. **Tien**, imper. sing. of *tenir*, q.v., and var. of *tuen*, q.v., infl. by *mien* (*meum*). **Tienge**, 1 & 3 pr. subj. of *tenir*, q.v.

Tierce (Eccl. L. *tertia* (*hōra*), third hour), *sf.* terce, 9 a.m.

Tiesche, fem. of *tiois*, q.v. **Tieux,** var. of *teus, tex,* q.v.

Til (******tilium* on *tilia*), *sm.* linden, lime-tree.

Tinc, 1 pft., **Tindrent,** 6 pft. of *tenir*, q.v.

Tinel (******tignellum,* on *tignum,* beam, log), *sm.* club, large stick, staff.

Ting, 1 pft. of *tenir,* q.v.

Tinter (LL. *tinnĭtare,* on *tinnĭtus,* pp. of *tinnire*), *va.* sound ; *vn.* ring. *Ne t. mot :* not to utter a word.

Tiois (Germ., cf. Goth. *thiudisk*), *adj. & sm.* German, Teuton.

Tire, (1) (Fk. ******têri,* ornament), *sf.* order, rank, file, type. *A t.,* *T. a t. :* completely, on end ; (2) (*Tyrium,* of Tyre), *sm.* silk cloth.

Toaille (Fk. ******thwahlja*), *sf.* towel, cloth.

Tocher (******toccare,* onom. orig.), *va.* touch, urge on, prod, spur. *T. le feu :* set fire (to).

Toe, v. *toue.*

Toeil (on *toeillier* < *tudiculare,* crush), *sm.* trouble, confusion, movement, slaughter, battle.

Toi, 1 pft. of *taire,* q.v. **Toil,** 1 pr., **Toille,** 1 & 3 pr. subj. of *toldre,* q.v.

Toise (*tē*(*n*)*sa,* fem. pp. of *tendere,* stretch), *sf.* toise (about 6 ft.), stretch (of bow). *Also* 3 pr. of *teser,* q.v.

Toldre (*tollere*), *va.* take, take away, carry off ; *v. rfl.* go away, leave.

Toleit, pp. & 3 impft., **Tolge,** 1 & 3 pr. subj. of *toldre,* q.v. **Tolir,** remodelling of *toldre,*

q.v. **Tolt,** 3 pr., **Tolu,** pp. of *toldre,* q.v.

Tondu (pp. of *tondre* < LL. *tondere* for *-ēre*), *adj.* shaven, close-cropped.

Tonel (dimin. of *tone* < LL. *tunna,* Celt. orig., cf. Med. Ir. *tonn,* skin), *sm.* barrel.

Tooil, v. *toeil.*

Top (Germ. ******top,* cf. G. *Zopf,* tress of hair), *sm.* hair, top.

Tor, (1) (*taurum*), *sm.* bull ; (2) (*turrem*), *sf.* tower ; (3) (on *torner,* q.v.), *sm.* turn, twist.

Torbe, (1) (*turba*), *sf.* crowd ; (2) (Fk. ******turba*), *sm.* turf, peat, peat-bog.

Torber (*turbare,* disturb), *va.* trouble, annoy ; *v. rfl.* be worried or irritated.

Torbler, v. *trobler.*

Torçonier (on LL. *tortionare,* torment, on *tortio,* torture), *adj.* violent, cruel, unjust, harmful.

Tordre (******torcere* for *torquere*), *va.* twist, wring.

Torent, 6 pft. of *taire,* q.v.

Torfait, Torfet (*tort,* q.v., + *fait* < *factum*), *sm.* wrong, injustice, violence.

Torge, 1 & 3 pr. subj. of *tordre,* q.v.

Torment (*tormentum,* instrument of torture), *sm.* torment, anguish ; storm, whirlwind, shipwreck.

Tornele (dimin. of *tor* 2, q.v., infl. by *torner* for *-n*), *sf.* watch-tower, small tower.

Torner (*tornare,* make round, turn), *va.* turn ; *vn.* return, arrive, turn back, turn over,

go ; *v. rfl.* turn back, go away ;
v. impers. turn out. *En t. :*
depart. *S'en t. :* depart. *T.
a :* impute, interpret as. *T.
a mal a :* turn out badly for.

Tornoiement (on *tornoier,* q.v.),
sm. tournament, joust, combat.

Tornoier (on *torner,* q.v.), *vn.* engage in a tournament, joust,
turn, travel far and wide ; *va.*
turn ; *sm.* tournament, combat.

Torrai, 1 fut. of *toldre,* q.v., &
perh. of *torner,* q.v.

Tors, pp. of *tordre,* q.v. ; also
case in -s of *tort,* q.v.

Torsel (on *torse, sf.,* parcel,
on *torser,* q.v.), *sm.* bundle,
parcel.

Torser, v. *trosser.*

Tort (PL. *tortum,* pp. as noun),
sm. wrong, harm. *A t. o a
dreit :* rightly or wrongly.
Also 3 pr. of *tordre,* q.v., or 3
pr. subj. of *torner,* q.v.

Tortil, Tortin, Tortis (on *tort,* pp.
of *tordre,* q.v.), *sm.* torch.

Tost (PL. *tostum,* promptly), *adv.*
soon, quickly.

Tot (**tōttum* for *tōtum*), *adj. &
pron.* every, all, each, everything ; *adv.* quite, completely,
the length of. *De (Del) t. en
t. :* completely. *Del t. :* completely. *Ne . . . del t. :* not
entirely. *Tote veie :* all the
time. *Toz jors :* always. *Toz
tens :* always. *Also* 3 pft. of
taire, q.v.

Totdis, v. *toudiz.*

Totevoies (on *tot* + pl. of *voie,*
q.v.), *adv. & conj.* yet, however, always.

Touaille, v. *toaille.*

Toudiz (*tot* + *dis* < *dies,* days),
adv. ever, always. *A t. :* for
ever.

Toudre, v. *toldre.*

Toue (tonic form of *tua*), *fem.
poss. adj. & pron.* thine, thy.

Touillier, *vb.,* cf. *toeill, sm.*

Tourent, 6 pft. of *taire,* q.v.

Tournoier, v. *tornoier.* **Tourser,**
var. of *trosser,* q.v. **Tout,** v.
tot. **Toutdis,** v. *toudiz.* **Toz,**
form in -s of *tot, adj. & adv.,*
q.v., or var. of *tost,* q.v.

Trace, 1 & 3 pr. of *tracier,*
q.v., or form of pr. subj. of
traire, q.v.

Tracier (**tractiare,* on *tractus,* pp.
of *trahere*), *va.* seek, follow the
tracks of, travel over, efface ;
vn. track, search, journey.

Traient, 6 pr. & pr. subj. of
traire, q.v.

Train (on *traïner,* q.v.), *sm.*
wandering, trail, train (of
dress), delay ; company ; pursuit, carnage.

Traïner (**traginare,* on **tragere,*
v. *traire*), *va.* drag, drag along.

Traioie, 1 & 3 impft. of *traire,*
q.v.

Traïr (**tradīre* for **-ēre*), *va.*
betray.

Traire (**tragere* for *trahere,* pp.
tractus ; infl. by *agere,* pp.
actus, lead), *va.* pull, draw,
bring, tear (hair), rescue,
suffer, translate ; *vn.* shoot
(arrow, javelin, etc.) ; *v. rfl.*
go, move, withdraw. *Ça vos
traiez :* come here, come along.
Faire t. : send for, cause to be
brought. *Se t. vers (a) :* go

towards. *T. a chief :* complete successfully, give satisfaction. *T. avant :* bring forward, come forward. 3 pft. : **Traist.**

Trait (*tractum*, pp. of *trahere*, draw), *sm.* pull, dart, shot, range (arrow, etc.). · *A t. :* slowly, deliberately. *Also* pp. & 3 pr. *traire*, q.v.

Traitis (on pp. of *traire*, q.v.), *adj.* well-fashioned, slender, graceful, delightful.

Traitor (*traditōrem*, infl. by *trair*, q.v.), *sm.* traitor. *Nom. sing. :* **Traitre(s)** (*traditor*).

Trametre (*transmittere*), *va.* send. 3 pft. : **Tramist.**

Travaillier, Traveillier (**tripaliare*, with change of init. vowel, on PL. *tripalium*, instrument of torture, *lit.* made of three stakes), *va.* torment, harass, weary ; *vn.* ˙suffer, worry ; *v. rfl.* tire oneself, toil, make an effort. *Traveillié*, pp. *adj.* : weary, exhausted.

Tré, v. *tref.*

Trecherie (on *trechier*, q.v.), *sf.* deceit, guile, treachery.

Trechier, v. *trichier.*

Trecier (etym. obsc., perh. on **tricia*, Gk. *tricha*, three-fold), *va.* plait.

Tref (*trabem*), *sm.* beam, tent, sail, mast.

Treillis, alter. of *tresliz*, q.v.,·infl. by **treille** (*trichila*), arbour. **Treliz,** v. *tresliz.* **Tremper,** metathesised form of *temprer*, q.v.

Trepeil, Trepel (on *trepeillier*, on *treper*, q.v.), *sm.* noise, clash, battle, trouble, confusion.

Treper (Fk. **trippôn*, jump), *vn.* stamp, jump, dance.

Trere, v. *traire.*

Tres (*tra(n)s*, beyond), *adv.* very, right ; *prep.* through, across, near, behind, since, until. *T. que,* v. *tresque. Also* form in *-s* of *tref*, q.v.

Tres-. Add the idea of " completely," " right through," etc. to the simple form.

Tresallir, v. *tressaillir.*

Tresche (on *treschier*, q.v.), *sf.* dance, leap, round.

Treschier (Germ., cf. Goth. *thriskan*, thresh), *vn.* leap, dance. *Also adj.* = *tres chier*, very dear.

Tresgeter (*tres*, q.v., + *geter*, v. *jeter*), *va.* transport, cross ; throw out, cast in a mould ; cast (a spell). *Tresgeté*, pp. *adj.* : sculptured, cast in a mould, engraved.

Treske, v. *tresque* or *tresche.*

Tresliz (alter. of *treliz* < **trilīcium*, on *trilix*, having three threads), *adj.* of interwoven mail ; *sm.* trellis.

Trespas (on *trespasser*, q.v.), *sm.* passage ; space of time ; sin, transgression. *T. de vent :* breeze.

Trespasser (*tres*, q.v., + *passer*, q.v.), *va.* pass, traverse, undergo, infringe, surpass ; *vn.* pass, pass by, traverse, transgress, die, recover. *T. de :* leave. *Trespassé en eage :* advanced in years.

Trespenser (*tres*, q.v., + *penser*, q.v.), *vn. & rfl.* think, reflect, worry.

Tresprendre (*tres*, q.v., + *prendre*, q.v.), *va*. seize.

Tresque (*tres*, q.v., + *que*), *prep*. right up to, as far as ; *conj.* as soon as, until. *T. a* (*en*) : as far as.

Tressaillir (*tres*, q.v., + *saillir*, q.v.), *va*. jump over, sin against ; *vn*. tremble, start, jump up.

Tressuer (*tres*, q.v., + *suer* < *sŭdare*, perspire), *vn*. perspire profusely, be greatly disturbed.

Trestor (on *trestorner*, q.v.), *sm*. detour, obstacle, turn, return, trick, cessation.

Trestorner (*tres*, q.v., + *torner*, q.v.), *va*. turn, turn aside, overturn, overthrow, change, hide ; *vn*. return, escape ; *v. rfl.* turn away. *Ja nen ert trestorné* : without fail.

Trestot (*tres*, q.v., + *tot*, q.v.), *adj*. all ; *adv*. completely.

Trestourner, Trestout, v. *trestorner, trestot*. **Trestuit,** nom. pl. of *trestot*, q.v. **Trestuz,** for *trestoz*, case in -*s* of *trestot*, q.v. **Tretis,** v. *traitis*.

Treü (*trĭbūtum*), *sm*. tribute, tax, toll. *Syn. :* **Treüage.**

Treuve, 1 & 3 pr. of *trover*, q.v. **Treve,** v. *trive*. **Trez,** for *tres*, case in -*s* of *tref*, q.v.

Tricheor (on *trichier*, q.v.), *sm*. deceiver, traitor, trickster.

Tricherie, v. *trecherie*.

Trichier (etym. unkn.), *va*. deceive, trick.

Trichierre, nom. of *tricheor*, q.v. **Tries,** v. *tres*. **Trieve,** v. *trive*.

H

Trifoir (on *trifoire*, q.v.), *adj*. in open-work, inlaid, carved.

Trifoire (on Med. L. *triforia*, n. pl., three openings), *sf*. carving, open-work, inlaid work.

Tripot (etym. obsc.), *sm*. trick, intrigue, difficulty.

Tristor (on *triste*, b. *tristem*), *sf*. sadness, grief.

Trive (Fk. **triuwa*, pledge), *sf*. truce, respite.

Trobler (**turbulare*, on **turbulus* for *turbidus*), *va*. disturb, harass, trouble, cloud (sight) ; *vn*. become troubled.

Troer (on *trou*, 8th c. L. *traugum*, etym. unkn.), *va*. make holes in, pierce, break.

Tronçoner (on *tronçon* < **truncĭōnem*, on *truncus*, dismembered), *va*. cut, mutilate, shatter ; *vn*. splinter, shatter.

Trop (Fk. **thorp*, quantity), *adv*. much, very, enough, too, too much, long, too long.

Tros (*thyrsum*, stalk), *sm*. stump, piece, trunk.

Trosque (on *intrŏ* + *ŭsque?*), *adv*. until, as far as ; *conj.* until.

Trosser (perh. **torciare*, twist), *va*. load, parcel.

Trou-, try under **Tro-.**

Troveor (on *trover*, q.v.), *sm*. trouvere (poet), story-teller. *Nom. sing. :* **Trovere.**

Trover (perh. **tropare*, on *tropus*, figure of speech, and, in LL., melody), *va*. find, invent, discover, compose, arrange.

Truant (Gaul. **trŭganto-*, cf. W. *tru, truan* & Ir. *truag*, unfortunate), *sm*. vagabond, wretch ; *adj*. miserable, wretched.

Truesque, v. *trosque*. **Trueve**, v. *treuve*. **Truis**, 1 pr., **Truisse**, 1 & 3 pr. subj., **Truist**, 3 pr. subj. of *trover*, q.v.

Tuen (tonic form of *tuum*), *adj. & pron.* thy, thine.

Tuert, 3 pr. of *tordre*, q.v. **Tuit**, nom. pl. of *tot*, q.v. **Tum** = *tu me*.

Tumer (Fk. **tumôn*), *vn.* leap, fall, dance ; *va.* cast down.

Tur, v. *tor*. **Tut**, v. *tot*. **Turnelz**, var. of *torneis*, *tournois*, tourney, cf. *tornoier*. **Tuz**, v. *toz*. **Ty-**, try under **Ti-**.

U

U-, try also under **O-** or **Ou-**, e.g. **Uan**, v. *ouan*.

U = *ou*, var. of *el* = *en le* : also form of *o* (*aut*), or.

Ueil (*oculum*), *sm.* eye.

Üel = *oel*, v. *ivel*. **Uelent**, 6 pr. of *oloir*, q.v. **Uelz**, form in *-s* of *ueil*, q.v. **Uen**, v. *huem*.

Ues (*opus*), *sm.* need, use, work. *A* (*Ad*) *o.* : for the use of, for. *Also* form in *-s* of **Uef** (**ovum* for *ōvum*), *sm.* egg.

Uevre, v. *oevre* ; *also* 1 & 3 pr. & pr. subj. of *ovrer*, q.v., or of *ovrir*, q.v. **Ui**, v. *hui*.

Uidme (**octimum* for *octavum*), *adj.* eighth.

Uile (*olea*, in PL., olive oil), *sf.* oil.

Uis (LL. *ūstium* for *ōstium*), *sm.* door.

Uiseuse, v. *oiseuse*.

Uisset (dimin. of *uis*, q.v.), *sm.* small door.

Uissier (on *uis*, q.v.), *sm.* door-keeper, porter ; ship with a door in the side allowing horses to be transported.

Uitante (*octōginta*), *num.* eighty.

Uller (**ŭrulare* for *ululare*), *vn.* howl, roar.

Unc, v. *onc*. **Uncques, Unkes, Unques**, v. *onques*. **Unt**, var. of *ont* (*unde*), q.v., or 6 pr. of *avoir*.

Us (*ūsum*) *sm.* use, custom. *Aveir en us :* be accustomed to. *En us :* in common use.

User (**ūsare*, on *ūsus*, pp. of *ūti*, use), *va.* use, pass (time, life, etc.). *Usé*, pp. **adj.** : customary, skilled.

V

Vadlet, v. *vaslet*.

Vaillant (pr. p. of *valoir*, q.v.), *prep.* worth, to the value of ; *adj.* valiant, valuable, worthwhile.

Vaillissant (inchoat. pr. p. of *valoir*, q.v.), *adj. & prep.* worth, to the value of ; *sm.* value.

Vain (*vanum*), *adj.* empty, weak, foolish, vain.

Vair (*varium*, variegated), *adj.* changing, variegated, bright (eyes), dappled (horse), vair (*heraldic*) ; *sm.* fur, miniver.

Valdrai, 1 fut. of *valoir*, q.v. **Vallet**, v. *vaslet*.

Valoir (*valēre*, be strong, be of avail), *va. & n.* be worth, be of avail.

Valor (*valōrem*), *sf.* worth, reputation. *Aveir v. :* be of avail.

Valsis, form of 2 pft. of *valoir*, q.v. **Valui,** 1 pft. of *valoir*, q.v. **Vanjoison,** v. *vengison*.

Vantance(on*vanter*< LL.*vanitare*, be vain), *sf.* boast, bragging.

Varlet, v. *vaslet*.

Vaslet (Gallo-Rom. **vassellitum*, Celt. orig., cf. *vassal*), *sm.* young noble, squire, youth, servant.

Vassal (Merov. L. *vassallum*, on *vassus*, Celt. orig., cf. W. *gwas* & Ir. *foss*, servant), *adj. & sm.* vassal, true knight, valiant. *Form in -s :* **Vassax.**

Vasselage (on *vassal*, q.v.), *sm.* valour, nobility, prowess.

Vaucel, *sm.*, **Vaucelle,** *sf.* (dimins. of *val* < *vallem*), valley.

Vaucrer (Germ., cf. Eng. *walk*), *vn.* drift (on the sea), wander.

Vaurai, 1 fut., **Vausis,** 2 pft. of *valoir*, q.v., or of *voloir*, q.v.

Vavassor (Merov. L. *vassus vassorum*, cf. *vassal*), *sm.* vavasour, lesser vassal.

Veable (on *vëoir*, q.v.), *adj.* visible.

Veant (pr. p. of *vëoir*, q.v.), *sm.* sight, presence ; *prep.* in the presence of, before.

Vedeir, v. *vëoir*. **Vedis,** v. *vëis*. **Vedisse,** v. *vëisse*.

Vedve (*vidua*, fem. adj., deprived), *sf.* widow.

Veer (*vetare*), *va.* refuse, deny, prevent, forbid, violate (law, custom). *V. son escu a :* refuse to fight.

Vei, imper. sing. & 1 pr. of *vëoir*, q.v. **Veie,** 1 & 3 pr. subj. of *vëoir*, q.v., and var. of *voie*, *sf.*, q.v. **Veier,** v.

voier. **Veigne,** 1 & 3 pr. subj. of *venir*, q.v.

Veillier (*vigilare*), *va.* watch, lie in wait for ; *vn.* keep watch, keep vigil.

Veintre (*vincere*), *va.* conquer, vanquish, win.

Veir, v. *voir.* **Veirement,** v. *voirement.* **Veirent,** 6 pft., **Veis,** 2 pft. of *vëoir*, q.v.

Veisdie, cf. *boisdie.* **Veisse,** 1 impft. subj., **Veit,** 3 pr., **Veit,** 3 pft. of *vëoir*, q.v.

Vels (*vel* + adv. *-s*), *adv.* at least.

Velt, 3 pr. of *voloir*, q.v.

Veltre (**veltrum* for LL. *vertragum*, of Celt. orig.), *sm.* hound.

Vench-, v. **Veng-. Vencu,** pp. of *veintre*, q.v. **Vendrai,** 1 fut. of *venir*, q.v., or of *vendre* (*vendere*), sell.

Veneör (*vënatörem*), *sm.* hunter.

Vengeresse (on *vengier* < *vindicare*), *adj. f.* avenging.

Vengieres, nom. of **Vengeor** (on *vengier* < *vindicare*), *sm.* avenger.

Vengison, Vengeison (on *vengier* < *vindicare*), *sf.* vengeance.

Venir (*venire*), *vn. & rfl.* come, happen, become ; *sm.* coming, return. *Bien viegne . . . :* welcome to. . . . *(S')En venir :* return, come, come up, come round. *V. mielz :* be (more) fitting, be preferable.

Venis, 2 pft. of *venir*, q.v. **Venjoison,** v. *vengison.* **Venqui,** 1 pft. of *veintre*, q.v. **Venrai,** 1 fut. of *venir*, q.v.

Ventaille (on *vent* < *ventum*, wind), *sf.* aventail (movable part of hauberk covering the face), visor.

Venter (on *vent* < *ventum*, wind), *va.* scatter to the wind, blow; *vn.* blow (wind).

Ventreillier (on *ventriculum*, dimin. of *venter*, belly), *vn.* lie on the stomach; *v. rfl.* wallow.

Vĕoir (*vidēre*), *va.* see; *sm.* sight. *Veschi, Vei ci, Vez ci :* here is.

Veons, imper. & 4 pr. of *vĕoir*, q.v.

Ver (*verrem*), *sm.* wild boar. *Also* var. of *voir*, q.v., or of *vair*, q.v.

Verai (perh. **vēracum* for *vērax*, *-acem*), *adj.* true, truthful. *Also* 1 fut. of *vĕoir*, q.v.

Vergié (**viridiatum* for *viridatum*, pp., made green), *adj.* enamelled.

Vergier (*viridiarium*, pleasure garden), *sm.* garden. *Also* syn. of *vergié*, q.v.

Vergoignier (on *vergoigne* < *verē-cundia*, shame), *va.* dishonour; *v. rfl.* be ashamed.

Vergonder (on *vergonde*, var. of *vergoigne*, cf. *vergoignier*), *va.* shame, dishonour; *vn. & rfl.* be ashamed, be afraid.

Vermeil (*vermiculum*, little worm; in LL., the cochineal insect), *adj.* scarlet, red.

Vers (*versus*, adv., towards), *prep.* towards, about, against.

Verser (*versare*, turn), *va.* turn, overthrow, cause to turn, pour; *vn.* be overthrown, overturn.

Verté (*vēritatem*), *sf.* truth.

Vertir (**vertīre* for *-ere*), *va.* turn, change; *vn.* turn, return, be

changed; *v. rfl.* return, turn away, abandon oneself to.

Vertu (*virtūtem*, manliness), *sf.* courage, prowess, force, strength, power, miracle. *De Deu aiez v. :* God grant you power or strength. *De v. :* with force. *Par v. :* with force.

Vespre (*vesperem*), *sm. & f.* evening, night. (*Syn. :* **Vespree**); *pl.* (Eccl. L. *vesperas*, on *vespera*, evening), vespers.

Vesqui, 1 pft. of *vivre*, q.v.

Vesteüre (on *vestir*, q.v., or LL. *vestitūra*), *sf.* clothing, dress, garment.

Vestir (*vestīre*), *va.* dress, wear, put on, don, cover, occupy (town), invest (with a fief); *vn.* dress; *v. rfl.* clothe oneself.

Vet = *vait*, 3 pr. of *aler*, go.

Veü, pp. of *vĕoir*, q.v.

Veüe (fem. pp. of *vĕoir*, q.v.), *sf.* sight.

Veul, 1 pr. of *voloir*, q.v.

Vez (imper. of *vĕoir*, q.v.), *adv. & interj.* behold, lo, here is. *Vez ci, Veschi :* here is. *Vez me ci :* here I am.

Vezié (*vitiatum*, pp., corrupted; perh. some confusion with *veisdie*, v. *boisdie*), *adj.* scoundrel, base, villainous, skilful, crafty. *V. de :* clever at, skilled in.

Vi, 1 pft. of *vĕoir*, q.v., or var. of *vif*, q.v.

Viaire (form obsc.), *sm.* face, countenance. *Ço m'est v. :* it seems to me, I think. *Venir a v. :* commend itself.

Vialt, form of *velt*, q.v.

Viande (**vivanda* for *vivenda*, n. pl. as sf.), *sf.* food; *later*, flesh.

Viaus, form of 2 pr. of *voloir*, q.v., or var. of *vels*, adv., q.v. **Viaut,** form of *velt*, q.v. **Vic,** 1 pr. of *vivre*, q.v. **Viegne,** 1 & 3 pr. subj. of *venir*, q.v.

Vieil (PL. *veclum* for *vetulum*), *adj.* old.

Vieler (on *viele*, sort of fiddle, orig. obsc.), *va.* play the "viele," fiddle.

Vielle, fem. of *vieil*, q.v. **Vielz,** form in -s of *vieil*, q.v. **Vienc, Vieng,** 1 pr. of *venir*, q.v. **Viés,** v. *viez*. **Vies-,** try under **Ves-**. **Vieut,** v. *velt*. **Viex,** case in -s of *vieil*, q.v., or 2 pr. of *voloir*, q.v.

Viez (*vetus*), *adj. m. & f.* old.

Vif (*vivum*), *adj.* living, alive, lively. *Also* 1 pr. of *vivre*, q.v.

Vil (*vilem*, cheap), *adj.* common, wretched, vile. *Aveir v. :* hold cheap.

Vilain (LL. *villanum*, farm-dweller), *sm.* peasant, commoner, wretch, knave; *adj.* boorish, unseemly.

Vilenaille (on *vilain*, q.v.), *sf.* rabble, populace.

Vilenie, Vilonie (on *vilain*, q.v.), *sf.* shame, dishonour, slander, coarse behaviour, uncourtly behaviour.

Viltage, *sm.*, **Viltance,** *sf.*, **Vilté,** *sf.* (on *vil*, q.v.), shame, dishonour.

Vinc, Ving, 1 pft. of *venir*, q.v.

Virge (b. *virginem*), *sf.* maiden, the Virgin. *Early form :* **Virgene.**

Vis, (1) (*visum*, sight), *sm.* face; (2) (PL. (*mihi*) *est visum* for (*mihi*) *videtur*). *Ço m'est v., Ço m'est a v. :* it seems to me, I think; (3) Form in -s of *vif*, q.v.

Visder (*visitare*), *va.* visit.

Vitaille (LL. *vict(u)alia*, on *victus*, food), *sf.* food, victuals.

Vivendier (alter. of *vivandier*, on *viande*, q.v., infl. by the Cl. L.), *adj.* hospitable, generous.

Vivre, *sf.*, v. *guivre; also vn.*, (*vivere*), live. **Viz,** v. *vis*.

Vo-, try also **Vu-**.

Vochier (*vocare*), *va.* call, call upon, denounce.

Voer (**votare*, or on *votum*, vow), *va. & n.* make a vow, swear.

Voi, v. *vei*. **Voidie,** v. *voisdie*. **Voidier,** v. *vuidier*.

Voie (*via*), *sf.* way, road. *Metre en v. :* persuade, influence, train. *Tote v. :* all the while. *Totes voies*, v. *totevoies*.

Voier, (1) (*vicarium* substitute), *sm.* provost-marshal; (2) (on *voie*, q.v.), *va.* guide; *vn.* travel; (3) (on root *voi-* of *vëoir*, q.v.), *va.* see, examine.

Voil, (1) 1 pr. of *voloir*, q.v.; (2) Var. of *vuel*, sm., q.v.; (3) (*vēlum*), *sm.* veil, sail.

Voir (*vērum*), *adj.* true; *sm.* the truth; *adv.* (*sometimes with* adv. -s, **Voirs**), truly, in truth, truthfully. *A v. :* truthful, serious. *De v. :* truly, in truth.

Voire (*vēra*, n.pl.), *adv.* truly, in truth; *sf.* truth; (2) (*vitrum*), *sm.* glass.

Voirement (on *voir*, adj. q.v.), adv. truly, assuredly.

Voirs, v. *voir*. **Vois**, v. *voiz ;* also 1 pr. of *aler*, go ; *later* 1 pr. of *vēoir*, q.v. **Voisdie**, cf. *boisdie*. **Voise**, 1 & 3 pr. subj., **Voist**, 3 pr. subj. of *aler*, go.

Voisous (*vitiōsum*, wicked), adj. cunning, clever.

Voitrer, alter. of *voutrer*, q.v.

Voiz (*vōcem*), sf. voice, sound. *A v. :* loudly, aloud. *Faire v. :* give tongue. *Also* 2 pr. of *vēoir*, q.v.

Vol (on *voler* < *volare*, fly), sm. flight ; adj. winged, light, swift. *Also* var. of *vuel*, sm., q.v., or of *voil*, q.v., or 1 pr. of *voler*, see above.

Voldrent, 6 pft. of *voloir*, q.v.

Voloir (**volēre* for *velle*), va. & n. wish, desire, be willing ; sm. wish, will.

Volrent, v. *voldrent*. **Vols**, form in *-s* of *volt*, q.v. **Volsis**, 2 pft., **Volsisse**, 1 impft. subj., **Volst**, 3 pft. of *voloir*, q.v.

Volt, (1) (*vōltum*), sm. face, countenance ; (2) (**volvitum*, pp. of *volvere*), adj. vaulted, arched ; (3) 3 pft. of *voloir*, q.v.

Volti, Voltis (on *volt* 2, q.v.), adj. vaulted, arched. *Escu v.,* v. *escu.* *Fem. of voltis :* **Voltice**.

Voltrer, v. *voutrer*. **Volz**, form in *-s* of *volt*, q.v. **Vorrai**, form of 1 fut. of *voloir*, q.v. **Voti, Votis**, v. *volti, voltis*. **Vous**, form in *-s* of *volt*, q.v., or *pers. pron.*, you. **Vout**, 3 pft. of *voloir*, q.v. or var. of *volt*, q.v.

Voutrer (perh. **voltulare*, on **voltus*, pp. of *volvere*, turn), va., n., & rfl. wallow.

Vreté, v. *verté*. **Vueil**, v. *vuel*.

Vuel (on *voloir*, q.v.), sm. will, wish. (*Par*) *Mon v. :* with my consent, if I had my way. *Also* 1 pr. of *voloir*, q.v.

Vuelent, 6 pr. of *voloir*, q.v.

Vuels, 2 pr. of *voloir*, q.v., or form in *-s* of *vuel*, sm., q.v. **Vuide**, fem. of *vuit*, q.v.

Vuidier (**vocitare*, on **vocitus*, cf. *vuit*), va. empty, abandon (city) ; vn. depart, leave. *V. les arçons, la sele* or *les estriers :* topple from one's horse.

Vuit (**vocitum*, on **voc(u)us* for *vacuus*, cf. *vocivus* in Terence), adj. empty, bereft. *Vuide terre :* fallow land.

W

Try under **V-** or **G(u)-**, e.g. **Wacrer, Walcrer, Waucrer**, v. *vaucrer*.

Wast, v. *gast ;* etc.

Y

Try also under **I-**.

Yaue = *eaue*, v. *eve*.

Ydre, v. *idle*.

Ymés, v. *huimais*.